The O'Leary Series

Microsoft® Access 2002

Brief Edition

Timothy J. O'Leary
Arizona State University

Linda I. O'Leary

InformationTechnology

McGraw-Hill Irwin

Boston   Burr Ridge, IL   Dubuque, IA   Madison, WI   New York
San Francisco   St. Louis   Bangkok   Bogotá   Caracas   Kuala Lumpur
Lisbon   London   Madrid   Mexico City   Milan   Montreal   New Delhi
Santiago   Seoul   Singapore   Sydney   Taipei   Toronto

McGraw-Hill Higher Education

*A Division of The **McGraw-Hill** Companies*

MICROSOFT® ACCESS 2002, BRIEF EDITION
Published by McGraw-Hill/Irwin, an imprint of the McGraw-Hill Companies, Inc. 1221 Avenue of the Americas, New York, NY, 10020. Copyright © 2002 by the McGraw-Hill Companies, Inc. All rights reserved.

Some ancillaries, including electronic and print components, may not be available to customers outside the United States.

Disclaimer: This book is designed to help you improve your computer use. However, the author and publisher assume no responsibility whatsoever for the uses made of this material or for decisions based on their use, and make no warranties, either expressed or implied, regarding the contents of this book, its merchantability, or its fitness for any particular purpose.

Neither the publisher nor anyone else who has been involved in the creation, production, or delivery of this product shall be liable for any direct, incidental, or consequential damages, such as, but not limited to, loss of anticipated profits or benefits or benefits resulting from its use or from any breach of warranty. Some states do not allow the exclusion or limitation of direct, incidental, or consequential damages, so the above disclaimer may not apply to you. No dealer, company, or person is authorized to alter this disclaimer. Any representation to the contrary will not bind the publisher or author.

This book is printed on acid-free paper.

domestic   3 4 5 6 7 8 9 0 QPD/QPD 0 9 8 7 6 5 4 3 2
international   2 3 4 5 6 7 8 9 0 QPD/QPD 0 9 8 7 6 5 4 3 2 1

ISBN 0-07-247243-X

Publisher: *George Werthman*
Sponsoring editor: *Danial Silverburg*
Developmental editor: *Sarah Wood*
Senior marketing manager: *Jeffrey Parr*
Project manager: *James Labeots*
Manager, new book production: *Melonie Salvati*
Media producer: *David Barrick*
Freelance design coordinator: *Gino Cieslik*
Lead supplement coordinator: *Marc Mattson*
Photo research coordinator: *David A. Tietz*
Cover & interior design: *Maureen McCutcheon*
Cover image: *Digitalvision*
Typeface: *10.5/13 New Aster*
Compositor: *Rogondino & Associates*
Printer: *Quebecor World Dubuque Inc.*

Library of Congress Control Number 2001092431

INTERNATIONAL EDITION ISBN 0-07-112354-7

www.mhhe.com

InformationTechnology

Information Technology at McGraw-Hill/Irwin

At McGraw-Hill Higher Education, we publish instructional materials targeted at the higher education market. In an effort to expand the tools of higher learning, we publish texts, lab manuals, study guides, testing materials, software, and multimedia products.

At McGraw-Hill/Irwin (a division of McGraw-Hill Higher Education), we realize that technology has created and will continue to create new mediums for professors and students to use in managing resources and communicating information to one another. We strive to provide the most flexible and complete teaching and learning tools available as well as offer solutions to the changing world of teaching and learning.

McGraw-Hill/Irwin is dedicated to providing the tools for today's instructors and students to successfully navigate the world of Information Technology.

- **Seminar Series** McGraw-Hill/Irwin's Technology Connection seminar series offered across the country every year demonstrates the latest technology products and encourages collaboration among teaching professionals.

- **McGraw-Hill/Osborne** This division of The McGraw-Hill Companies is known for its best-selling Internet titles, *Internet & Web Yellow Pages* and the *Internet Complete Reference*. For more information, visit Osborne at **www.osborne.com**.

- **Digital Solutions** McGraw-Hill/Irwin is committed to publishing digital solutions. Taking your course online doesn't have to be a solitary adventure, nor does it have to be a difficult one. We offer several solutions that will allow you to enjoy all the benefits of having your course material online.

- **Packaging Options** For more information about our discount options, contact your McGraw-Hill/Irwin Sales representative at 1-800-338-3987 or visit our web site at **www.mhhe.com/it**.

Brief Contents

Detailed Contents

Lab 2 — Modifying a Table and Creating a Form   AC2.1

Lab 3 — Analyzing Data and Creating Reports   AC3.1

Acknowledgments

The new edition of The O'Leary Series has been made possible only through the enthusiasm and dedication of a great team of people. Because the team spans the country, literally from coast to coast, we have utilized every means of working together including conference calls, FAX, e-mail, and document collaboration. We have truly tested the team approach and it works!

Leading the team from McGraw-Hill/Irwin are George Werthman, Publisher and Alexandra Arnold, Developmental Editor. Their renewed commitment, direction, and support have infused the team with the excitement of a new project.

The production staff is headed by James Labeots, Project Manager, whose planning and attention to detail has made it possible for us to successfully meet a very challenging schedule. Members of the production team include: Gino Cieslik, Designer; Pat Rogondino, Compositor; Susan Defosset, Copy Editor; Melonie Salvati, Production Supervisor; Marc Mattson, Supplement Coordinator; and David Barrick, Media Producer. We would particularly like to thank Pat and Susan—team members for many past editions whom we can always depend on to do a great job.

Finally, we are particularly grateful to a small but very dedicated group of people who helped us develop the manuscript. Colleen Hayes, Susan Demar, and Kathy Duggan have helped on the last several editions and continue to provide excellent developmental and technical support. To Steve Willis and Carol Cooper who provide technical expertise, youthful perspective, and enthusiasm, my thanks for helping get the manuscripts out the door and meeting the deadlines.

Preface

Introduction

The 20th century not only brought the dawn of the Information Age, but also rapid changes in information technology. There is no indication that this rapid rate of change will be slowing— it may even be increasing. As we begin the 21st century, computer literacy will undoubtedly become prerequisite for whatever career a student chooses. The goal of the O'Leary Series is to assist students in attaining the necessary skills to efficiently use these applications. Equally important is the goal to provide a foundation for students to readily and easily learn to use future versions of this software. This series does this by providing detailed step-by step instructions combined with careful selection and presentation of essential concepts.

About the Authors

Tim and Linda O'Leary live in the American Southwest and spend much of their time engaging instructors and students in conversation about learning. In fact, they have been talking about learning for more than 25 years. Something in those early conversations convinced them to write a book, to bring their interest in the learning process to the printed page. Today, they are as concerned as ever about learning, about technology, and about the challenges of presenting material in new ways, both in terms of content and the method of delivery.

A powerful and creative team, Tim combines his years of classroom teaching experience with Linda's background as a consultant and corporate trainer. Tim has taught courses at Stark Technical College in Canton, Ohio, Rochester Institute of Technology in upper New York state, and is currently a professor at Arizona State University in Tempe, Arizona. Tim and Linda have talked to and taught students from ages 8 to 80, all of them with a desire to learn something about computers and the applications that make their lives easier, more interesting, and more productive.

About the Book

Times are changing, technology is changing, and this text is changing, too. Do you think the students of today are different from yesterday? There is no doubt about it—they are. On the positive side, it is amazing how much effort students will put toward things they are convinced are relevant to them. Their effort directed at learning application programs and exploring the Web seems at times limitless. On the other hand, students can often be shortsighted, thinking that learning the skills to use the application is the only objective. The mission of the series is to build upon and extend this interest by not only teaching the specific application skills but by introducing the concepts that are common to all applications, providing students with the confidence, knowledge, and ability to easily learn the next generation of applications.

What's New in This Edition?

- **Introduction to Computer Essentials**—A brief introduction to the basics of computer hardware and software (Appears in Office XP, Volume I only).

- **Introduction to Windows 2000**—Two hands-on labs devoted to Windows 2000 basics (Appears in Office XP, Volume I only).

- **Introduction to the WWW: Internet Explorer and E-mail**—Hands-on introductions for using Internet Explorer to browse the WWW and using e-mail (Appears in Office XP, Volume I only).

- **Topic Reorganization**—The text has been reorganized to include main and subtopic heads by grouping related tasks. For example, tasks such as changing fonts and applying character effects appear under the "Formatting" topic head. This results in a slightly more reference-like approach, making it easier for students to refer back to the text to review. This has been done without losing the logical and realistic development of the case.

- **Clarified Marginal Notes**—Marginal notes have been enhanced by more clearly identifying the note content with box heads and the use of different colors.

    Additional Information—Brief asides with expanded discussion of features.

    Having Trouble?—Procedural tips advising students of possible problems and how to overcome.

    Another Method—Alternative methods of performing a procedure.

- **Larger Screen Figures**—Make it easier to identify elements and read screen content.

- All **Numbered Steps** and bullets appear in left margin space making it easy not to miss a step.

- A **MOUS (*Microsoft Office User Specialist*) Skills** table, appearing at the end of each lab, contains page references to MOUS skills learned in the lab.

- **Two New References** are included at the end of each text.

    Data File List—Helps organize all data and solution files.

    MOUS (*Microsoft Office User Specialist*) Skills—Links all MOUS objectives to text content and end-of-chapter exercises.

Same Great Features as the Office 2000 Series

- **Relevant Cases**—Four separate running cases demonstrate the features in each application. Topics are of interest to students—At Arizona State University, over 600 students were surveyed to find out what topics are of interest to them.

- **Focus on Concepts**—Each chapter focuses on the concepts behind the application. Students learn the essentials, so they can succeed regardless of the software package they might be using.

- **Steps**—Numbered procedural steps clearly identify each hands-on task needed to complete the step.

- **Screens**—Plentiful screen illustrations illustrate the completion of each numbered step to help students stay on track.

- **Callouts**—Meaningful screen callouts identify the results of the steps as well as reinforce the associated concept.

- **End-of-Chapter Material**

  Terminology—Questions and exercises test recall of the basic information and terminology in the lab.

  - Screen Identification
  - Matching
  - Multiple Choice

  Concepts—Questions and exercises review students' understanding of concepts and ability to integrate ideas presented in different parts of the lab.

  - Fill-In
  - Discussion Questions

  Hands-On Practice Exercises—Students apply the skills and concepts they learned to solve case-based exercises. Many cases in the practice exercises tie to a running case used in another application lab. This helps to demonstrate the use of the four applications across a common case setting. For example, the Adventure Travel Tours case used in the Word labs is continued in practice exercises in Excel, Access, and PowerPoint.

  - Step-by-Step
  - On Your Own
  - On The Web

- **Rating System**—The 3-star rating system identifies the difficulty level of each practice exercise in the end-of-chapter materials.

- **Working Together Labs**—At the completion of the brief and introductory texts, a final lab demonstrates the integration of the MS Office applications and the WWW.

Instructor's Guide

We understand that, in today's teaching environment, offering a textbook alone is not sufficient to meet the needs of the many instructors who use our books. To teach effectively, instructors must have a full complement of supplemental resources to assist them in every facet of teaching from preparing for class, to conducting a lecture, to assessing students' comprehension. *The O'Leary Series* offers a fully-integrated supplements package and Web site, as described below.

Instructor's Resource Kit

The **Instructor's Resource Kit** contains a computerized Test Bank, an Instructor's Manual, and PowerPoint Presentation Slides. Features of the Instructor's Resource Kit are described below.

- **Instructor's Manual**   The Instructor's Manual contains lab objectives, concepts, outlines, lecture notes, and command summaries. Also included are answers to all end-of chapter material, tips for covering difficult materials, additional exercises, and a schedule showing how much time is required to cover text material.

- **Computerized Test Bank**   The test bank contains over 1,300 multiple choice, true/false, and discussion questions. Each question will be accompanied by the correct answer, the level of learning difficulty, and corresponding page references. Our flexible Diploma software allows you to easily generate custom exams.

- **PowerPoint Presentation Slides**   The presentation slides will include lab objectives, concepts, outlines, text figures, and speaker's notes. Also included are bullets to illustrate key terms and FAQs.

Online Learning Center/Web Site

Found at **www.mhhe.com/oleary**, this site provides additional learning and instructional tools to enhance the comprehension of the text. The OLC/Web Site is divided into these three areas:

- **Information Center**   Contains core information about the text, supplements, and the authors.

- **Instructor Center**   Offers instructional materials, downloads, additional exercises, and other relevant links for professors.

- **Student Center**   Contains data files, chapter competencies, chapter concepts, self-quizzes, flashcards, projects, animations, additional Web links, and more.

Skills Assessment

SimNet (Simulated Network Assessment Product) provides a way for you to test students' software skills in a simulated environment. SimNet is available for Microsoft Office 97, Microsoft Office 2000, and Microsoft Office XP. SimNet provides flexibility for you in your course by offering:

- Pre-testing options
- Post-testing options
- Course placement testing
- Diagnostic capabilities to reinforce skills
- Proficiency testing to measure skills
- Web or LAN delivery of tests.
- Computer-based training tutorials (new for Office XP)
- MOUS preparation exams

For more information on skills assessment software, please contact your local sales representative, or visit us at **www.mhhe.com/it**.

Digital Solutions to Help You Manage Your Course

PageOut is our Course Web Site Development Center that offers a syllabus page, URL, McGraw-Hill Online Learning Center content, online exercises and quizzes, gradebook, discussion board, and an area for student Web pages.

Available free with any McGraw-Hill/Irwin product, PageOut requires no prior knowledge of HTML, no long hours of coding, and a way for course coordinators and professors to provide a full-course web site. PageOut offers a series of templates—simply fill them with your course information and click on one of 16 designs. The process takes under an hour and leaves you with a professionally designed Web site. We'll even get you started with sample web sites, or enter your syllabus for you! PageOut is so straightforward and intuitive, it's little wonder why over 12,000 college professors are using it. For more information, visit the PageOut Web site at **www.pageout.net**.

Online courses are also available. Online Learning Centers (OLCs) are your perfect solutions for Internet-based content. Simply put, these Centers are "digital cartridges" that contain a book's pedagogy and supplements. As students read the book, they can go online and take self-grading quizzes or work through interactive exercises. These also provide students appropriate access to lecture materials and other key supplements.

Online Learning Centers can be delivered through any of these platforms:

McGraw-Hill Learning Architecture (TopClass)

Blackboard.com

Ecollege.com (formerly Real Education)

WebCT (a product of Universal Learning Technology)

McGraw-Hill has partnerships with WebCT and Blackboard to make it even easier to take your course online. Now you can have McGraw-Hill content delivered through the leading Internet-based learning tool for higher education. At McGraw-Hill, we have the following service agreements with WebCT and Blackboard:

Instructor Advantage Instructor Advantage is a special level of service McGraw-Hill offers in conjuction with WebCT designed to help you get up and running with your new course. A team of specialists will be immediately available to ensure everything runs smoothly through the life of your adoption.

Instructor Advantage Plus Qualified McGraw-Hill adopters will be eligible for an even higher level of service. A certified WebCT or Blackboard specialist will provide a full day of on-site training for you and your staff. You will then have unlimited e-mail and phone support through the life of your adoption. Please contact your local McGraw-Hill representative for more details.

Technology Connection Seminar Series

McGraw-Hill/Irwin's Technology Connection seminar series offered across the country every year demonstrates the latest technology products and encourages collaboration among teaching professionals.

Computing Essentials

Available alone, or packaged with the O'Leary Series, *Computing Essentials* offers a unique, visual orientation that gives students a basic understanding of computing concepts. *Computing Essentials* is one of the few books on the market that is written by a professor who still teaches the course every semester and loves it! While combining current topics and technology into a highly illustrated design geared to catch students' interest and motivate them in their learning, this text provides an accurate snapshot of computing today. When bundled with software application lab manuals, students are given a complete representation of the fundamental issues surrounding the personal computing environment.

The text includes the following features:

- **A "Learn By Doing" approach** encourages students to engage in activity that is more interactive than the traditional learning pattern students typically follow in a concepts course. The exercises, explorations, visual orientation, inclusion of screen shots and numbered steps, and integrated internet references combine several methods to achieve an interactive learning environment for optimum reinforcement.

- **Making IT Work For You** sections visually demonstrate how technology is used in everyday life. Topics covered include how find a job online and how to protect a computer against viruses. These "gallery" style boxes combine text and art to take students step-by-step through technological processes that are both interesting and useful. As an added bonus, the *CE 2001-2002 Making IT Work Video Series* has been created to compliment the topics presented throughout the text.

- **On the Web Explorations** appear throughout the margins of the text and encourage students to go to the Web to visit several informative and established sites in order to learn more about the chapter's featured topic.

- **On the Web Exercises** present thought-provoking questions that allow students to construct articles and summaries for additional practice on topics relevant to that chapter while utilizing Web resources for further research. These exercises serve as additional reinforcement of the chapter's pertinent material while also allowing students to gain more familiarity with the Web.

- **A Look to the Future** sections provide insightful information about the future impact of technology and forecasts of how upcoming enhancements in the world of computing will play an important and powerful role in society.

- **Colorful Visual Summaries**, appearing at the end of every chapter, provide dynamic, graphical reviews of the important lessons featured in each chapter for additional reinforcement.

- **End-of-Chapter Review** material follows a three-level format and includes exercises that encourage students to review terms, concepts, and applications of concepts. Through matching, true/false, multiple choice, short answer completion, concept matching, and critical thinking questions, students have multiple review opportunities.

PowerWeb

PowerWeb is an exciting new online product available from McGraw-Hill. A nominally priced token grants students access through our web site to a wealth of resources—all corresponding to computer literacy. Features include an interactive glossary; current events with quizzing, assessment, and measurement options; Web survey; links to related text content; and WWW searching capability via Northern Lights, an academic search engine. Visit the PowerWeb site at **www.dushkin.com/powerweb**.

Interactive Companion CD-ROM

This free student CD-ROM, designed for use in class, in the lab, or at home by students and professors alike, includes a collection of interactive tutorial labs on some of the most popular and difficult topics in information technology. By combining video, interactive exercises, animation, additional content, and actual "lab" tutorials, we expand the reach and scope of the textbook. The lab titles are listed below.

- Binary Numbers
- Basic Programming
- Computer Anatomy
- Disk Fragmentation
- E-mail Essentials
- Multimedia Tools
- Workplace Issues (ergonomics/privacy/security)
- Introduction to Databases
- Programming II
- Network Communications
- Purchasing Decisions
- User Interfaces
- File Organization
- Word Processing and Spreadsheets
- Internet Overview
- Photo Editing
- Presentation Techniques
- Computer Troubleshooting
- Programming Overview
- SQL Queries

Student's Guide

As you begin each lab, take a few moments to read the **Case Study** and the **Concept Overview**. The case study introduces a real-life setting that is interwoven throughout the entire lab, providing the basis for understanding the use of the application. Also, notice the **Additional Information**, **Having Trouble?**, and **Another Method** boxes scattered throughout the book. These tips provide more information about related topics, help to get you out of trouble if you are having problems and offer suggestions on other ways to perform the same task. Finally, read the text between the steps. You will find the few minutes more it takes you is well worth the time when you are completing the practice exercises.

Many learning aids are built into the text to ensure your success with the material and to make the process of learning rewarding. The pages that follow call your attention to the key features in the text.

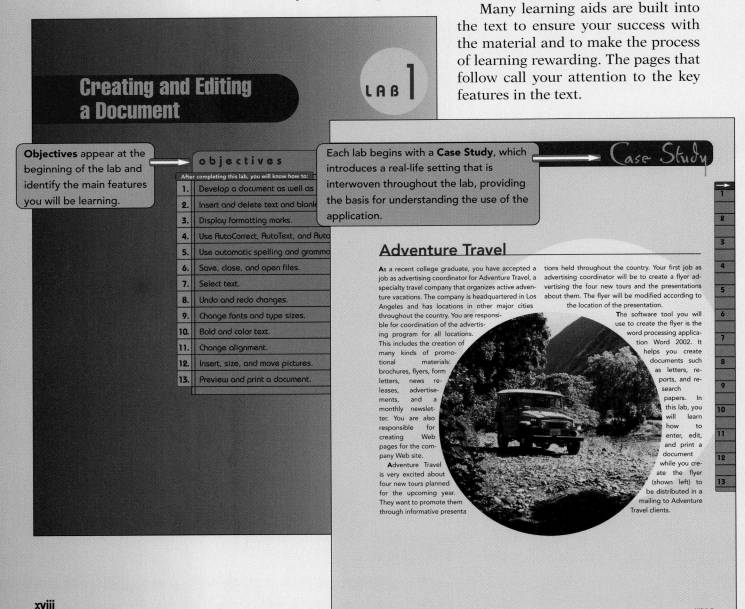

Creating and Editing a Document

LAB 1

Objectives appear at the beginning of the lab and identify the main features you will be learning.

objectives

After completing this lab, you will know how to:

1.	Develop a document as well as
2.	Insert and delete text and blank
3.	Display formatting marks.
4.	Use AutoCorrect, AutoText, and Auto
5.	Use automatic spelling and gramma
6.	Save, close, and open files.
7.	Select text.
8.	Undo and redo changes.
9.	Change fonts and type sizes.
10.	Bold and color text.
11.	Change alignment.
12.	Insert, size, and move pictures.
13.	Preview and print a document.

Each lab begins with a **Case Study**, which introduces a real-life setting that is interwoven throughout the lab, providing the basis for understanding the use of the application.

Case Study

Adventure Travel

As a recent college graduate, you have accepted a job as advertising coordinator for Adventure Travel, a specialty travel company that organizes active adventure vacations. The company is headquartered in Los Angeles and has locations in other major cities throughout the country. You are responsible for coordination of the advertising program for all locations. This includes the creation of many kinds of promotional materials: brochures, flyers, form letters, news releases, advertisements, and a monthly newsletter. You are also responsible for creating Web pages for the company Web site.

Adventure Travel is very excited about four new tours planned for the upcoming year. They want to promote them through informative presenta

tions held throughout the country. Your first job as advertising coordinator will be to create a flyer advertising the four new tours and the presentations about them. The flyer will be modified according to the location of the presentation.

The software tool you will use to create the flyer is the word processing application Word 2002. It helps you create documents such as letters, reports, and research papers. In this lab, you will learn how to enter, edit, and print a document while you create the flyer (shown left) to be distributed in a mailing to Adventure Travel clients.

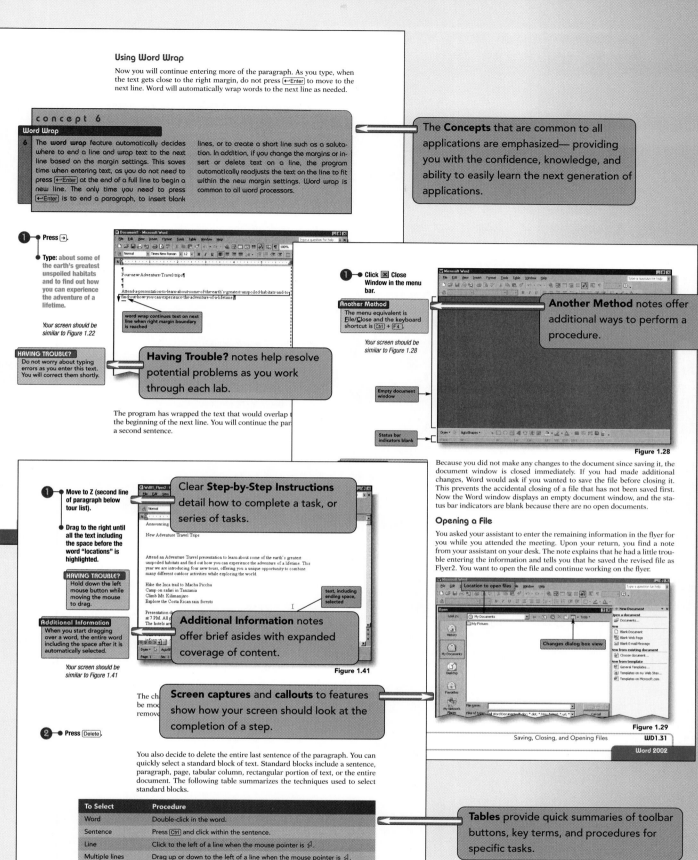

Using Word Wrap

Now you will continue entering more of the paragraph. As you type, when the text gets close to the right margin, do not press ←Enter to move to the next line. Word will automatically wrap words to the next line as needed.

concept 6

Word Wrap

6 The **word wrap** feature automatically decides where to end a line and wrap text to the next line based on the margin settings. This saves time when entering text, as you do not need to press ←Enter at the end of a full line to begin a new line. The only time you need to press ←Enter is to end a paragraph, to insert blank lines, or to create a short line such as a salutation. In addition, if you change the margins or insert or delete text on a line, the program automatically readjusts the text on the line to fit within the new margin settings. Word wrap is common to all word processors.

The **Concepts** that are common to all applications are emphasized— providing you with the confidence, knowledge, and ability to easily learn the next generation of applications.

1 ► Press →.

► **Type:** about some of the earth's greatest unspoiled habitats and to find out how you can experience the adventure of a lifetime.

Your screen should be similar to Figure 1.22

HAVING TROUBLE?
Do not worry about typing errors as you enter this text. You will correct them shortly.

word wrap continues text on next line when right margin boundary is reached

Having Trouble? notes help resolve potential problems as you work through each lab.

The program has wrapped the text that would overlap the beginning of the next line. You will continue the par a second sentence.

1 ► Click ☒ Close Window in the menu bar.

Another Method
The menu equivalent is **File/Close** and the keyboard shortcut is Ctrl + F4.

Your screen should be similar to Figure 1.28

Another Method notes offer additional ways to perform a procedure.

Empty document window

Status bar indicators blank

Figure 1.28

Because you did not make any changes to the document since saving it, the document window is closed immediately. If you had made additional changes, Word would ask if you wanted to save the file before closing it. This prevents the accidental closing of a file that has not been saved first. Now the Word window displays an empty document window, and the status bar indicators are blank because there are no open documents.

Opening a File

You asked your assistant to enter the remaining information in the flyer for you while you attended the meeting. Upon your return, you find a note from your assistant on your desk. The note explains that he had a little trouble entering the information and tells you that he saved the revised file as Flyer2. You want to open the file and continue working on the flyer.

1 ► Move to Z (second line of paragraph below tour list).

► Drag to the right until all the text including the space before the word "locations" is highlighted.

HAVING TROUBLE?
Hold down the left mouse button while moving the mouse to drag.

Additional Information
When you start dragging over a word, the entire word including the space after it is automatically selected.

Your screen should be similar to Figure 1.41

Clear **Step-by-Step Instructions** detail how to complete a task, or series of tasks.

Announcing

New Adventure Travel Trips

Attend an Adventure Travel presentation to learn about some of the earth's greatest unspoiled habitats and find out how you can experience the adventure of a lifetime. This year we are introducing four new tours, offering you a unique opportunity to combine many different outdoor activities while exploring the world.

Hike the Inca trail to Machu Picchu
Camp on safari in Tanzania
Climb Mt. Kilimanjaro
Explore the Costa Rican rain forests

text, including ending space, selected

Presentation d... at 7 P.M. All p... The hotels ar...

Additional Information notes offer brief asides with expanded coverage of content.

Figure 1.41

Location to open files

Changes dialog box view

Figure 1.29

Saving, Closing, and Opening Files   **WD1.31**

Word 2002

The ch... be mo... remo...

Screen captures and **callouts** to features show how your screen should look at the completion of a step.

2 ► Press Delete.

You also decide to delete the entire last sentence of the paragraph. You can quickly select a standard block of text. Standard blocks include a sentence, paragraph, page, tabular column, rectangular portion of text, or the entire document. The following table summarizes the techniques used to select standard blocks.

To Select	Procedure
Word	Double-click in the word.
Sentence	Press Ctrl and click within the sentence.
Line	Click to the left of a line when the mouse pointer is ⌐.
Multiple lines	Drag up or down to the left of a line when the mouse pointer is ⌐.
Paragraph	Triple-click on the paragraph or double-click to the left of the paragraph when the mouse pointer is a ⌐.
Multiple paragraphs	Drag to the left of the paragraphs when the mouse pointer is ⌐.
Document	Triple-click or press Ctrl and click to the left of the text when the mouse pointer is ⌐.
	Use Edit/Select All or the keyboard shortcut Ctrl + Alt.

Tables provide quick summaries of toolbar buttons, key terms, and procedures for specific tasks.

Each lab ends with a **Concept Summary** that reinforces the concepts presented throughout.

LAB 1
eating and Editing a Document

Template (WD1.7)

A template is a document file that includes predefined settings that are used as a pattern to create many common types of documents.

Automatic Grammar Check (WD1.18)

The automatic grammar-checking feature advises you of incorrect grammar as you create and edit a document, and proposes possible corrections.

Auto Text and Auto Complete (WD1.20)

The **AutoText** feature includes entries, such as commonly used phrases, that can be quickly inserted into a document. If the **AutoComplete** feature

A **Key Terms** section, a **MOUS Skills** guide, and a **Command Summary** table provide a list of page-referenced terms and keyboard and toolbar shortcuts, which can be a useful study aid.

Terminology is reinforced through **Screen Identification, Matching, Multiple Choice**, and **True/False** questions.

Terminology

screen identification

In the following Word screen, screen element in the space pro

Concepts are reinforced in **Fill-In** and **Discussion** questions.

Attend-an-Adventure-Travel
unspoiled-habitats-and-find-ou
year-we-are-introducing-four-v
many-different-outdoor-activi

Hike-the-I
Camp-ov
Climb-M
Explore

Presentat
All-preser
hotels-are

Call-1-80

lab exercises

Concepts

Fill-in questions

1. A small blue box appearing under a word or cha_____ feature was applied

2. If a word is underlined with purple dots, this in_____

Hands-on Exercises develop critical thinking skills and offer step-by-step practice. These exercises have a rating system from easy to difficult, and test your ability to apply the knowledge you have gained in each lab.

new tex

ht side

s openi

keep y

w displa

10. The _____ feature inclu can be quickly inserted into a document.

discussion questions

1. Discuss several uses you may have for a word pr to create a document.

2. Discuss how the AutoCorrect and Spelling and G What types of corrections does the AutoCorrect

3. Discuss how word wrap works. What happens w removed?

4. Discuss three ways you can select text. Discuss w methods.

5. Describe how the Undo and Redo features work.

6. Discuss how graphics can be used in a document to a document? Can the use of a graphic change

A. _____
B. _____
C. _____
D. _____
E. _____

I.
J.

lab review

LAB 2
Organizing Your Work

key terms

alignment	WN1.53	end-of-file marker	WN1.5	picture	WN1.55
AutoComplete	WN1.20	font	WN1.46	points	WN1.46
AutoCorrect	WN1.2	font size	WN1.46	ruler	WN1.5
automatic grammar check	WN1.8	format	WN1.	sans serif font	WN1.46
automatic spelling check	WN1.23	formatting mark	WN1.3	select	WN1.4
AutoText	WN1.20	Formatting toolbar	WN1.5	selection rectangle	WN1.5
character formatting	WN1.45	global template	WN1.7	serif font	WN1.46
clip art	WN1.55	graphic	WN1.55	sizing handles	WN1.5
cursor	WN1.3	Insert mode	WN1.5	SmartTag	WN1.27
custom dictionary	WN1.23	insertion point	WN1.5	source program	WN1.55
default	WN1.7	main dictionary	WN1.23	Standard toolbar	WN1.5
drawing object	WN1.55	Normal template	WN1.7	template	WN1.7
Drawing toolbar	WN1.6	object	WN1.55	TrueType	WN1.47
edit	WN1.	Overtype mode	WN1.3	typeface	WN1.46
embedded object	WN1.55	paragraph formatting	WN1.45	word wrap	WN1.26

MOUS Skills

The Microsoft Office User Specialist (MOUS) certification program is designed to measure your proficiency in performing basic tasks using the Office 2002 applications. Getting certified demonstrates that you have the skills and provides a valuable industry credential for employment. After completing this lab, you have learned the following Word Microsoft Office User Specialist skills:

Skill	Description	Page
Inserting and	Insert text	39
Modifying text	Use spelling and grammar checking	23
	Apply and modify character formats	45
	Apply and modify font formats	45
	character effects	45
	aragraph formats (alignment)	53
	Preview	61

Hands-On Exercises

step-by-step

★ **Writing a Memo**

1. Universal Industries is starting a casual Friday policy. Ms. Jones, the Vice President of Human Resources, has sent a memo informing employees of this new policy. Your completed memo is shown here.

   a. Open a blank Word document and create the memo with the following text. Press Tab twice ater you type colons (:) in the To, From, Date, and RE lines. This will make the information following the colons line up evenly. Enter a blank line below the RE line and between paragraphs.

   ```
   To:     [Your Name]
   From:   Ms. Jones
   Date:   [Current date]
   RE:     Business Casual Dress Code
   ```

   Effective next Friday, business casual will be allowed in the corporate facility on Fridays and the day before a holiday break. Business casual is sometimes difficult to interpret. For men, it is a collared shirt and tailored trousers. For women, it is a pantsuit or tailored trousers or skirt. Business casual is not jeans, t-shirts, or exercise clothes. A detailed dress code will be available on the company intranet.

   Thank you for your cooperation in this matter.

   CSJ/xxx

   b. Correct any spelling and grammar errors that are identified.
   c. Change the font for the entire memo to 14 pt.
   d. Change the alignment of the memo body to justified.
   e. Insert a blank line under the Date line and insert the AutoText reference line "RE:".
   f. Press Tab and type "Business Casual Dress Code".
   g. Save the document as Dress Code on your data disk.
   h. Preview and print the document.

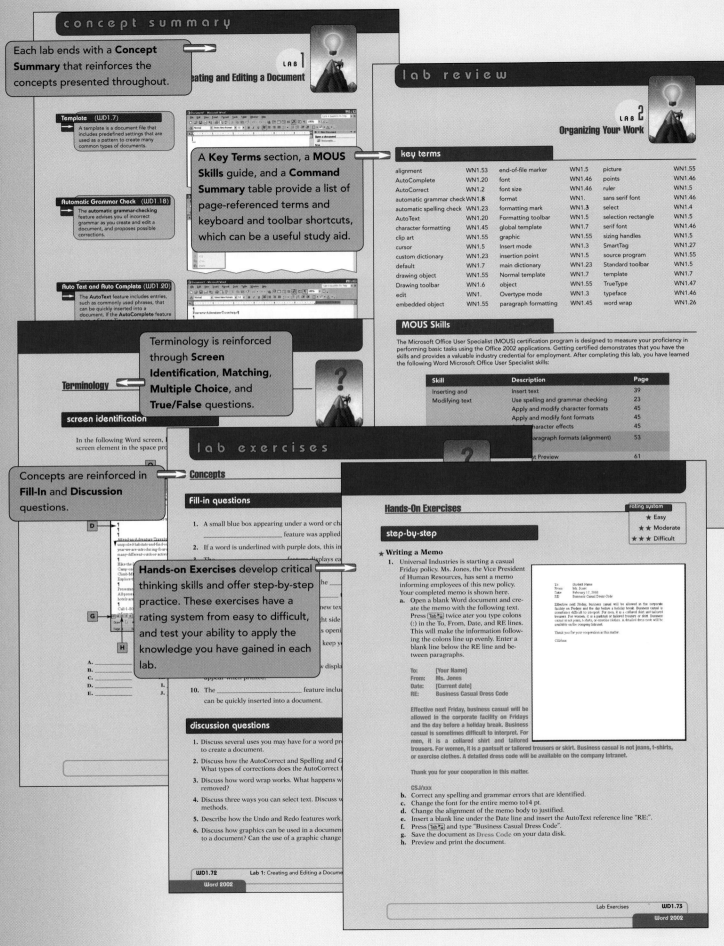

Introduction to Microsoft Office XP

What is Office XP?

Microsoft Office XP is a suite of applications that can be used individually and that are designed to work together seamlessly. The applications include tools used to create, discuss, communicate, and manage projects. If you share a lot of documents with other people, these features facilitate access to common documents. This version has expanded and refined the communication and collaboration features and integration with the World Wide Web. In addition, several new interface features are designed to make it easier to perform tasks and help users take advantage of all the features in the applications.

The Office XP suite is packaged in different combinations of components. The major components and a brief description are provided in the following table.

Component	Description
Word 2002	Word processor
Excel 2002	Spreadsheet
Access 2002	Database manager
PowerPoint 2002	Presentation graphics
Outlook 2002	Desktop information manager
FrontPage 2002	Web page authoring
Publisher	Desktop publishing
SharePoint	Team Web sites

The four main components of Office XP—Word, Excel, Access, and PowerPoint—are described in more detail in the following sections.

Word 2002

Word 2002 is a word processing software application whose purpose is to help you create text-based documents. Word processors are one of the most flexible and widely used application software programs. A word processor can be used to manipulate text data to produce a letter, a report, a memo, an e-mail, message or any other type of correspondence. Two documents you will produce in the first two Word labs, a letter and flyer, are shown here.

February 18, 2001

Dear Adventure Traveler,

Imagine hiking and paddling your way through the rain forests of Costa Rica, under the stars in Africa, or following in the footsteps of the ancient Inca as you backp the Inca trail to Machu Picchu. Turn these dreams of adventure into memories you w forever by joining Adventure Travel Tours on one of our four new adventure tours.

To tell you more about these exciting new adventures, we are offerin presentations in your area. These presentations will focus on the features and cultu region. We will also show you pictures of the places you will visit and activities participate in, as well as a detailed agenda and package costs. Plan on attending c following presentations:

Date	Time	Location	Room
January 5 ----- 7:00 PM ----------- Town Center Hotel ------- Room 284B
February 3 ---- 7:30 PM ----------- Airport Manor ------------- Conference Room A
March 8 ------- 7:00 PM ----------- Country Inn ---------------- Mountainside Room

In appreciation of your past patronage, we are pleased to offer you a 10% disco price of any of the new tour packages. You must book the trip at least 60 days pr departure date. Please turn in this letter to qualify for the discount.

Our vacation tours are professionally developed solely for your enjoyment. W almost everything in the price of your tour while giving you the best possible value dollar. All tours include:

- **Professional tour manager and local guides**
- **All accommodations and meals**
- **All entrance fees, excursions, transfers and tips**

We hope you will join us this year on another special Adventure Travel Tour Your memories of fascinating places and challenging physical adventures should li long, long time. For reservations, please see your travel agent, or contact Adventure Tra at 1-800-777-0004. You can also visit our new Web site at www.AdventureTravelTours

Best regards,

Student Name

A letter containing a tabbed table, indented paragraphs, and text enhancements is quickly created using basic Word features.

Announcing
New Adventure Travel Tours

This year we are introducing four new tours, offering you a unique opportunity to combine many different outdoor activities while exploring the world.

Hike the Inca trail to Machu Picchu
Camp on safari in Tanzania
Climb Mt. Kilimanjaro
Explore the Costa Rican rain forests

Attend an Adventure Travel presentation to learn about some of the earth's greatest unspoiled habitats and find out how you can experience the adventure of a lifetime.

Presentation dates and times are January 5 at 7 PM, February 3 at 7:30 PM, and March 8 at 7 PM. All presentations are held at convenient hotel locations located in downtown Los Angeles, Santa Clara and at the airport.

Call us at 1-800-777-0004 for presentation locations, a full color brochure, and itinerary information, costs, and tour dates.

Visit Our
Web site at
AdventureTravelTours.com

A flyer incorporating many visual enhancements such as colored text, varied text styles, and graphic elements is both eye-catching and informative.

The beauty of a word processor is that you can make changes or corrections as you are typing. Want to change a report from single spacing to double spacing? Alter the width of the margins? Delete some paragraphs and add others from yet another document? A word processor allows you to do all these things with ease.

Word 2002 includes many group collaboration features to help streamline how documents are developed and changed by group members. You can also create and send e-mail messages directly from within Word using all its features to create and edit the message. You can also send an entire document as your e-mail message, allowing the recipient to edit the document directly without having to open or save an attachment.

Word 2002 is also closely integrated with the World Wide Web, detecting when you type a Web address and automatically converting it to a hyperlink. You can also create your own hyperlinks to locations within documents, or to other documents, including those at external locations such as a Web site or file server. Its many Web-editing features, including a Web Page Wizard that guides you step by step, help you quickly create a Web page. You will see how easy it is when you create the Web page shown below in the Working Together tutorial.

A Web page created in Word and displayed in the Internet Explorer browser.

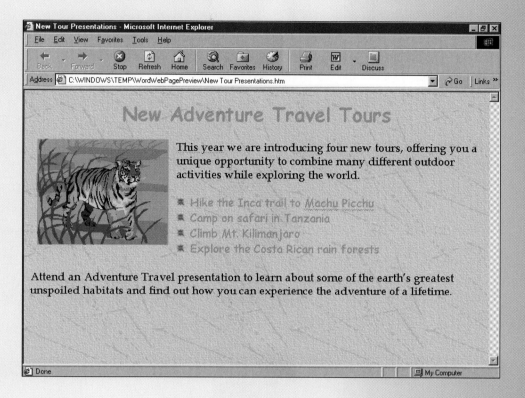

Excel 2002

Excel 2002 is an electronic worksheet that is used to organize, manipulate, and graph numeric data. Once used almost exclusively by accountants, worksheets are now widely used by nearly every profession. Marketing professionals record and evaluate sales trends. Teachers record grades and calculate final grades. Personal trainers record the progress of their clients. Excel includes many features that not only help you create a well-designed worksheet, but one that produces accurate results. Formatting features include visual enhancements such as varied text styles, colors, and graphics. Other features help you enter complex formulas and identify and correct formula errors. You can also produce a visual display of data in the form of graphs or charts. As the values in the worksheet change, charts referencing those values automatically adjust to reflect the changes.

Excel also includes many advanced features and tools that help you perform what-if analysis and create different scenarios. And like all Office XP applications, it is easy to incorporate data created in one application into another. Two worksheets you will produce in Labs 2 and 3 of Excel are shown here.

A worksheet showing the quarterly sales forecast containing a graphic, text enhancements, and a chart of the data is quickly created using basic Excel features.

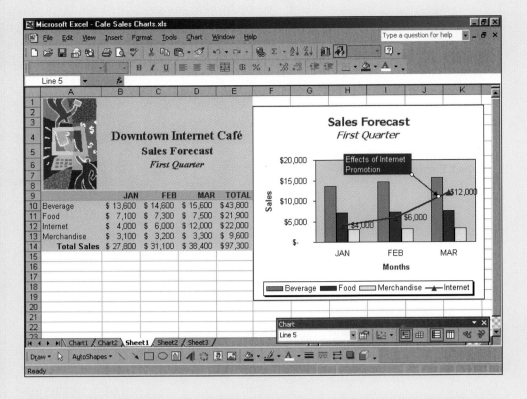

A large worksheet incorporating more complex formulas, visual enhancements such as colored text, varied text styles, and graphic elements is both informative and attractive.

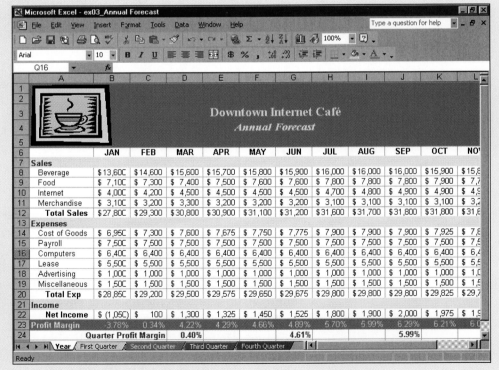

You will see how easy it is to analyze data and make projections using what-if analysis and what-if graphing in Lab 3 and to incorporate Excel data in a Word document as shown in the figures below.

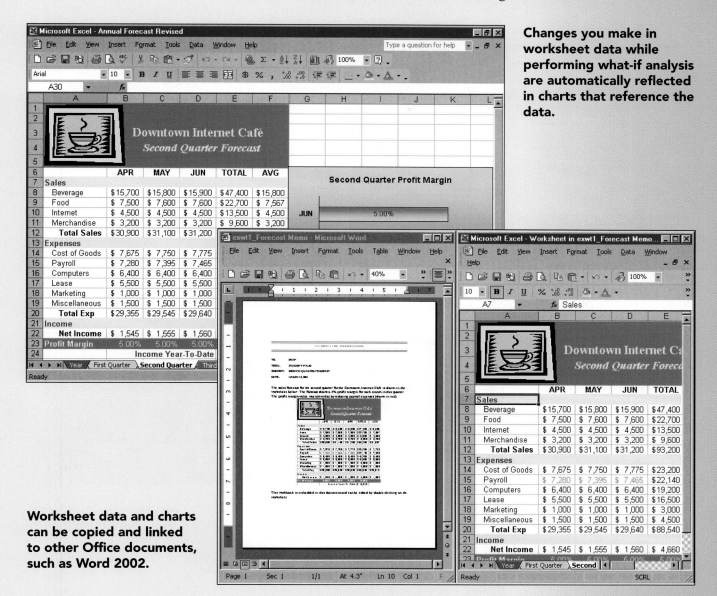

Changes you make in worksheet data while performing what-if analysis are automatically reflected in charts that reference the data.

Worksheet data and charts can be copied and linked to other Office documents, such as Word 2002.

Access 2002

Access 2002 is a relational database management application that is used to create and analyze a database. A database is a collection of related data. In a relational database, the most widely used database structure, data is organized in linked tables. Tables consist of columns (called fields) and rows (called records). The tables are related or linked to one another by a common field. Relational databases allow you to create smaller and more manageable database tables, since you can combine and extract data between tables.

The program provides tools to enter, edit, and retrieve data from the database as well as to analyze the database and produce reports of the output. One of the main advantages of a computerized database is the ability to quickly add, delete, and locate specific records. Records can also be easily rearranged or sorted according to different fields of data, resulting in multiple table arrangements that provide more meaningful information for different purposes. Creation of forms makes it easier to enter and edit data as well. In the Access labs you will create and organize the database table shown below.

A relational database can be created and modified easily using basic Access features.

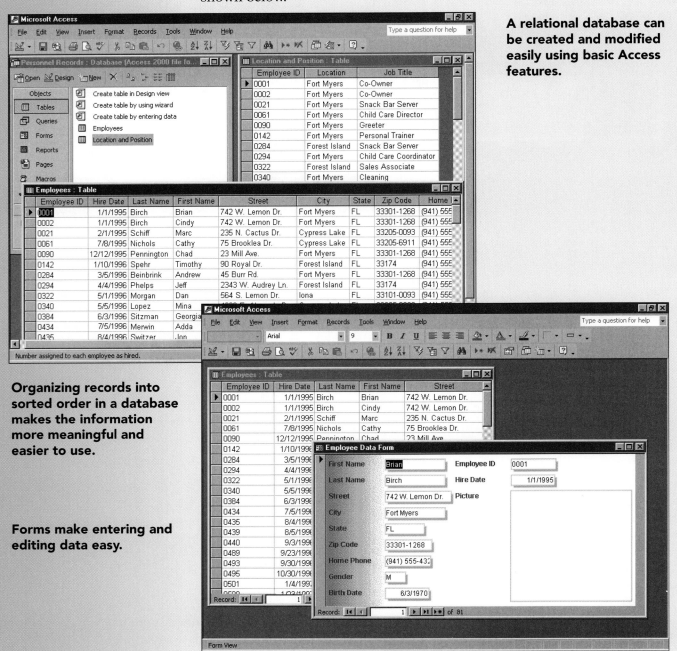

Organizing records into sorted order in a database makes the information more meaningful and easier to use.

Forms make entering and editing data easy.

Another feature is the ability to analyze the data in a table and perform calculations on different fields of data. Additionally, you can ask questions or query the table to find only certain records that meet specific conditions to be used in the analysis. Information that was once costly and time-consuming to get is now quickly and readily available. This information can then be quickly printed out in the form of reports ranging from simple listings to complex, professional-looking reports in different layout styles, or with titles, headings, subtotals, or totals.

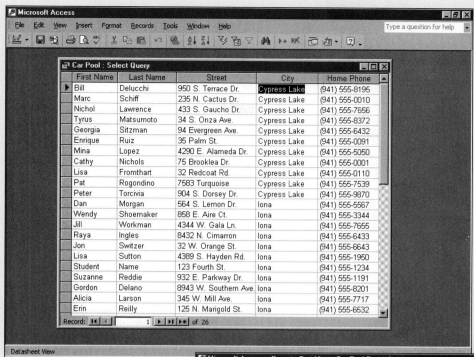

A database can be queried to locate and display only specified information.

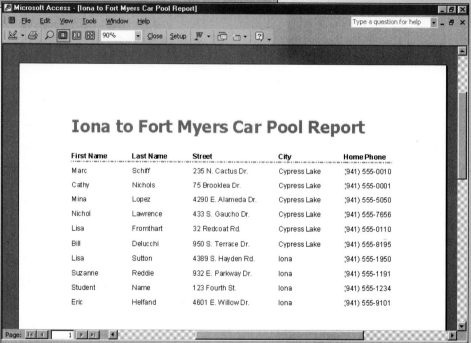

A professional-looking report can be quickly generated from information contained in a database.

PowerPoint 2002

PowerPoint 2002 is a graphics presentation program designed to help you produce a high-quality presentation that is both interesting to the audience and effective in its ability to convey your message. A presentation can be as simple as overhead transparencies or as sophisticated as an on-screen electronic display. In the first two PowerPoint labs you will create and organize the presentation shown on the next page.

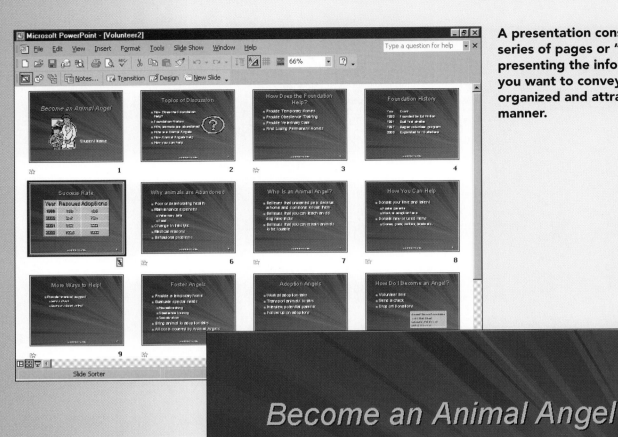

A presentation consists of a series of pages or "slides" presenting the information you want to convey in an organized and attractive manner.

When running an onscreen presentation, each slide of the presentation is displayed full-screen on your computer monitor or projected onto a screen.

Common Office XP Features

Now that you know a little about each of the applications in Microsoft Office XP, we will take a look at some of the features that are common to all Office applications. This is a hands-on section that will introduce you to the features and allow you to get a feel for how Office XP works. Although Word 2002 will be used to demonstrate how the features work, only common features will be addressed. These features include using menus, the Office Assistant and Office Help, task panes, toolbars, and starting and exiting an application. The features that are specific to each application will be introduced individually in each lab.

Starting an Office Application

There are several ways to start an Office application. One is to use the New Office Document command on the Start menu and select the type of document you want to create. Another is to use the Documents command on the Start menu and select the document name from the list of recently used documents. This starts the associated application and opens the selected document at the same time. The two most common ways to start an Office XP application are by choosing the application name from the Start menu or by clicking a desktop shortcut for the program if it is available.

① • Click **Start** to display the Start menu.

• Select Programs.

• Choose 📝 Microsoft Word.

or

① • Double-click the 📝 Microsoft Word shortcut on the desktop.

② • If necessary, click ☐ in the title bar to maximize the window.

Your screen should be similar to Figure 1

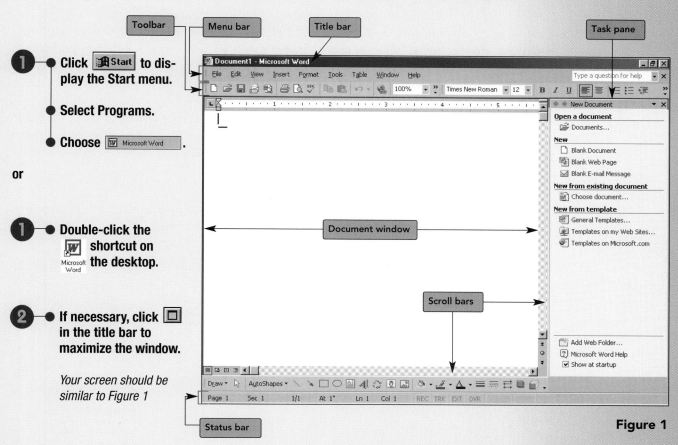

Figure 1

The Word program is started and displayed in a window on the desktop. The left end of the application window title bar displays the file name followed by the program name, Microsoft Word. The right end of the title bar displays the ☐ Minimize, ☐ Restore, and ☒ Close buttons. They perform the same functions and operate in the same way as in Windows 98 and 2000.

The **menu bar** below the title bar displays the application's program menu. The right end displays the document window's ☒ Close button. As you use the Office applications, you will see that the menu bar contains many of the same menus, such as File, Edit, and Help. You will also see several menus that are specific to each application.

The **toolbars** located below the menu bar contain buttons that are mouse shortcuts for many of the menu items. Commonly, the Office applications will display two toolbars when the application is first opened: Standard and Formatting. They may appear together on one row (as in Figure 1), or on separate rows.

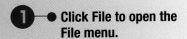
Use <u>V</u>iew/Tas<u>k</u> Pane to hide and display task panes.

The large center area of the program window is the **document window** where open application files are displayed. Currently, there is a blank Word document open. The **task pane** is displayed on the right side of the document window. Task panes provide quick access to features as you are using the application. As you perform certain actions, different task panes automatically open. In this case, since you just started an application, the New Document task pane is automatically displayed, providing different ways to create a new document or open an existing document.

The **status bar** at the bottom of the window displays location information and the status of different settings as they are used. Different information is displayed in the status bar for different applications.

On the right and bottom of the document window, are vertical and horizontal scroll bars. A **scroll bar** is used with a mouse to bring additional lines of information into view in a window. The vertical scroll bar is used to move up or down, and the horizontal scroll bar moves side to side in the window.

As you can see, many of the features in the Word window are the same as in other Windows applications. The common user interface makes learning and using new applications much easier.

Using Menus

A **menu** is one of many methods you can use to accomplish a task in a program. When opened, a menu displays a list of commands.

1 ● **Click File to open the File menu.**

Your screen should be similar to Figure 2

HAVING TROUBLE?
If Office is set to display full menus, your menu will look like that shown in Figure 3.

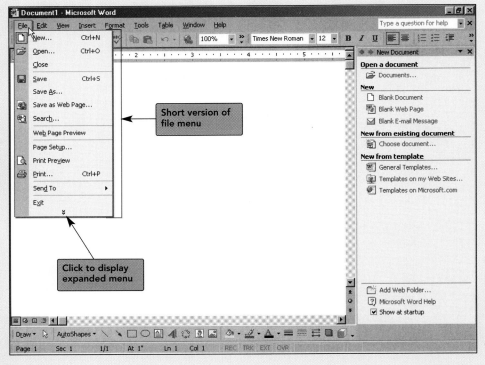

Figure 2

Additional Information
If you do not want to wait for the expanded menu to appear, you can click ✕ at the bottom of the menu or double-click the menu name to display the full menu immediately.

When an Office program menu is first opened, it may display a short version of commands. The short menu is a personalized version of the menu that displays basic and frequently used commands and hides those used less often. An expanded version will display automatically after the menu is open for a few seconds (see Figure 3).

Your screen should be similar to Figure 3

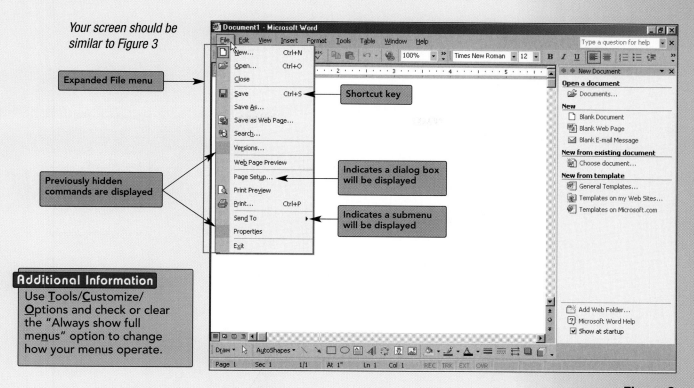

Expanded File menu

Previously hidden commands are displayed

Shortcut key

Indicates a dialog box will be displayed

Indicates a submenu will be displayed

Figure 3

When the menu is expanded the hidden commands are displayed. Once one menu is expanded, others are expanded automatically until you choose a command or perform another action.

2 • Point to each menu in the menu bar to see the full menu for each.

• Point to the File menu again.

Many commands have images next to them so you can quickly associate the command with the image. The same image appears on the toolbar button for that feature. Menus may include the following features (not all menus include all features):

Feature	Meaning
Ellipsis (...)	Indicates a dialog box will be displayed
▶	Indicates a submenu will be displayed
Dimmed	Indicates the command is not available for selection until certain other conditions are met
Shortcut key	A key or key combination that can be used to execute a command without using the menu
Checkmark	Indicates a toggle type of command. Selecting it turns the feature on or off. A checkmark indicates the feature is on.

Once a menu is open, you can select a command from the menu by pointing to it. A colored highlight bar, called the **selection cursor**, appears over the selected command.

3 ● **Point to the Send To command to select it and display the submenu.**

Your screen should be similar to Figure 4

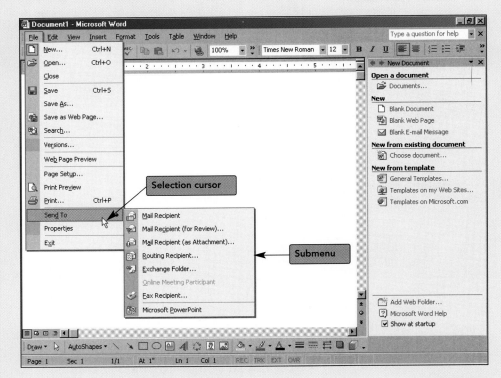

Figure 4

Then to choose a command, you click on it. When the command is chosen, the associated action is performed. You will use a command in the Help menu to access the Microsoft Office Assistant and Help features.

Note: If your screen displays the Office Assistant character as shown in Figure 5, skip step 4.

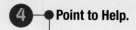

4 **Point to Help.**

Click Show the Office Assistant to choose the command.

Your screen should be similar to Figure 5

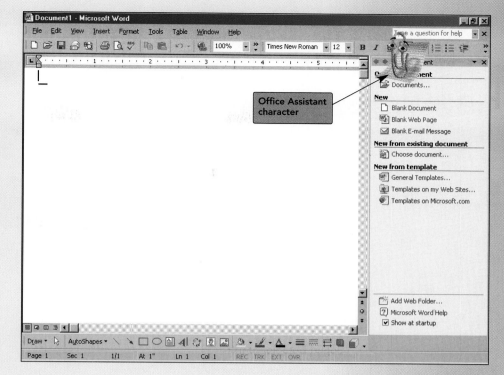

Office Assistant character

Figure 5

HAVING TROUBLE?

If the Assistant does not appear, this feature has been disabled. If this is the case, choose Help/Microsoft Word Help or press F1 and skip to the section "Using Help."

The command to display the Office Assistant has been executed, and the Office Assistant character is displayed. The default Assistant character is Clippit shown in Figure 5. Because there are eight different characters from which you can select, your screen may display a different Assistant character.

Using the Office Assistant

When the Office Assistant is on, it automatically suggests help topics as you work. It anticipates what you are going to do and then makes suggestions on how to perform a task. In addition, you can activate the Assistant at any time to get help on features in the Office application you are using. Clicking on the Assistant character activates it and displays a balloon in which you can type the topic you want help on. You will ask the Office Assistant to provide information on the different ways you can get help while using the program.

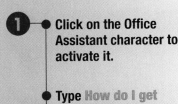

1 ● **Click on the Office Assistant character to activate it.**

● **Type** How do I get help? **in the text box.**

● **Click** Search .

Another Method

You could also press ←Enter to begin the search.

Your screen should be similar to Figure 6

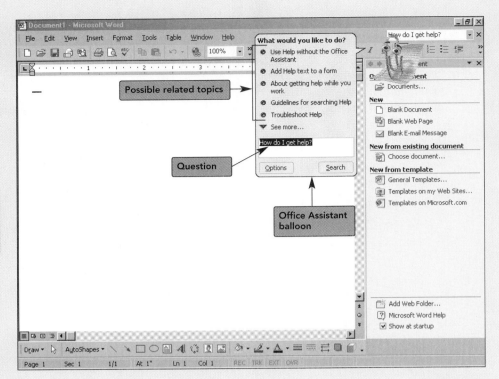

Figure 6

The balloon displays a list of related topics from which you can select.

2 ● **Select "About getting help while you work."**

Additional Information

Clicking See more... displays additional topics.

Your screen should be similar to Figure 7

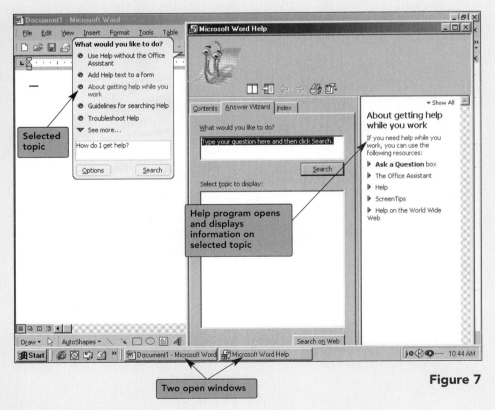

Figure 7

Another Method

You can also choose <u>H</u>elp/Microsoft Word <u>H</u>elp, or click 🔲 or press F1 to start Help.

The Help program opens and displays the selected topic. Because Word Help is a separate program within Office, it appears in its own window. The Help window overlaps the Word window so that it is easy to read the information in Help while referring to the application window. The taskbar displays a button for both open windows.

Now that Help is open, you no longer need to see the Assistant. To access commands to control the Office Assistant, you will display the object's shortcut menu by right-clicking on the Assistant character. **Shortcut menus** display the most common menu options related to the selected item only.

3 ● Right-click the Assistant to display the shortcut menu.

● Choose Options.

● Click **U**se the Office Assistant to clear the option.

● Click [OK].

● Click 🔲 to maximize the Help window.

● If necessary, click ◁▤ to display the Tabs frame.

Your screen should be similar to Figure 8

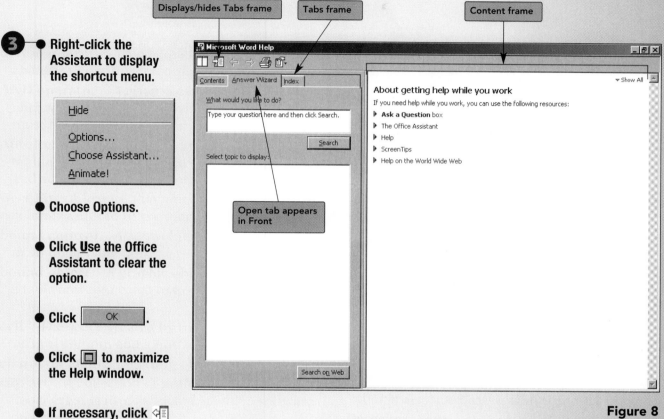

Figure 8

Using Help

In the Help window, the toolbar buttons help you use different Help features and navigate in Help.

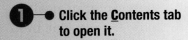

Additional Information

You can drag the frame divider line to adjust the width of the frames. When the Tab frame is too narrow ◄ and ► appear to scroll the tabs into view.

The Help window is divided into two vertical frames. **Frames** divide a window into separate, scrollable areas that can display different information. The left frame in the Help window is the Tabs frame. It contains three folder-like tabs, Contents, Answer Wizard, and Search, that provide three different means of getting Help information. The open tab appears in front of the other tabs and displays the available options for the feature. The right frame is the content frame where the content for the selected topic is displayed.

1 ● **Click the Contents tab to open it.**

HAVING TROUBLE?

If you cannot see the Contents tab, click the ◄ tab scroll button to bring it into view.

Your screen should be similar to Figure 9

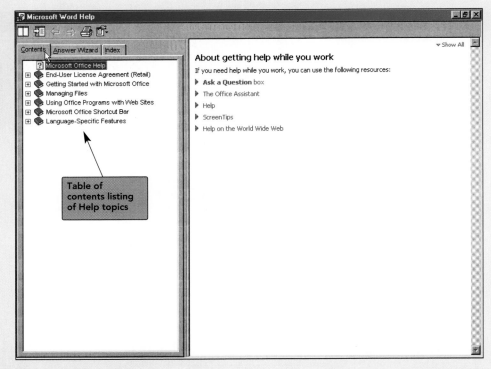

Figure 9

Using the Contents Tab

The Contents tab displays a table of contents listing of topics in Help. Clicking on an item preceded with a ⊞ opens a "chapter," which expands to display additional chapters or specific Help topics.

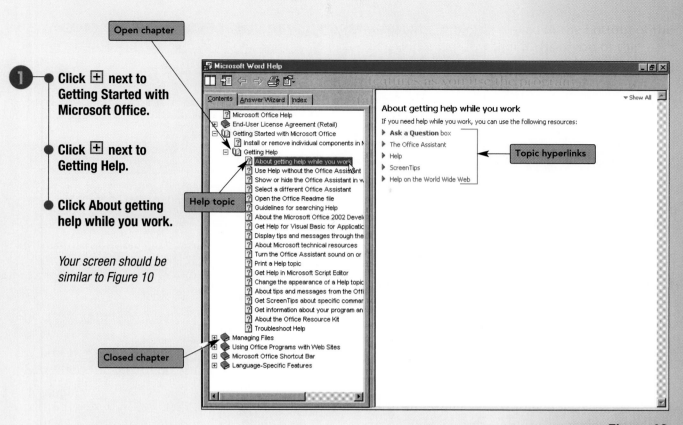

Figure 10

You have opened two chapters and selected a Help topic. Open chapters are preceded with a 📖 icon and topics with a ❓ icon.

Using a Hyperlink

The Help topic tells you about five resources you can use to get help. Each resource is a **hyperlink** or connection to additional information in the current document, in online Help, or on the Microsoft Office Web site. It commonly appears as colored or underlined text. Clicking the hyperlink accesses and displays the information associated with the hyperlink. A hyperlink preceded with a ▶ indicates clicking the link will display additional information about the topic.

1 ● **Click the "Ask a Question box" hyperlink.**

● **Click the "The Office Assistant" hyperlink.**

Your screen should be similar to Figure 11

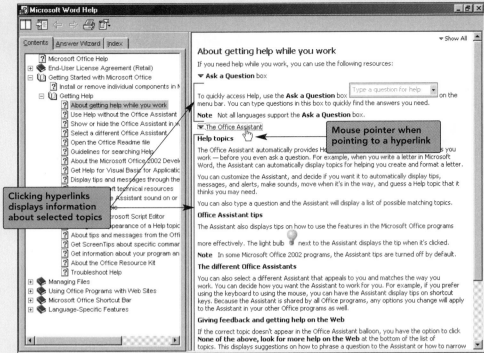

Figure 11

Additional Information

Clicking the scroll arrows scrolls the text in the frame line by line, and dragging the scroll box up or down the scroll bar moves to a general location within the frame area.

The content frame displays additional information about the two selected topics. Now, because there is more information in the content frame than can be displayed at one time, you will need to use the vertical scroll bar to scroll the additional information into the frame as you read the Help information. Also, as you are reading help, you may see text that appears as a hyperlink. Clicking on the text will display a definition of a term.

2 ● **Using the scroll bar, scroll the content frame to read the information on this topic.**

● **Click the "shortcut keys" hyperlink.**

Your screen should be similar to Figure 12

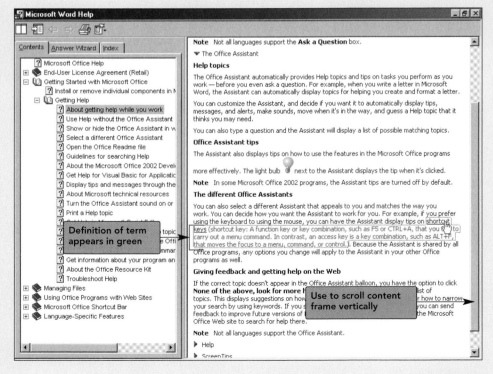

Figure 12

Scrolling the frame displays the information at the bottom of the frame while the information at the top of the frame is no longer visible. The end of the Help information is displayed in the frame. A definition of the term "shortcut keys" is displayed in green text.

3 ● **Click on the definition to clear it.**

● **Click on the Use Help without the Office Assistant topic in the Contents tab.**

Additional Information

Pointing to a topic in the content frame that is not fully visible displays the full topic in a ScreenTip box.

Your screen should be similar to Figure 13

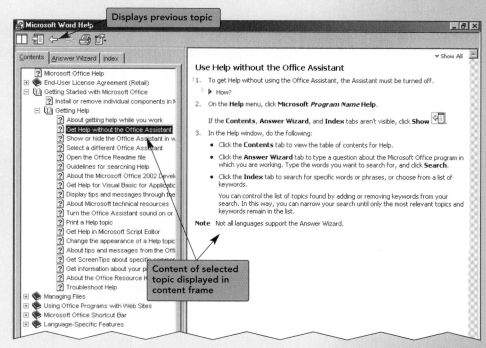

Figure 13

The content frame now displays the Help information about the selected topic. To quickly return to the previous topic,

4 ● **Click ⇦ Back.**

Your screen should be similar to Figure 14

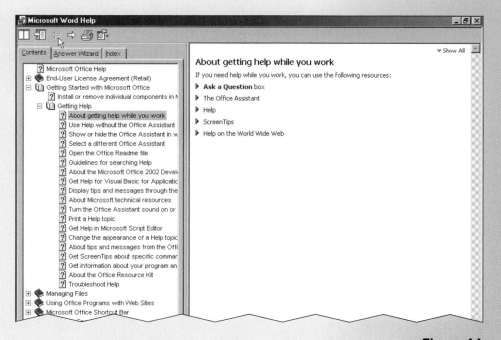

Figure 14

The topic is redisplayed as it originally appeared, without the topic selections expanded.

Using the Index Tab

To search for Help information by entering a word or phrase for a topic, you can use the Index tab.

1 ● **Open the Index tab.**

HAVING TROUBLE?
If the Index tab is not visible in the frame, click the ▶ scroll button to display it.

Your screen should be similar to Figure 15

Enter word or phrase to locate

Alphabetical list of keywords

Open tab

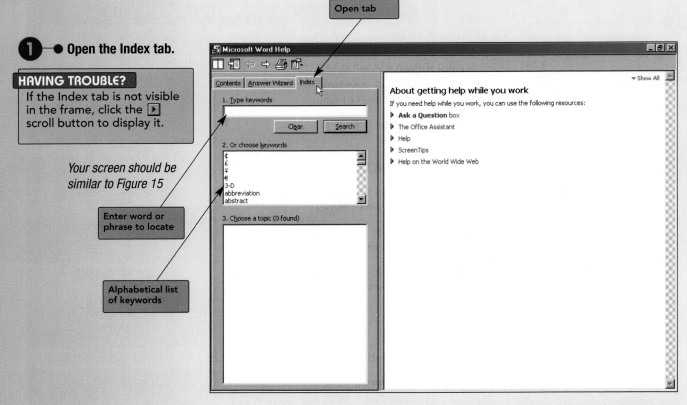

Figure 15

The Index tab consists of a text box where you can type a word or phrase that best describes the topic you want to locate. Below it is a list box displaying a complete list of Help keywords in alphabetical order. You want to find information about using the Index tab.

2

● Type **index** in the text box.

● Click [Search].

Your screen should be similar to Figure 16

19 Help topics containing keyword "index"

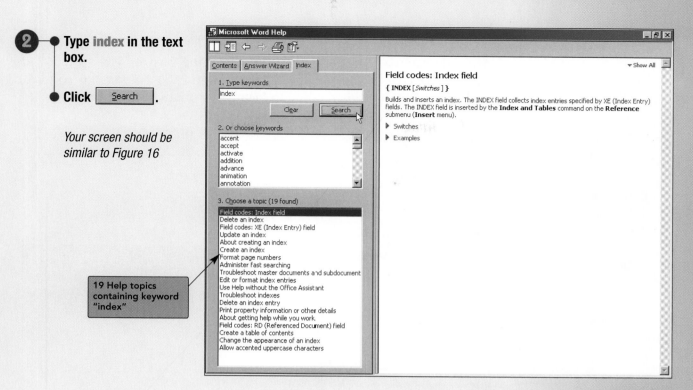

Figure 16

The topic list displays 19 Help topics containing this word, and the content frame, displays the information on the first topic. However, many of the located topics are not about the Help Index feature. To narrow the search more, you can add another word to the keyword text box.

3

● Click in the text box.

● Type **help** following the word "index."

● Click [Search].

Your screen should be similar to Figure 17

Two topics contain both keywords

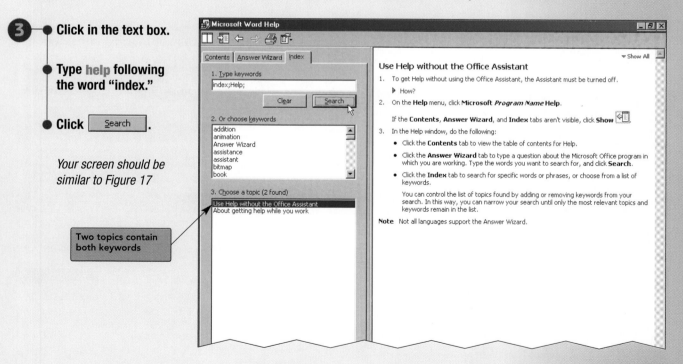

Figure 17

Now only two topics were located that contain both keywords. The first topic in the list is selected and displayed in the content frame.

Using the Answer Wizard

Another way to locate Help topics is to use the Answer Wizard tab. This feature works just like the Office Assistant and the Answer box to locate topics. You will use this method to locate information on toolbars.

1 ● **Open the Answer Wizard tab.**

● **Type** How do I use toolbars? **in the text box.**

● **Click** Search .

Your screen should be similar to Figure 18

Topics related to your search

Additional Information
The search term does not need to be worded as a question. It can also be a word or phrase.

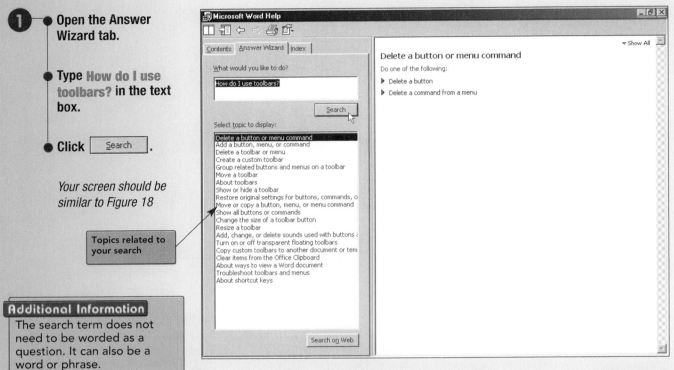

Figure 18

The topic list box displays all topics that the Answer Wizard considers may be related to the question you entered.

2 ● **Select "About toolbars" from the topic list.**

● **Click Show All.**

Your screen should be similar to Figure 19

Selected topic

Selected topic is displayed in Content frame

Displays/hides all topic information

Topic information fully displayed

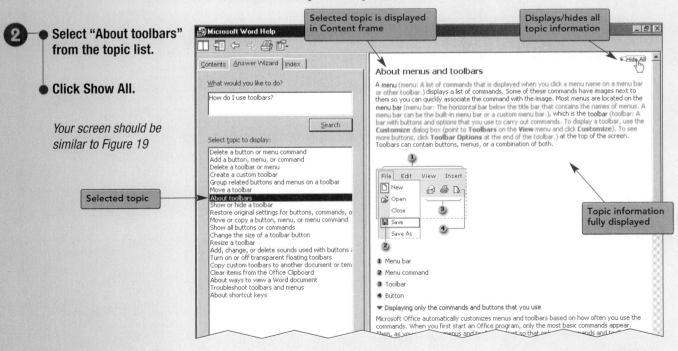

Figure 19

All topics are expanded and definitions displayed.

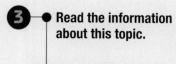

Read the information about this topic.

Click ⊠ to close Help.

Your screen should be similar to Figure 20

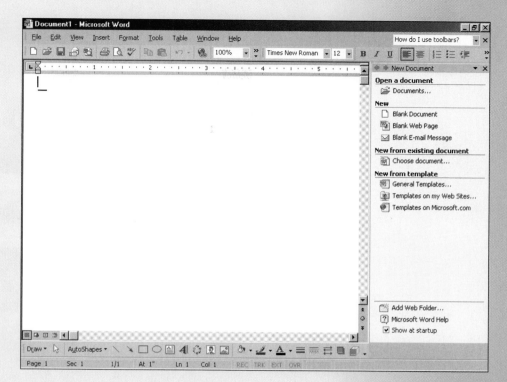

Figure 20

The Help window is closed, and the Word window is displayed again.

HAVING TROUBLE?

Your system must have an Internet connection to access the Microsoft Office Web site. If you do not have that, skip this section.

Getting Help on the Web

A final source of Help information is the Microsoft Office Web site. If a Help topic begins with "Web," clicking it takes you to the Web site and displays the topic in your Help window. You can also connect directly to this site from any Office application using the Help menu.

1 • Choose **H**elp/Office on the **W**eb.

• If necessary, enter your user information and make the appropriate selections to connect to the Internet.

• If necessary, click United States.

Your screen should be similar to Figure 21

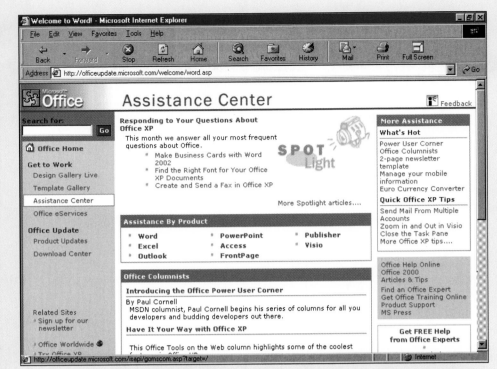

Figure 21

The browser application on your system is started and displays the Microsoft Office Web site. Now you could select any of the hyperlinks to further explore the site.

2 • Read the information on this page.

• Click ☒ Close to close the browser.

• If necessary, disconnect from the Internet.

The Word application window is displayed again.

Using Toolbars

While using Office XP, you will see that many toolbars open automatically as different tasks are performed. Toolbars initially display the basic buttons. Like menus, they are personalized automatically, displaying those buttons you use frequently and hiding others. The More Buttons ⯆ button located at the end of a toolbar displays a drop-down button list of those buttons that are not displayed. When you use a button from this list, it then is moved to the toolbar, and a button that has not been used recently is moved to the More Buttons list.

Initially, Word displays two toolbars, Standard and Formatting, on one row below the menu bar (see Figure 22). The Standard toolbar contains buttons that are used to complete the most frequently used menu commands. The Formatting toolbar contains buttons that are used to change the appearance or format of the document.

HAVING TROUBLE?
Your screen may display different toolbars in different locations. This is because the program displays the settings that were in effect when it was last exited.

1 ● **Right-click on any toolbar to display the shortcut menu.**

Your screen should be similar to Figure 22

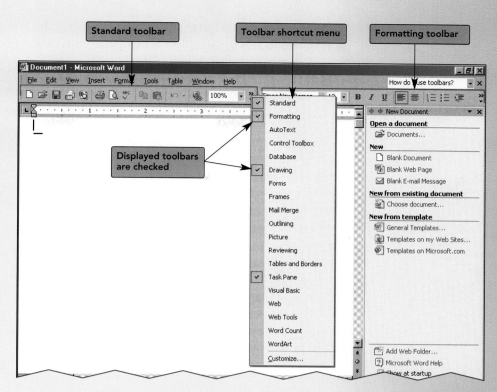

Standard toolbar

Toolbar shortcut menu

Formatting toolbar

Displayed toolbars are checked

Figure 22

The toolbar shortcut menu displays a list of toolbar names. The Formatting, Standard, and Task Pane options should be checked, indicating they are displayed. Clicking on a toolbar from the list will display it on-screen. Clicking on a checked toolbar will hide the toolbar.

2 ● **Click Task Pane to clear the checkmark.**

Your screen should be similar to Figure 23

Docked toolbars display move handle

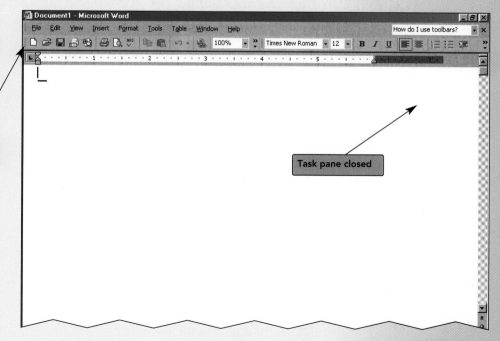

Task pane closed

Figure 23

The task pane is closed. When a toolbar is open, it may appear docked or floating. A docked toolbar is fixed to an edge of the window and displays a vertical bar ‖ called the move handle, on the left edge of the toolbar. Dragging this bar up or down allows you to move the toolbar. If multiple toolbars share the same row, dragging the bar left or right adjusts the size of the toolbar. If docked, a toolbar can occupy a row by itself, or several can be on a row together. A floating toolbar appears in a separate window.

3 ● Drag the move handle of the Standard toolbar into the document window.

Another Method

You can also double-click the top or bottom edge of a docked toolbar to change it to a floating toolbar.

Your screen should be similar to Figure 24

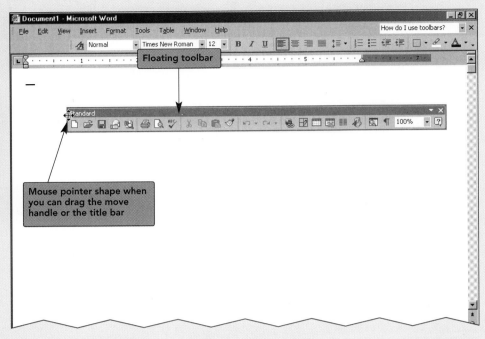

Figure 24

The Standard toolbar is now floating and can be moved to any location in the window by dragging the title bar. If you move it to the edge of the window, it will attach to that location and become a docked toolbar. A floating toolbar can also be sized by dragging the edge of toolbar.

4 ● Drag the title bar of the floating toolbar to move it to the row below the Formatting toolbar.

● Move the Formatting toolbar below the Standard toolbar.

Your screen should be similar to Figure 25

Additional Information

You can permanently display the toolbars on two rows using **T**ools/**C**ustomize/**O**ptions or by choosing **C**ustomize/**O**ptions from the toolbar shortcut menu and selecting "Show Standard and Formatting toolbars on two rows."

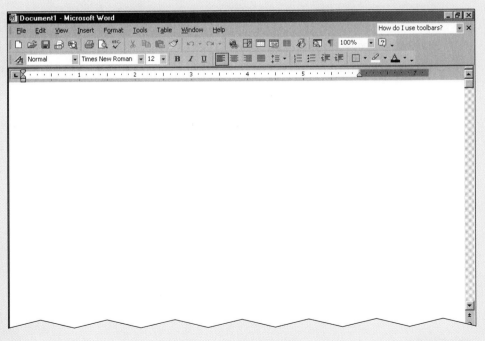

Figure 25

The two toolbars now occupy two rows. To quickly identify the toolbar buttons, you can display the button name by pointing to the button.

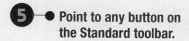

Point to any button on the Standard toolbar.

Your screen should be similar to Figure 26

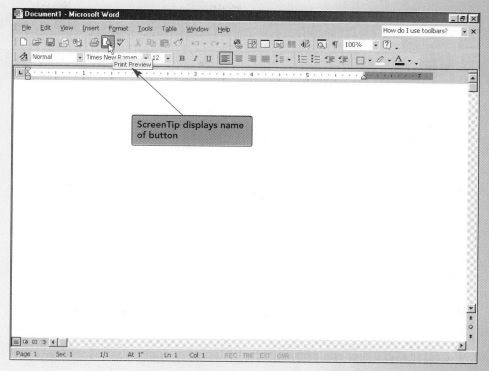

ScreenTip displays name of button

Figure 26

A ScreenTip containing the button name appears next to the mouse pointer.

Exiting an Office Application

The Exit command on the File menu can be used to quit most Windows programs. Alternatively, you can click the ☒ Close button in the program window title bar.

Click ☒ Close.

The program window is closed and the desktop is visible again.

lab review

Starting an Office Application

key terms

document window   I.10
frame   I.16
hyperlink   I.17
menu   I.10
menu bar   I.9
scroll bar   I.10
selection cursor   I.12
shortcut menu   I.15
status bar   I.10
task pane   I.10
toolbar   I.9

command summary

Command	Shortcut	Button	Action
⊞Start /Programs			Opens program menu
File/E**x**it	Alt + F4		Exits Office program
View/**T**oolbars			Hides or displays toolbars
View/Tas**k** Pane			Hides or displays task pane
Tools/**C**ustomize/**O**ptions			Changes settings associated with toolbars and menus
Help/Microsoft Word **H**elp	F1	?	Opens Help window
Help/Show the **O**ffice Assistant			Displays Office Assistant

Overview to Microsoft Access 2002

What Is a Database?

Somewhere at home, or maybe in your office, you probably have a file cabinet or desk drawer filled with information. Perhaps you have organized the information into drawers of related information, and further categorized that information into file folders. This is a database.

As organized as you might be, it takes time to locate a specific piece of information by manually opening drawers and searching through the folders. You can just imagine how much time would be required for a large company to manually search through its massive amounts of data. These companies use electronic database management systems. Now you too can use electronic database management systems to store, organize, access, manipulate, and present information in a variety of ways.

In this series of labs you will learn how to design and create a computerized database using Access 2002 and you will quickly appreciate the many advantages of a computerized database.

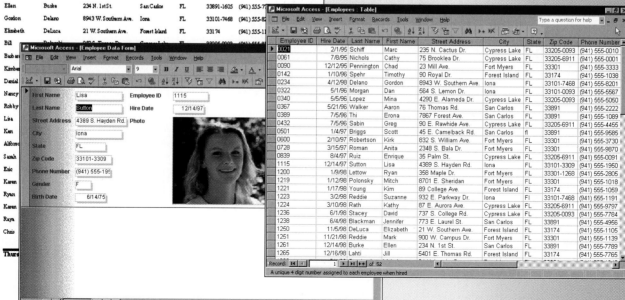

Access 2002 Features

Access 2002 is a relational database management system. In relational database systems, data is organized in tables that are related or linked to one another. Each table consists of rows, called records, and columns, called fields.

For example, a state's motor vehicle department database might have an address table. Each row (record) in the table would contain address information about one individual. Each column (field) would contain just one piece of information, for example, zip codes. The address table would be linked to other tables in the database by common fields. For example, the address table might be linked to a vehicle owner's table by name and linked to an outstanding citation table by license number (see example below).

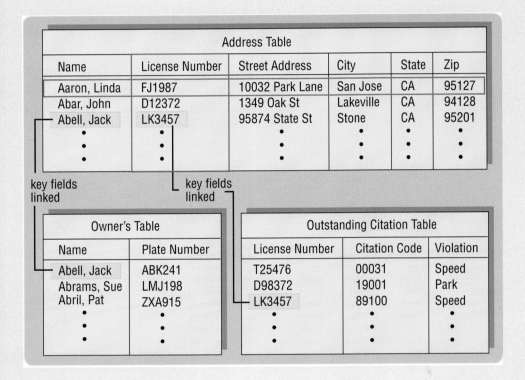

Address Table

Name	License Number	Street Address	City	State	Zip
Aaron, Linda	FJ1987	10032 Park Lane	San Jose	CA	95127
Abar, John	D12372	1349 Oak St	Lakeville	CA	94128
Abell, Jack	LK3457	95874 State St	Stone	CA	95201

key fields linked

key fields linked

Owner's Table

Name	Plate Number
Abell, Jack	ABK241
Abrams, Sue	LMJ198
Abril, Pat	ZXA915

Outstanding Citation Table

License Number	Citation Code	Violation
T25476	00031	Speed
D98372	19001	Park
LK3457	89100	Speed

Access 2002 is a powerful program with numerous easy-to-use features including the ability to quickly locate information, add, delete, modify and sort records, analyze data, and produce professional-looking reports. Some of the basic Access 2002 features are described next.

Find Information

Once you enter data into the database table, you can quickly search the table to locate a specific record based on the data in a field. In a manual system, you can usually locate a record by knowing one key piece of information. For example, if the records are stored in a file cabinet alphabetically by last name, to quickly find a record you must know the last name. In a computerized database, even if the records are sorted or organized by last name, you can still quickly locate a record using information in another field.

Add, Delete, and Modify Records

Using Access, it is also easy to add and delete records from the table. Once you locate a record, you can edit the contents of the fields to update the record or delete the record entirely from the table. You can also add new records to a table. When you enter a new record, it is automatically placed in the correct organizational location within the table.

Sort Records

The capability to arrange or sort records in the table according to different field can provide more meaningful information. You can organize records by name, department, pay, class, or any other category you need at a particular time. Sorting the records in different ways can provide information to different departments for different purposes.

Analyze Data

Using Access, you can analyze the data in a table and perform calculations on different fields of data. Instead of pulling each record from a filing cabinet, recording the piece of data you want to use, and then performing the calculation on the recorded data, you can simply have the database program perform the calculation on all the values in the specified field. Additionally, you can ask questions or query the table to find only certain records that meet specific conditions to be used in the analysis. Information that was once costly and time-consuming to get is now quickly and readily available.

Generate Reports

Access includes many features that help you quickly produce reports ranging from simple listings to complex, professional-looking reports. You can create a simple report by asking for a listing of specified fields of data and restricting the listing to records meeting designated conditions. You can create a more complex professional report using the same restrictions or conditions as the simple report, but you can display the data in different layout styles, or with titles, headings, subtotals, or totals.

Case Study for Labs 1–3

You have recently accepted a job as employment administrator for Lifestyle Fitness Club. The club has recently purchased Microsoft Access 2002, and you are using it to update their manual system for recording employee information.

Lab 1: You will learn how to design and create the structure for a computerized database and how to enter and edit records in the database. You will also print a simple report of the records you enter in the database file.

Lab 2: You will continue to build, modify, and use the employee database of records. You will learn how to sort the records in a database file to make it easier to locate records. Additionally, you will create a form to make it easier to enter and edit data in the database file.

Lab 3: You will learn how to query the database to locate specific information. You will also learn how to create a report and link multiple tables.

Working Together: You will learn how to share information between applications by incorporating database information from Access into a Word memo.

Before You Begin

To the Student

The following assumptions have been made:

- Microsoft Access 2002 has been properly installed on the hard disk of your computer system.
- The data files needed to complete the series of labs and practice exercises are supplied by your instructor.
- You have completed the O'Leary Series Windows 98 or 2000 modules or you are already familiar with how to use Windows and a mouse.

To the Instructor

It is assumed that the complete version of the program has been installed prior to students using the labs. In addition, please be aware that the following settings are assumed to be in effect for the Access 2002 program. These assumptions are necessary so that the screens and directions in the manual are accurate.

- The New File Task Pane is displayed on startup (use Tools/Options/View).
- The status bar is displayed (use Tools/Options/View).
- The New Object shortcuts are displayed in the Object list (use Tools/Options/View).
- The Database toolbar is displayed (use Tools/Customize/Options).
- Full menus are always displayed (use Tools/Customize/Options).
- The ScreenTips feature is active (use Tools/Customize/Options).
- The Office Assistant feature is not on (click on the Assistant, click [Options], and clear the Use the Office Assistant option).
- All default datasheet settings are in effect, including font settings of Arial 10 pt.

In addition, all figures in the manual reflect the use of a standard VGA display monitor set at 800 by 600. If another monitor setting is used, there may be more or fewer lines displayed in the windows than in the figures. This setting can be changed using Windows setup.

Microsoft Office Shortcut Bar

The Microsoft Office Shortcut Bar (shown below) may be displayed automatically on the Windows desktop. Commonly, it appears in the right side of the desktop; however, it may appear in other locations, depending upon your setup. The Shortcut Bar on your screen may display different buttons. This is because the Shortcut Bar can be customized to display other toolbar buttons.

The Office Shortcut Bar makes it easy to open existing documents or to create new documents using one of the Microsoft Office applications. It can also be used to send e-mail, add a task to a to-do list, schedule appointments using Schedule[+], or access Office Help.

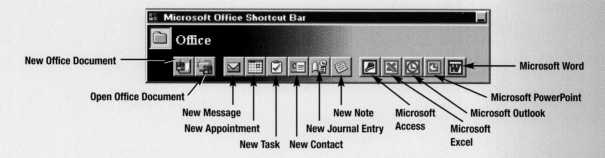

Instructional Conventions

Hands-on instructions you are to perform appear as a sequence of numbered steps. Within each step, a series of bullets identifies the specific actions that must be performed. Step numbering begins over within each topic heading throughout the lab.

Command sequences you are to issue appear following the word "Choose." Each menu command selection is separated by a /. If the menu command can be selected by typing a letter of the command, the letter will appear underlined and bold. Items that need to be highlighted will follow the word "Select." You can select items with the mouse or directional keys. (See Example A.)

Example A

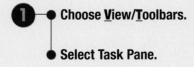

1 ● Choose **V**iew/**T**oolbars.

● Select Task Pane.

Commands that can be initiated using a button and the mouse appear following the word "Click." The icon (and the icon name if the icon does not include text) is displayed following "Click." The menu equivalent and keyboard shortcut appear in a margin note when the action is first introduced. (See Example B.)

Example B

1 ● Click  Open.

Another Method

The menu equivalent is
File/Open and the keyboard
shortcut is Ctrl + O.

Plain blue text identifies file names you need to open. Information you are asked to type appears in blue and bold. (See Example C.)

Example C

1 ● Click  Open.

● **Select** Employee Records.

● **Move to a new blank record.**

● **Type** Smith.

The O'Leary Series

Microsoft®
Access 2002

Brief Edition

Creating a Database

LAB 1

objectives

After completing this lab, you will know how to:

1.	Plan and create a database.
2.	Create a table.
3.	Define field names, data types, field properties, and primary key fields.
4.	Save the table structure.
5.	Change views.
6.	Enter and edit data in Datasheet view and Data Entry.
7.	Insert a picture.
8.	Adjust column widths.
9.	Use the Best Fit feature.
10.	Delete records.
11.	Preview and print a table.
12.	Change page orientation.
13.	Close and open a table and database.

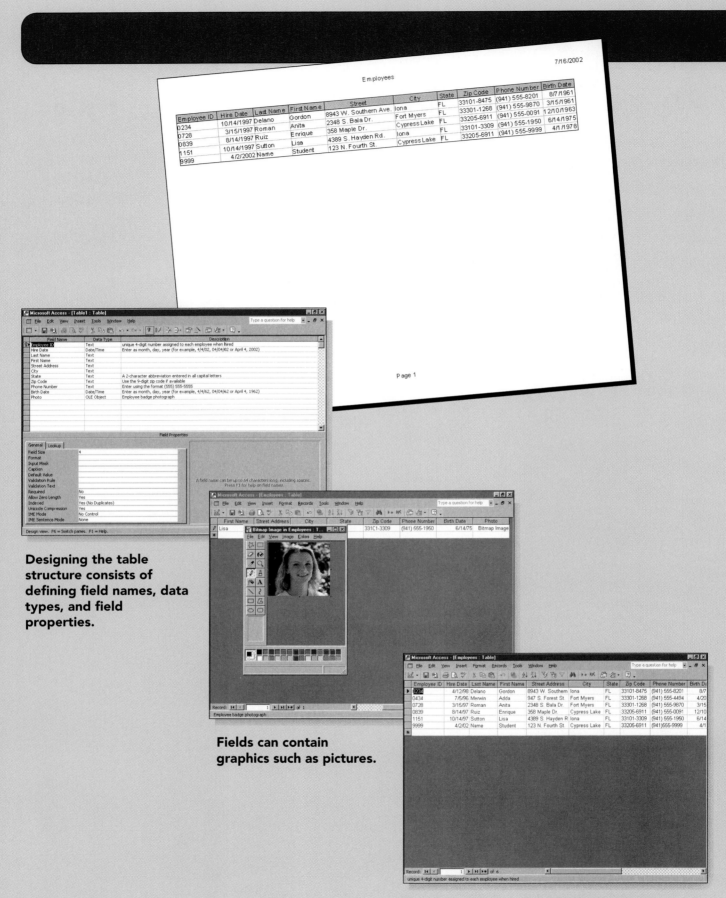

Designing the table structure consists of defining field names, data types, and field properties.

Fields can contain graphics such as pictures.

Entering data in a table creates records of information.

Lifestyle Fitness Club

You have recently accepted a new job as employment administrator with Lifestyle Fitness Club. Like many fitness centers, Lifestyle Fitness Club includes exercise equipment, free weights, aerobic classes, tanning and massage facilities, swimming pool, steam room and sauna, and child care facilities. In addition, they promote a healthy lifestyle by including educational seminars on good nutrition and proper exercise. They also have a small snack bar that serves healthy drinks, sandwiches, and snacks.

The Lifestyle Fitness Clubs are a franchised chain of clubs that are individually owned. You work at a club owned by Brian and Tami Birch, who also own two others in Florida. Accounting and employment functions for all three clubs are handled centrally at the Fort Myers location.

You are responsible for maintaining the employment records for

all employees, as well as records for traditional employment activities such as hiring and benefits. Currently the Club employment records are maintained on paper forms and stored in file cabinets organized alphabetically by last name. Although the information is well organized, it still takes time to manually leaf through the folders to locate the information you need and to compile reports from this data.

The Club has recently purchased new computers, and the owners want to update the employee record-keeping system to an electronic database management system. The software tool you will use to create the database is the database application Microsoft Access 2002. In this lab, you will learn about entering, editing, previewing, and printing a database while you create it and a table of basic employee information.

© Corbis

1	**Database**	A database is an organized collection of related information. Typically, the information in a database is stored in a table consisting of vertical columns and horizontal rows.
2	**Object**	An object is an item, such as a table or report, that can be created, selected, and manipulated as a unit.
3	**Field Name**	A field name is used to identify the data stored in the field.
4	**Data Type**	The data type defines the type of data the field will contain.
5	**Field Property**	A field property is a characteristic that helps define a field. A set of field properties is associated with each field.
6	**Primary Key**	A primary key is a field that uniquely identifies each record.
7	**Graphic**	A graphic is a non-text element or object, such as a drawing or picture, which can be added to a table.
8	**Column Width**	Column width refers to the size of a field column in a datasheet. It controls the amount of data you can see on the screen.

Introducing Access 2002

The Lifestyle Fitness Club recently purchased the Microsoft Office XP application software suite. You are very excited to learn how to use this new and powerful application to store and maintain the club's records.

Starting Access

You will use the Access database management program to create several different databases of information.

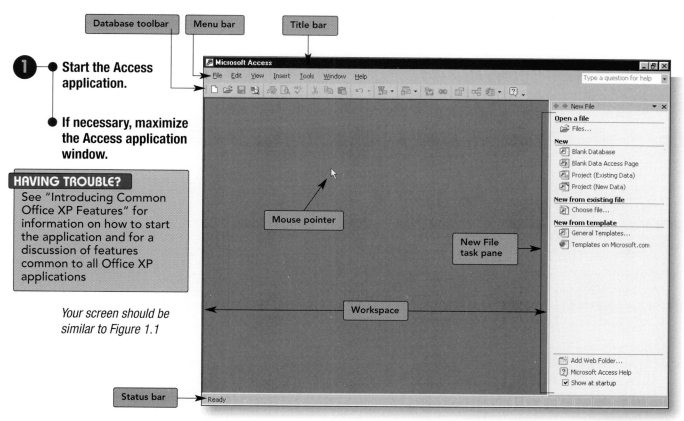

Figure 1.1

1 ● Start the Access application.

● If necessary, maximize the Access application window.

HAVING TROUBLE?
See "Introducing Common Office XP Features" for information on how to start the application and for a discussion of features common to all Office XP applications

Your screen should be similar to Figure 1.1

HAVING TROUBLE?
If your screen looks slightly different, this is because Access remembers settings that were on when the program was last used.

HAVING TROUBLE?
If the New File task pane is not displayed, choose View/Toolbars/Task Pane.

Another Method
The File/New command or the keyboard shortcut Ctrl + N also opens the New File task pane.

The Access application window, with the New File task pane open in it, is displayed.

Exploring the Access Window

The menu bar below the title bar displays the Access program menu. It consists of seven menus that provide access to the commands and features you will use to create and modify a database. The menus and commands that are available at any time vary with the task you are performing.

Toolbars, normally located below the menu bar, contain buttons that are mouse shortcuts for many of the menu items. Access uses many different toolbars. Most toolbars appear automatically as you perform different tasks and open different windows. The **Database toolbar** is initially displayed and contains buttons that are used to access basic database features. Your screen may display other toolbars if they were on when the program was last exited.

The task pane is displayed on the right side of the window. Different task panes are displayed depending on the task being performed. Because you just started Access, the New File task pane is automatically displayed, providing different ways to create a new database file or open an existing file.

The large area to the left of the task pane is the **workspace**, where different Access windows are displayed as you are using the program. Just below the workspace, the status bar provides information about the task you are working on and the current Access operation. In addition, the status bar displays messages such as instructions to help you use the program more efficiently.

The mouse pointer appears as ▷ on your screen. The mouse pointer changes shape depending upon the task you are performing or where the pointer is located on the window.

Creating a New Database

The Lifestyle Fitness Club plans to use Access 2002 to maintain several different types of databases.

---

concept 1

Databasse

1 A **database** is an organized collection of related information. Typically, the information in a database is stored in a **table** consisting of vertical columns and horizontal rows. Each row contains a **record**, which is all the information about one person, thing, or place. Each column is a **field**, which is the smallest unit of information about a record. Access databases can contain multiple tables that can be linked to produce combined output form all tables. This type of database is called a **relational database**. See the "Overview to Access 2002" for more information about relational databases.

The database you will create will contain information about each Club employee. Other plans for using Access include keeping track of members and inventory. To keep the different types of information separate, the club plans to create a database for each group.

Creating a new database follows several basic steps: plan, create, enter and edit, and preview and print.

Step	Description
Plan	The first step in the development of a database is to understand the purpose of the database.
Create	After planning the database, you create tables to hold data by defining the table structure.
Enter and Edit	After setting up the table, you enter the data to complete each record. While entering data, you may make typing and entry errors that need to be corrected. This is one type of editing. Another is to revise the structure of the tables by adding, deleting, or redefining information in the table.
Preview and Print	The last step is to print a hard copy of the database or report. This step includes previewing the document onscreen as it will appear when printed. Previewing enables you to check the document's overall appearance and to make any final changes needed before printing.

You will find that you will generally follow these steps in order as you create your database. However, you will probably retrace steps as the final database is developed.

Planning a Database

Your first step is to plan the design of your database tables: how many tables, what data they will contain, and how they will be related. You need to decide what information each table in the employee database should contain and how it should be structured or laid out.

You can obtain this information by analyzing the current record-keeping procedures used throughout the company. You need to understand the existing procedures so your database tables will reflect the information that is maintained by different departments. You should be aware of the forms that are the basis for the data entered into the department records, and of the information that is taken from the records to produce periodic reports. You also need to find out what information the department heads would like to be able to obtain from the database that may be too difficult to generate using their current procedures.

After looking over the existing record-keeping procedures and the reports that are created from the information, you decide to create several separate tables of data in the database file. Creating several smaller tables of related data rather than one large table makes it easier to use the tables and faster to process data. This is because you can join several tables together as needed.

The main table will include the employee's basic information, such as employee number, name, birth date, and address. Another will contain work location information only. A third will contain data on pay rate and hours worked each week. To clarify the organization of the database, you sketched out the structure for the employee database as shown below.

Employee Database

Employee Table

Emp #	Last Name	First Name	Street	City	State	Zipcode	Phone	Birth Date
7721	Brown	Linda	—	—	—	—	—	—
7823	Duggan	Michael	—	—	—	—	—	—
⋮	⋮	⋮	⋮	⋮	⋮	⋮	⋮	⋮

link on common field

link on common field

Location

Emp #	Location
7721	Iona
7823	Fort Myers
⋮	⋮

Pay Rate

Emp #	Pay	Hours
7721	8.25	30
7823	7.50	20
⋮	⋮	⋮

Creating and Naming the Database File

Now that you have decided on the information you want to include in the tables, you are ready to create a new database to hold the table information.

1 ● **Click**  **in the New File task pane.**

Your screen should be similar to Figure 1.2

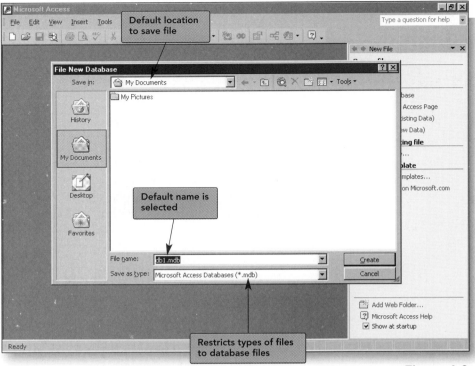

Figure 1.2

The File New Database dialog box is displayed. The first step is to specify a name for the database file and the location where you want the file saved. By default, Access opens the My Documents folder as the location to save the file. The file list section of the dialog box displays the names of folders and database files in the default location. Only database file names are displayed because the file type is restricted to Access Databases in the Save As Type text box. The default file name db1 appears in the File Name text box. You want the program to store the database on your data disk using the name Lifestyle Fitness Employees. Notice that the default name is highlighted, indicating it is selected and will be replaced as you type the new name.

2 **Type** Lifestyle Fitness Employees.

Additional Information

Windows files can have up to 215 characters in the file name. Names can contain letters, numbers, and spaces; the symbols \, /, ?, :, *, ", <, > cannot be used. The file name can be entered in either uppercase or lowercase letters and will appear exactly as you type it.

Your screen should be similar to Figure 1.3

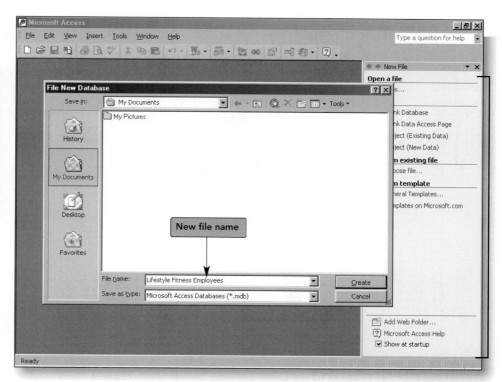

Figure 1.3

Additional Information

You can also click the ⬅ button in the toolbar to return to folders that were previously opened during the current session.

The default file name is replaced with the new file name. Next you need to change the location to the appropriate location for your data files. You can do this by selecting the location from the Save In drop-down list or from the icons in the Places bar along the left side of the dialog box. The icons bring up a list of recently accessed files and folders (History), the contents of the My Documents and Favorites folders, and the Windows Desktop. When you select a folder from one of these lists, the display changes to that location.

3 **Open the Save In list box and change the Save In location to the appropriate drive for your system.**

Your screen should be similar to Figure 1.4

HAVING TROUBLE?

If your screen does not display the extensions, your Windows program has this option deactivated.

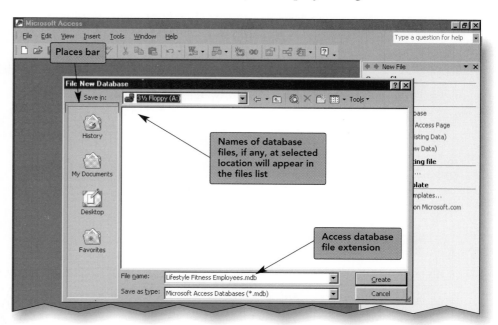

Figure 1.4

Now the file list section displays the names of all Access files on your data disk. Notice that the program added the .mdb file extension to the file name. This is the default extension for Access database files.

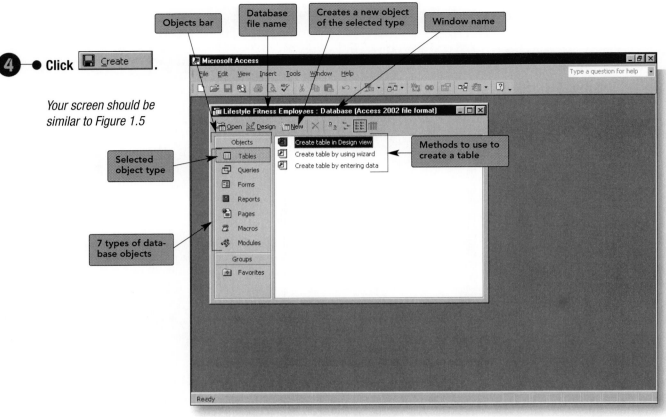

Figure 1.5

The Database window opens in the workspace and displays the name of the database, Lifestyle Fitness Employees, followed by the name of the window in the window title bar.

Creating a Table

The Database window is used to help you quickly create, open, or manage database objects.

concept 2

Object

2 An Access database is made up of several types of **objects**, such as a table or report, consisting of many elements. An object can be created, selected, and manipulated as a unit. The database objects are described below.

Object	Use
Table	Stores data
Query	Finds and displays selected data
Form	View, add, and update data in tables
Report	Analyze and print data in a specific layout

The table object is the basic unit of a database and must be created first, before any other types of objects are created. Access displays each different type of object in its own window. You can display multiple object windows in the workspace; however, you cannot open more than one database file at a time.

The Objects bar along the left edge of the Database window organizes the database objects into object types and groups, and is used to quickly access the different database objects. The currently selected object is Tables. The object list box to the right of the object bar displays three ways you can create a table. It will also display the names of objects of the selected object type once they are created.

After naming the database, your next step is to create the new table to hold the employee information by defining the structure of the table.

1 Click  .

Your screen should be similar to Figure 1.6

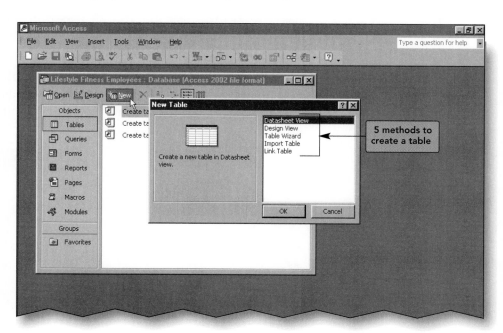

Figure 1.6

The New Table dialog box provides five different ways to create a table. The first three, Datasheet View, Design View, and Table Wizard, are the most commonly used. They are the same three methods that are listed in the object list box. The Datasheet and Design View options open different windows in which you can create a new custom table from scratch. The Table Wizard option starts the Table Wizard feature, which lets you select from predesigned database tables. The Wizard then guides you through the steps to create a table for you based upon your selections.

You will use the Design View option to create the table.

2
- Select Design View.

- Click ⬚ OK ⬚.

- If necessary, click 🔲 in the Table window title box to maximize the window.

Your screen should be similar to Figure 1.7

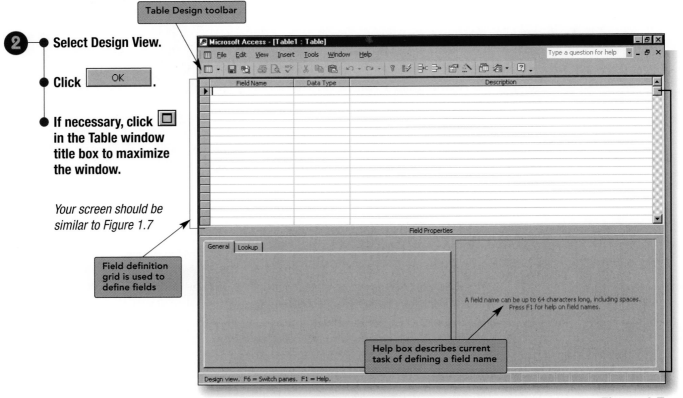

Figure 1.7

The Table Design window is opened and displayed over the Database window in the workspace. This window also has its own toolbar, the Table Design toolbar, which contains the standard buttons as well as buttons that are specific to this window.

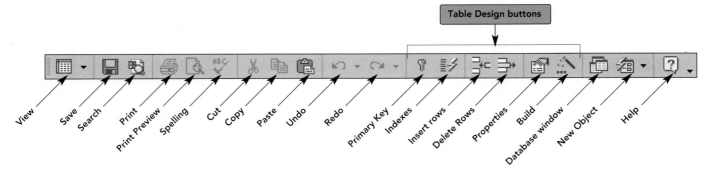

The upper section of the table Design window consists of a field definition grid where you define each field to include in the table. Each row in the grid is where a field is defined by entering the required information in each of the columns.

Defining Field Names

You decide to include the data currently maintained in the personnel folder on each employee in one table using the following 11 fields: Employee Number, Date Hired, Last Name, First Name, Street, City, State, Zip Code, Phone Number, Birth Date, and Picture. The first step is to give each field a field name.

concept 3

Field Name

3   A **field name** is used to identify the data stored in the field. A field name should be descriptive of the contents of the data to be entered in the field. It can be up to 64 characters long and can consist of letters, numbers, spaces, and special characters, except a period, an exclamation point, an accent grave (`), and brackets ([]). You also cannot start a field name with a space. Examples of field names are: Last Name, First Name, Address, Phone Number, Department, Hire Date, or other words that describe the data. It is best to use short field names to make the tables easier to manage.

In the lower right section of the table Design window, a Help box provides information on the task you are performing in the window. Because the insertion point is positioned in the Field Name text box, the Help box displays a brief description of the rules for entering a valid field name.

The first field of data you will enter in the table is the employee number, which is assigned to each employee when hired. Each new employee is given the next consecutive number, so no two employees can have the same number. It is a maximum of four digits. The ▶ to the left of the first row indicates the current field.

1 Type **Employee Number**.

Additional Information

The field name can be typed in uppercase or lowercase letters. It will be displayed in your database table exactly as you enter it.

Your screen should be similar to Figure 1.8

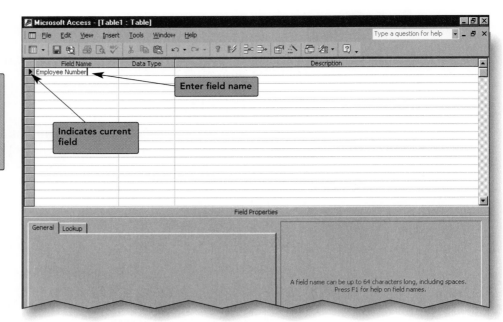

Enter field name

Indicates current field

Figure 1.8

You realize that "Employee ID" is the more common term used on company forms, so you decide to use this as the field name instead. To change the field name, you will edit the entry.

2 Press Backspace 6 times to delete the word "Number" (until only "Employee" and a space following it remain).

Another Method

You can also select (highlight by dragging or double-clicking on a word) the word "Number" and press the Delete key to erase it.

● Type **ID**.

● Press ←Enter.

Another Method

Using the Tab ⇥ or → key has the same effect as pressing ←Enter. It stores any entered data and moves the insertion point to the next column to the right. Pressing ⇧Shift + Tab ⇥ or ← moves the insertion point to the left one column.

Your screen should be similar to Figure 1.9

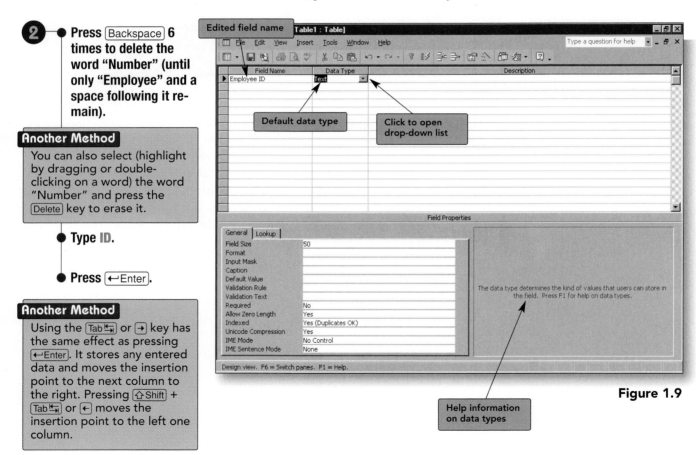

Edited field name

Default data type

Click to open drop-down list

Help information on data types

Figure 1.9

The insertion point has moved to the Data Type column, where the default data type of Text is automatically entered.

Defining Data Types

You know that the Employee ID will always be a number, so you decide to check out what other options there are for the Data Type field.

1 ● Click  to open the Data Type drop-down menu.

Your screen should be similar to Figure 1.10

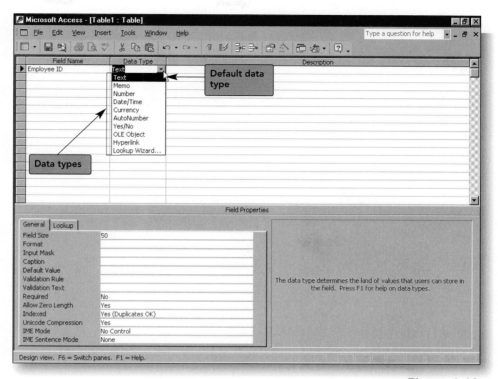

Figure 1.10

Data Type

4 The **data type** defines the type of data the field will contain. Access uses the data type to ensure that the right kind of data is entered in a field. It is important to choose the right data type for a field before you start entering data in the table. You can change a data type after the field con- tains data, but if the data types are not com- patible, such as a text entry in a field whose data type accepts numbers only, you may lose data. The data types are described in the fol- lowing table.

Data Type	Description
Text	Text entries (words, combinations of words and numbers, numbers that are not used in calculations) up to 255 characters in length. Names and phone numbers are examples of Text field entries. Text is the default data type.
Memo	Text that is variable in length and usually too long to be stored in a Text field. A maximum of 65,535 characters can be entered in a Memo field.
Number	Digits only. Number fields are used when you want to perform calculations on the values in the field. Number of Units Ordered is an example of a Number field entry.
Date/Time	Any valid date. Access allows dates from January 1, 100 to December 31, 9999. Access correctly handles leap years and checks all dates for validity.
Currency	Same as the Number field, but formatted to display decimal places and a currency symbol.
AutoNumber	A unique, sequential number that is automatically incremented by one when- ever a new record is added to a table. Once a number is assigned to a record, it can never be used again, even if the record is deleted.
Yes/No	Accepts only Yes or No, True or False, and On or Off entries.
OLE Object	An object, such as a graphic (picture), sound, document, or spreadsheet, that is linked to or embedded in a table.
Hyperlink	Accepts hyperlink entries that are paths to an object, document, Web page, or other destinations.
Lookup Wizard	Creates a Lookup field where you can enter a value or choose from a list of values from another table or query.

Even though a field such as the Employee ID field may contain numeric entries, unless the numbers are used in calculations, the field should be assigned the Text data type. This allows other characters, such as the parentheses or hyphens in a telephone number, to be included in the entry. Also, by specifying the type as Text, any leading zeros (for example, in the zip code 07739) will be preserved, whereas leading zeros in a Number type field are dropped (which would make this zip code incorrectly 7739).

2 ● Click ▼ to close the Data Type drop-down menu without changing the selection.

Another Method

You can also press Esc to close the menu.

Your screen should be similar to Figure 1.11

Default field properties for a Text data type

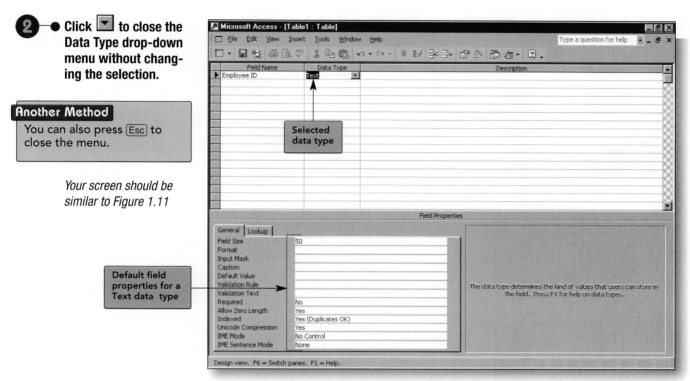

Figure 1.11

Defining Field Properties

In the Field Properties area of the dialog box, the General tab displays the default field property settings associated with the current data type (which in this case is Text).

concept 4

4   A **field property** is a characteristic that helps define a field. A set of field properties is associated with each field. Each data type has a different set of field properties. Setting field properties enhances the way your table works. Some of the more commonly used properties and their functions are described in the following table.

Field Property	Description
Field Size	Sets the maximum number of characters that can be entered in the field.
Format	Specifies how data displays in a table and prints.
Input Mask	Simplifies data entry by controlling what data is required in a field and how the data is to be displayed.
Caption	Specifies a field label other than the field name.
Default Value	Automatically fills in a certain value for this field in new records as you add to the table. You can override a default value by typing a new value into the field.
Validation Rule	Limits data entered in a field to values that meet certain requirements.
Validation Text	Specifies the message to be displayed when the associated Validation Rule is not satisfied.
Required	Specifies whether or not a value must be entered in a field.
Allow Zero Length	Specifies whether or not an entry containing no characters is valid.
Indexed	Sets a field as an index field (a field that controls the order of records). This speeds up searches on fields that are searched frequently.

First, you need to set the **field size** for the Employee ID field. By default, Access sets a Text field size to 50. Although Access uses only the amount of storage space necessary for the text you actually store in a Text field, setting the field size to the smallest possible size can decrease the processing time required by the program. Additionally, if the field data to be entered is a specific size, setting the field size to that number restricts the entry to the maximum number.

Since the employee ID will never be more than four digits long, you want to change the field size from the default of 50 to 4.

1 Click the **Field Size property** text box.

Another Method

You can also press the F6 key to switch between the upper and lower areas of the Table Design window.

● Double-click on **50** to select it.

● Type **4** to replace the default entry.

Your screen should be similar to Figure 1.12

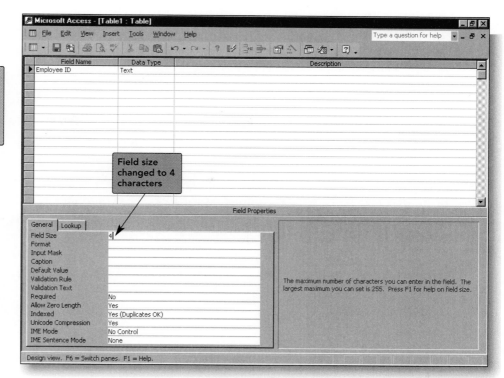

Field size changed to 4 characters

The maximum number of characters you can enter in the field. The largest maximum you can set is 255. Press F1 for help on field size.

Figure 1.12

Entering a Field Description

To continue defining the Employee ID field, you will enter a description of the field in the Description text box. Although it is optional, a field description makes the table easier to understand and update because the description is displayed in the status bar when you enter data into the table.

1 Click the **Description** text box for the Employee ID field.

● Type **A unique 4-digit number assigned to each employee when hired.**

Additional Information

The Description box scrolls horizontally as necessary to accommodate the length of the text entry.

Your screen should be similar to Figure 1.13

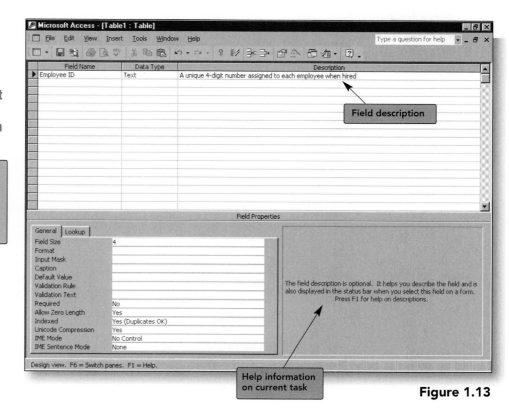

Field description

The field description is optional. It helps you describe the field and is also displayed in the status bar when you select this field on a form. Press F1 for help on descriptions.

Help information on current task

Figure 1.13

Defining a Primary Key Field

Next you want to make the Employee ID field a primary key field.

1 — ● Click  Primary Key.

Another Method
The menu equivalent is Edit/Primary Key.

Your screen should be similar to Figure 1.14

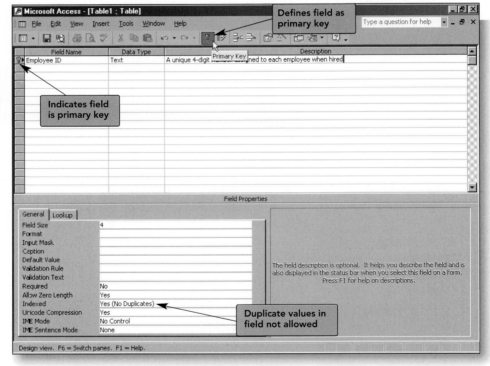

Figure 1.14

The icon appears in the column to the left of the field name, showing that this field is a primary key field. Now that this is the primary key field, the Indexed property setting has changed to Yes (No Duplicates). This setting prohibits duplicate values in a field.

Defining Additional Fields

The second field will display the date the employee started working at Lifestyle Fitness Club in the form of month/day/year.

1
- Press the ⏎Enter, Tab↹, or → key to move to the next row.

- Type **Hire Date**.

- Press ⏎Enter, Tab↹, or →.

- Select the Date/Time data type from the drop-down menu.

Another Method
You can also enter the data type by typing the first character of the type you want to use. For example, if you type D, the Date/Time data type will be automatically selected and displayed in the field.

Your screen should be similar to Figure 1.15

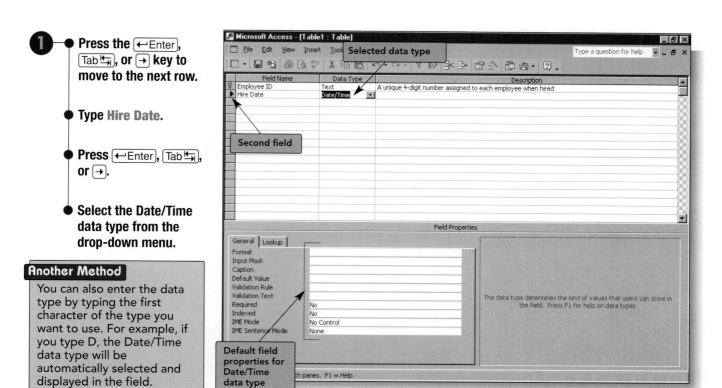

Figure 1.15

The default field properties for the selected data type are displayed. This time you want to change the format of the field so that the date will display as mm/dd/yyyy, regardless of how it is entered.

2
- Click in the Format property box.

- Click ▼ to open the drop-down list of Format options.

Your screen should be similar to Figure 1.16

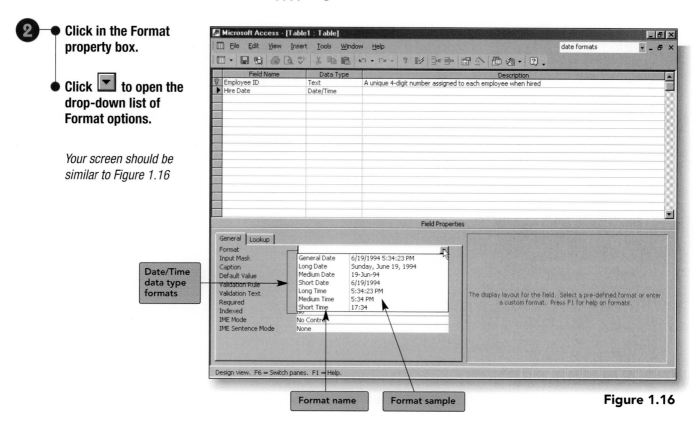

Figure 1.16

The names of the seven predefined layouts for the Date/Time field type are displayed in the list. An example of each layout appears to the right of the name. The General Date format is the default format. It displays dates using the Short Date format. If a time value is entered it will also display the time in the Long Time format.

3 ● **Choose General Date.**

● **In the Description text box of the Date Hired field, enter the following description: Enter as month, day, year (for example, 4/4/02, 04/04/02 or April 4, 2002).**

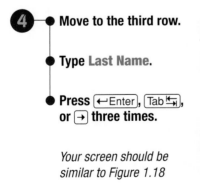

Additional Information

Access automatically assumes the first two digits of a year entry. If you enter a year that is between /30 and /99, Access reads this as a twentieth-century date (1930 to 1999). A year entry between /00 and /29 is assumed to be a twenty-first century date (2000 to 2029).

Your screen should be similar to Figure 1.17

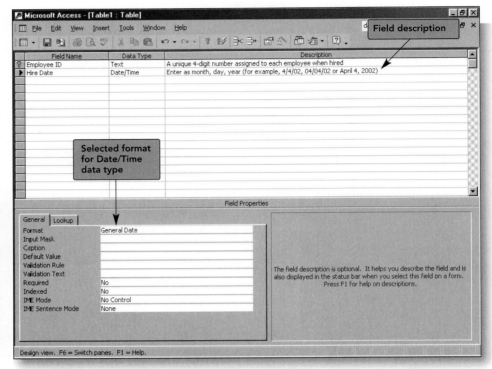

Figure 1.17

The third field is a Text field type that will contain the employee's last name. Because the field name is descriptive of the field contents, a description is not needed.

4 ● **Move to the third row.**

● **Type Last Name.**

● **Press** ⏎Enter, Tab↹, **or** → **three times.**

Your screen should be similar to Figure 1.18

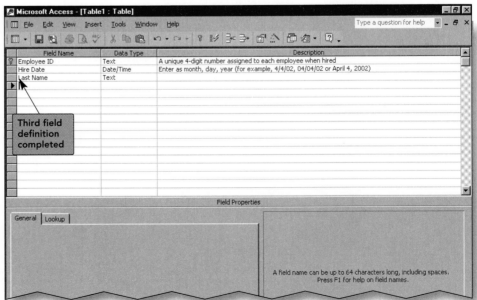

Figure 1.18

5 ● In the same manner, enter the information shown in the table on the right for the next eight fields.

HAVING TROUBLE?

If you make a typing mistake, use [Backspace] and [Delete] to correct errors.

When you have completed the eight additional fields, your field definition grid should be similar to Figure 1.19

Field Name	Data Type	Description	Field Size/ Format
First Name	Text		50
Street Address	Text		50
City	Text		50
State	Text	A 2-character abbreviation entered in all capital letters	2
Zip Code	Text	Use the 9-digit zip code if available	10
Phone Number	Text	Enter using the format (555) 555-5555	15
Birth Date	Date/Time	Enter as month, day, year (for example, 4/4/62, 04/04/62 or April 4, 1962)	General Date
Photo	OLE object	Employee badge photograph	

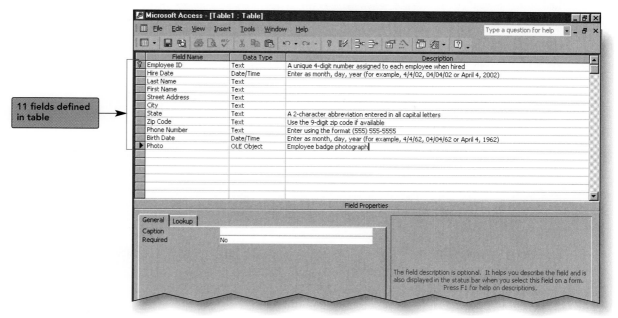

11 fields defined in table

Figure 1.19

Editing Field Definitions

After looking over the fields, you decide to change the field sizes of the Last Name, First Name, and City fields to 20-character entries. Positioning the insertion point in any column of a field will display the properties for that field.

1 • Move to any column in the Last Name field.

• Change the field size to **20**.

• In a similar manner, change the field size for the First Name and City fields to **20**.

• Carefully check your field definition grid to ensure that each field name and field type was entered accurately and make any necessary corrections.

Your screen should be similar to Figure 1.20

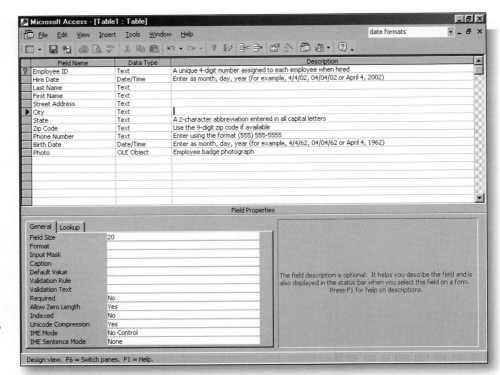

Figure 1.20

Saving the Table Structure

Once you are satisfied that your field definitions are correct, you save the table design by naming it.

1 • Click  Save.

Another Method

The menu equivalent is **File/Save** and the keyboard shortcut is Ctrl + S.

Your screen should be similar to Figure 1.21

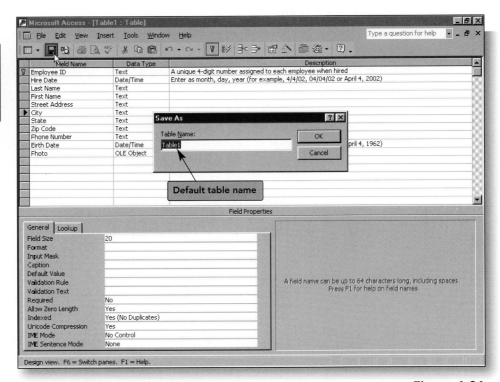

Figure 1.21

In the Save As dialog box, you want to replace the default name, Table1, with a more descriptive name. A table name follows the same set of standard naming conventions or rules that you use when naming fields. It is acceptable to use the same name for both a table and the database, although each table in a database must have a unique name. You will save the table using the table name "Employees."

2 ● **Type** Employees.

● **Click** OK .

The table structure is saved with the database file. You have created a table named "Employees" in the Lifestyle Fitness Employees database file.

Entering and Editing Table Data

Now that the table structure is defined and saved, you can enter the employee data into the new table, and change that data as necessary. In order to do this, you need to switch views.

Switching Views

Access uses several different window formats, called **views** to display and work with the objects in a database. Each view includes its own menu and toolbar designed to work with the object in the window. The views that are available change according to the type of object you are working with. The basic views are described in the following table.

View	Purpose
Design view	Used to create a table, form, query, or report.
Datasheet view	Provides a row-and-column view of the data in tables, forms, and queries.
Form view	Displays the records in a form.
Preview	Displays a form, report, table, or query as it will appear when printed.

The ▦▾ View button is a toggle button that switches between the different available views. The graphic in the button changes to indicate the view that will be displayed when selected. The View button appears as ⬟▾ for Design view and ▦▾ for Datasheet view. Clicking the ▾ in the View button displays a drop-down list of the available views from which you can choose.

You enter and display table data in Datasheet view, which is the view you will switch to right now.

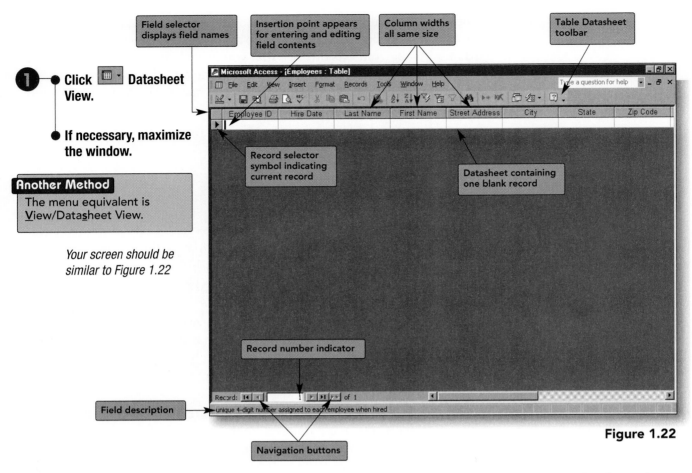

Field selector displays field names

Insertion point appears for entering and editing field contents

Column widths all same size

Table Datasheet toolbar

① ● Click [▦ ▾] **Datasheet View.**

● If necessary, maximize the window.

Record selector symbol indicating current record

Datasheet containing one blank record

Another Method

The menu equivalent is View/Datasheet View.

Your screen should be similar to Figure 1.22

Record number indicator

Field description

Navigation buttons

Figure 1.22

The Datasheet view window displays the table in a row-and-column format called a **datasheet**. Each field is a column of the table, and the field names you entered in Design view are displayed as column headings. The column heading area is called the **field selector** for each column. Below the field selector is a blank row where you will enter the data for a record. To the left of the row is the **record selector** symbol [▶], which indicates which record is the **current record**, or the record containing the insertion point.

The bottom of the window displays a horizontal scroll bar, navigation buttons, and a record number indicator. The **record number indicator** shows the number of the current record as well as the total number of records in the table. Because the table does not yet contain records, the indicator displays "Record: 1 of 1" in anticipation of your first entry. On both sides of the record number are the **navigation buttons**, which are used to move through records with a mouse.

In addition, this view displays a Table Datasheet toolbar containing the standard buttons as well as buttons (identified in the following illustration) that are specific to the Table Datasheet view window.

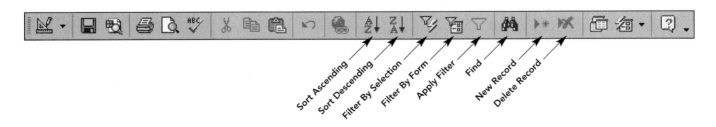

Sort Ascending — Sort Descending — Filter By Selection — Filter By Form — Apply Filter — Find — New Record — Delete Record

Notice also in this view that the column widths are all the same, even though you set different field sizes in the Table Design window. This is because the Table Datasheet view window has its own default column width setting.

Entering Data in Datasheet View

You can enter and delete records and edit field data in existing records using this view. The insertion point is positioned in the Employee ID field, indicating the program is ready to accept data in this field. The status bar displays the description you entered for the field. The data you will enter for the first record is shown in the following table. (Do not enter any of this data until you are instructed to do so in the following steps.)

Field Name	Data
Employee ID	1151
Hire Date	October 14,1997
Last Name	Sutton
First Name	Lisa
Street Address	4389 S. Hayden Rd.
City	Iona
State	FL
Zip Code	33101-3309
Phone Number	(941) 555-1950
Birth Date	June 14, 1975
Photo	Friend1.bmp

When you enter data in a record, it should be entered accurately and consistently. The data you enter in a field should be typed exactly as you want it to appear. This is important because any printouts of the data will display the information exactly as entered. It is also important to enter data in a consistent form. For example, if you decide to abbreviate the word "Street" as "St." in the Street field, then it should be abbreviated the same way in every record where it appears. Also be careful not to enter a blank space before or after a field entry. This can cause problems when using the table to locate information.

To see how field properties can help ensure data accuracy, you will first try to enter an Employee ID number that is larger than the field size of 4 that you defined in Table Design view.

1 ● **Type** 11510.

*Your screen should be
similar to Figure 1.23*

Identifies end of table
or where new record
can be entered

Additional Information

Notice that the current
record symbol has changed
to 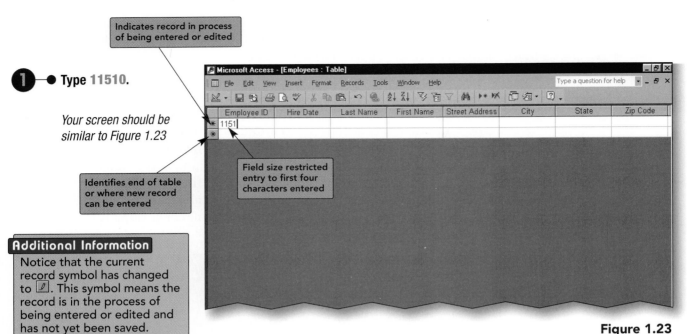. This symbol means the
record is in the process of
being entered or edited and
has not yet been saved.

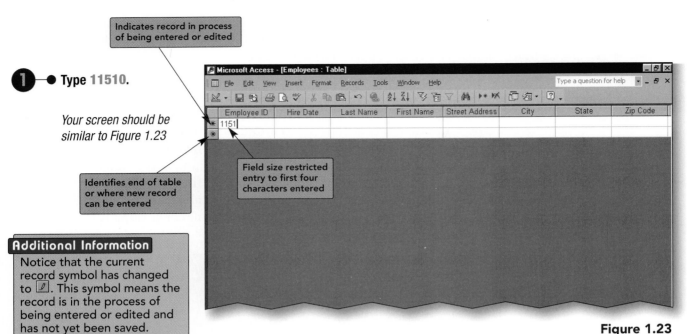

Field size restricted
entry to first four
characters entered

Figure 1.23

The program accepted only the first four digits, and would not let you type
a fifth. The field size restriction helps control the accuracy of data by not allowing an entry larger than specified.

Next, you will intentionally enter an invalid hire date to see what happens.

2 ● **Press** ←Enter, Tab,
or → **to move to the
Hire Date field.**

● **Type** 10/41/1997.

● **Press** ←Enter, Tab,
or →.

*Your screen should be
similar to Figure 1.24*

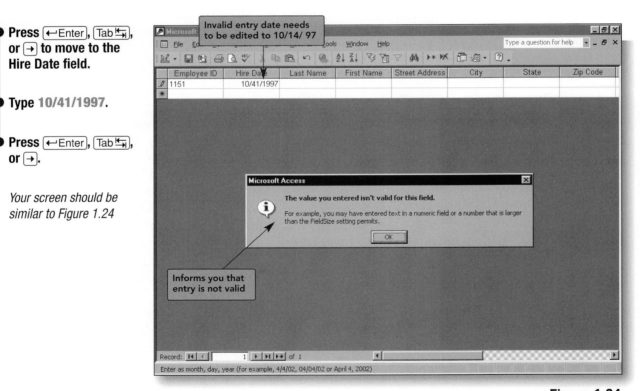

Invalid entry date needs
to be edited to 10/14/ 97

Informs you that
entry is not valid

Figure 1.24

An informational message box is displayed advising you that the entry is
not valid. In this case, the date entered (10/41/1997) could not be correct because there cannot be 41 days in a month. Access automatically performs
some basic validity checks on the data as it is entered based upon the field

type specified in the table design. This is another way Access helps you control data entry to ensure the accuracy of the data.

Editing Data

You will need to edit the date entry to correct it. To position the insertion point in the field entry, click at the location where you want it to appear. The keyboard keys shown in the table below can also be used to move the insertion point in an entry and to make changes to individual characters in the entry.

Key	Effect
← or →	Moves insertion point left or right one character.
Ctrl + ← or Ctrl + →	Moves insertion point left or right one word.
↓	Moves insertion point to current field in next record.
Home or End	Moves insertion point to beginning or end of field in single-line field.
Ctrl + Home or Ctrl + End	Moves insertion point to beginning or end of field in multiple-line field.
Delete	Deletes character to right of insertion point.
Backspace	Deletes character to left of insertion point.

1
- Click **OK** to close the message box.

- Press ← (5 times).

- Press Delete (2 times).

- Type **14**.

Additional Information
You can cancel changes you are making in the current field at any time before you move on to the next field. Just press Esc and the original entry is restored.

- Press Tab.

Your screen should be similar to Figure 1.25

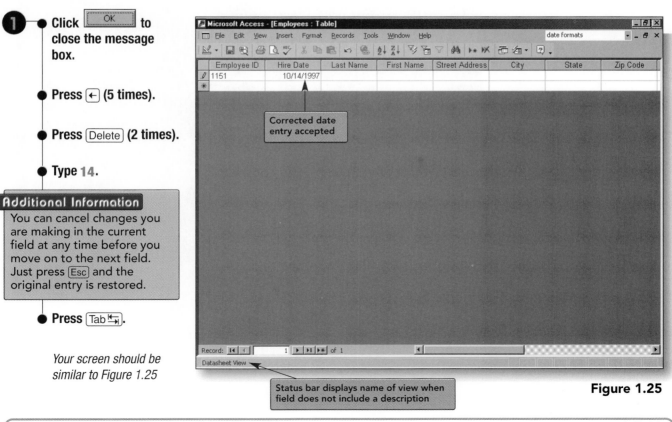

Corrected date entry accepted

Status bar displays name of view when field does not include a description

Figure 1.25

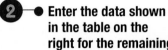

HAVING TROUBLE?
The date on your screen may appear with a two digit year, or in some other Short Date format. This is because the Short Date format is controlled by the date format settings in Windows.

The corrected date is accepted, and the insertion point moves to the Last Name field. The year in the date changed to four digits, which reflects the date format you specified in the field's property.

Because no description was entered for this field, the status bar displays "Datasheet View," the name of the current view, instead of a field description.

2 ● Enter the data shown in the table on the right for the remaining fields, typing the information exactly as it appears.

Additional Information
The fields will scroll on the screen as you move to the right in the record.

Your screen should be similar to Figure 1.26

Field Name	Data
Last Name	Sutton
First Name	Lisa
Street Address	4389 S. Hayden Rd.
City	Iona
State	FL
Zip Code	33101-3309
Phone Number	(941) 555-1950
Birth Date	6/14/75

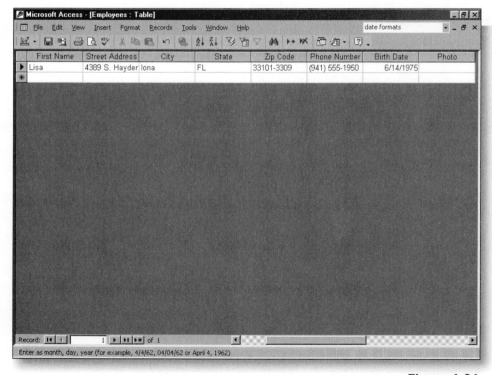

Figure 1.26

All the information for the first record is now complete, except for the Photo field.

Inserting a Picture

To complete the information for this record, you need to insert a picture of Lisa in the Photo field. A picture is one of several different types of graphic objects that can be added to a database table.

concept 8

Graphic

8 A **graphic** is a non-text element or object, such as a drawing or picture, which can be added to a table. A graphic can be a simple **drawing object** consisting of shapes such as lines and boxes that can be created using a drawing program such as Paint. A **picture** is an illustration such as a scanned photograph. Other types of graphic objects that can be added are a worksheet created in Excel or a Word document. Examples of several graphic objects are shown below.

Graphic objects can be inserted in a table as bound or unbound objects. A **bound object** is stored in a table and connected to a specific record and field. Each record can have its own graphic object. An **unbound object** is associated with the table as a whole, not with a specific record, and does not change when you move from record to record. An unbound object is often used to display decorative pictures, a background picture, or an informational text item, such as a company logo.

Photograph

Clip Art

Drawing Object

Picture files can be obtained from a variety of sources. Many simple drawings, called **clip art**, are available in the Clip Organizer that comes with Office XP. You can also create graphic files using a scanner to convert any printed document, including photographs, to an electronic format. Most images that are scanned and inserted into documents are stored as Windows bitmap files (.bmp). All types of graphics, including clip art, photographs, and other types of images, can be found on the Internet. These files are commonly stored as .jpg or .pcx files. Keep in mind that any images you locate on the Internet may be protected by copyright and should be used only with permission. You can also purchase CDs containing graphics for your use.

You have not organized the employees' badge photographs yet, but you want to demonstrate to the Club owners how this feature works, so you decide to insert a picture of a friend. Then, after the database design is completed, you will insert all the employees' photographs into the appropriate field. You have a recent picture of your friend that you scanned and saved in a file, which you will insert in the Photo field for Lisa Sutton.

1 ● If necessary, move to the Photo field.

● Choose **Insert/Object**.

Your screen should be similar to Figure 1.27

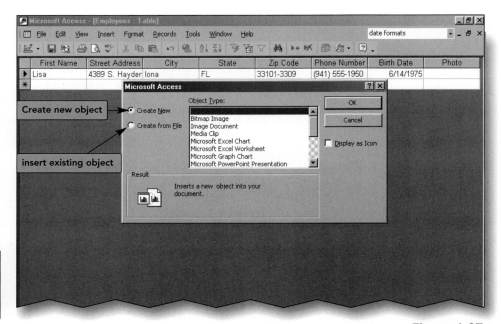

Figure 1.27

This dialog box asks you to specify whether you want to create a new object or insert an existing object. Because your friend's picture is already created and stored as a file, you will use the Create from File option and specify the location of the file.

2 ● Select **Create from File**.

● Click [Browse...].

Your screen should be similar to Figure 1.28

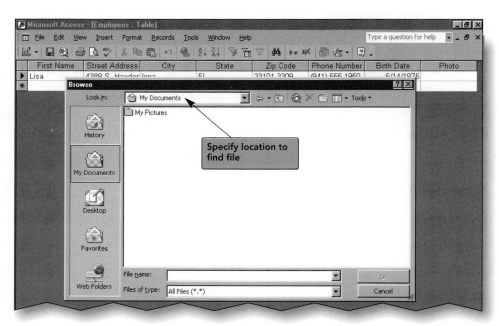

Figure 1.28

This Browse dialog box is used to locate and select the name of the file you want to insert. The Look In drop-down list box displays the location where the program will look for files, and the file list box displays the names of all files (if any) at that location. First you may need to change the location to the location containing your data files.

3 If necessary, open the Look In drop-down list box and specify the location of your data files.

Your screen should be similar to Figure 1.29

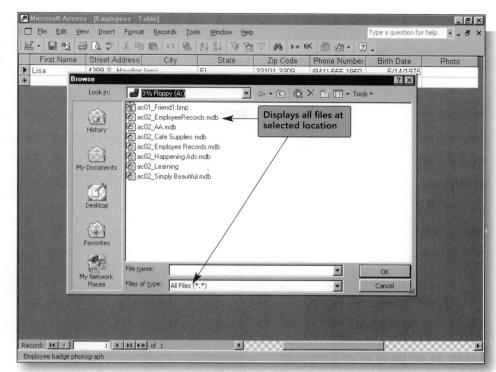

Figure 1.29

The Browse dialog box displays the names of all files on your data disk. When selecting a file to insert, it may be helpful to see a preview of the file first. To do this, you can change the dialog box view.

4 Open the 🖳 Views drop-down list.

● Choose Pre**v**iew.

● Click the file name ac01_Friend1 in the file list box.

HAVING TROUBLE?
If necessary, scroll the file list box to locate the file. If ac01_Friend1 is not displayed in the file list, ask your instructor for help.

Your screen should be similar to Figure 1.30

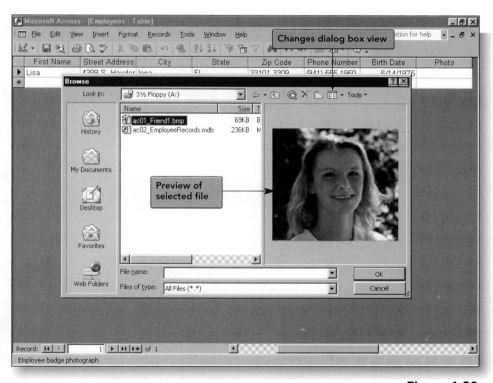

Figure 1.30

A preview of the file is displayed in the right side of the Browse dialog box.

You see that it is the picture you want, so you can select it as the object file to be inserted.

5 • **Change the dialog box view to List.**

• **Double-click the ac01_Friend1 file name.**

Your screen should be similar to Figure 1.31

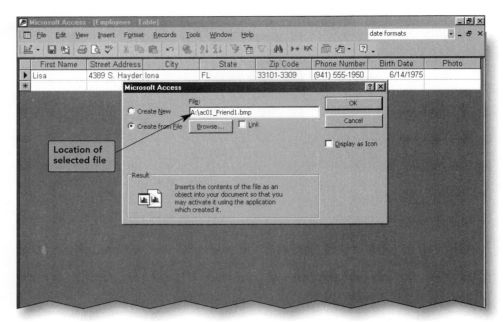

Figure 1.31

The object dialog box is displayed again with the path to the selected object displayed in the File text box. When inserting an object, you can specify if you want to display the object as an icon instead of the picture. Using this setting saves a lot of disk space, because only an icon appears for the object rather than the complete object. Although the future plan is to include a photograph for each employee and display it as an icon, for the test picture you want to display the photo itself.

6 • **Click** OK **.**

Your screen should be similar to Figure 1.32

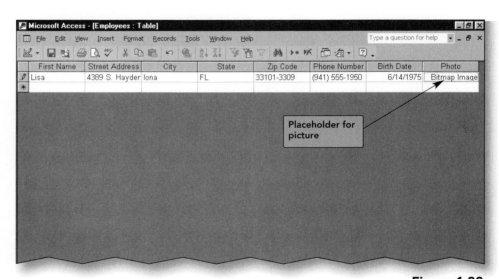

Figure 1.32

The picture object was inserted as a bound object, because it is associated with the Photo field. In Datasheet view, the field displays a text placeholder such as "Package" or "Bitmap Image" instead of the picture. The actual placeholder you will see will depend upon the software your computer used to import the image into Access.

You can now display the photograph from the Photo field to check that it has in fact been inserted there.

Double-click on the Photo field entry.

Your screen should be similar to Figure 1.33

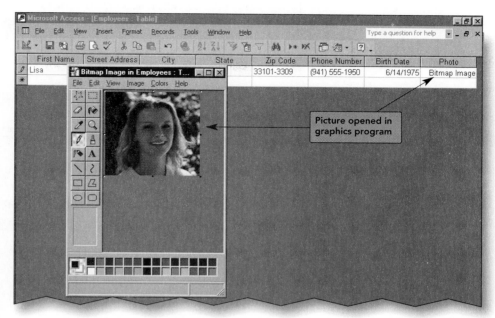

Figure 1.33

Additional Information

The graphic can be further manipulated using the graphics program features.

The picture object is opened and displayed in the associated graphics program, in this case, Paint. Yours may open and display in a different graphics program.

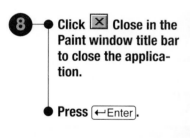
Click ☒ **Close in the Paint window title bar to close the application.**

● **Press** ↵Enter.

Your screen should be similar to Figure 1.34

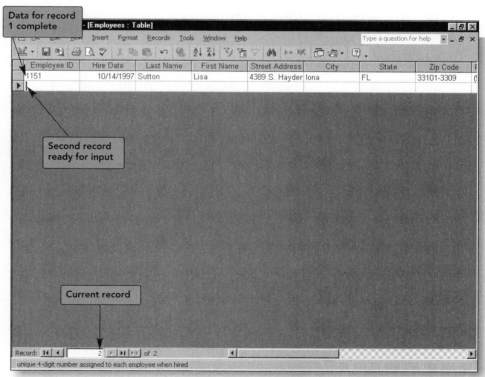

Figure 1.34

The data for the first record is now complete.

The insertion point moves to the first field on the next row and waits for input of the employee number for the next record. As soon as the insertion point moves to another record, the data is saved to the table file and the number of the new record appears in the status bar. The second record was automatically assigned the record number 2.

Navigating a Datasheet

Next you will check the first record for accuracy.

1 ● Point to the left end of the Employee ID field for the first record. When the mouse pointer appears as ⇩, click the mouse button.

Your screen should be similar to Figure 1.35

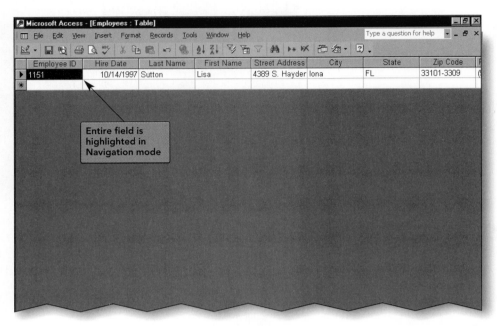

Figure 1.35

The entire field is selected (highlighted), and you have activated Navigation mode. In this mode you can quickly move from field to field in a datasheet using the keyboard keys shown in the following table.

Key	Moves highlight to
→ or Tab ↹	Next field
← or ⇧Shift + Tab ↹	Previous field
Home or End	First or last field in current record
↓	Current field in next record
↑	Current field in previous record
Home	First field in record
End	Last field in record

Because the entire field contents is selected, if you type, the selection will be replaced with the new text. If you use Delete or Backspace, the entire highlighted field contents are deleted. Next, you will select the Street Address field in order to check its contents.

2 • **Press** → **4 times.**

• **Click the Street Address field with the mouse pointer shape as an I-beam** .

Your screen should be similar to Figure 1.36

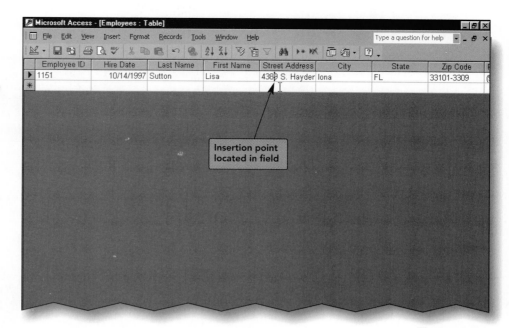

Figure 1.36

The insertion point is positioned in the field, and you could now edit the field contents if necessary. The beginning of the field looks fine, but because the column width is too narrow, you cannot see the entire entry. You will move the insertion point to the end of the address so you can check the rest of the entry.

3 • **Press** [End].

Your screen should be similar to Figure 1.37

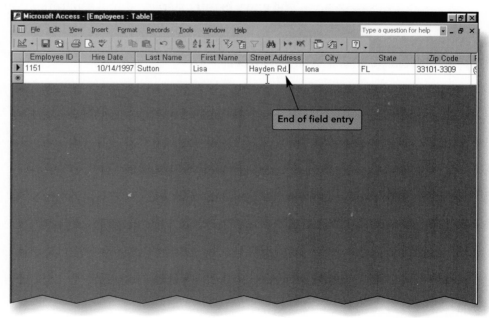

Figure 1.37

The text scrolled in the field, and the insertion point is positioned at the end of the entry. However, now you cannot see the beginning of the entry, which makes it difficult to edit.

Another way to view the field's contents is to expand the field.

4 ● Press ⬆Shift + F2 .

Your screen should be similar to Figure 1.38

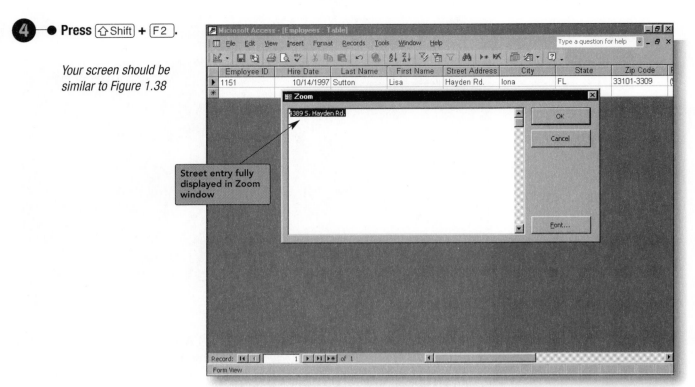

Street entry fully displayed in Zoom window

Figure 1.38

The entry is fully displayed in a separate Zoom window. You can edit in the window just as you would in the field.

5 ● If the entry contains an error, correct it.

● Click | OK |.

● Press Tab⇆ .

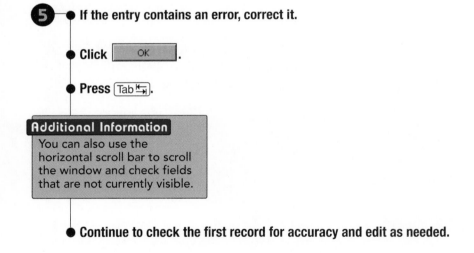

Additional Information

You can also use the horizontal scroll bar to scroll the window and check fields that are not currently visible.

● Continue to check the first record for accuracy and edit as needed.

6 • Enter the data shown in the table on the right for the second record.

• Press ⟨←Enter⟩ twice to skip the Photo field and complete the record.

• Check the second record for accuracy and edit it if necessary.

Your screen should be similar to Figure 1.39

Field Name	Data
Employee ID	0434
Hire Date	July 5, 1996
Last Name	Merwin
First Name	Adda
Street Address	947 S. Forest St.
City	Fort Myers
State	FL
Zip Code	33301-1268
Phone Number	(941) 555-4494
Birth Date	April 20, 1970

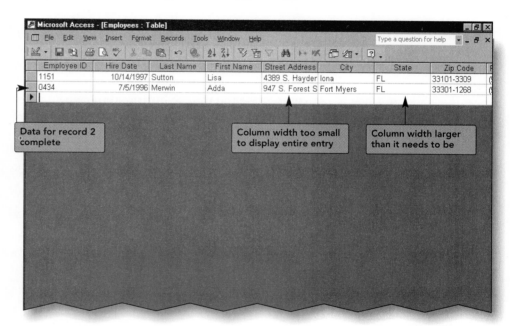

Figure 1.39

Notice that the dates changed automatically to the format set in the date property field.

Changing Column Width

Additional Information
You will learn how to do more table formatting in future labs.

The first thing you want to do is make the columns wider so you can see each complete field entry without having to move to the field and scroll or expand the field box. There are several ways that you can manipulate the rows and columns of a datasheet so that it is easier to view and work with the table data.

Resizing a Column

As you have noticed, some of the fields (such as the Street field) do not display the entire entry, while other fields (such as the State field) are much larger than the field's column heading or contents. This is because the default width of a column in the datasheet is not the same size as the field sizes you specified in Design view.

concept 9

Column Width

9 **Column width** refers to the size of a field column in a datasheet. The column width does not affect the amount of data you can enter into a field, but does affect the data that you can see. The default datasheet column width is set to display 15.6667 characters. You can adjust the column width to change the appearance of the datasheet. It is usually best to adjust the column width so the column is slightly larger than the column heading or longest field contents, whichever is longer. Do not confuse column width with field size. Field size is a property associated with each field; it controls the maximum number of characters that you can enter in the field. If you shorten the field size, you can lose data already entered in the field.

To quickly resize a column, simply drag the right column border line in the field selector in either direction to increase or decrease the column width. The mouse pointer shape is ↔ when you can drag to size the column. As you drag, a column line appears to show you the new column border. When you release the mouse button, the column width will be set. First you will increase the width of the Street field so the entire address will be visible.

1 • Point to the right column border line in the field selector for the Street Address field name.

  • When the mouse pointer is ↔, drag the border to the right until you think the column width will be long enough to display the field contents.

  • Adjust the column width again if it is too wide or not wide enough.

Another Method

You can also adjust the column width to a specific number of characters using Format/Column Width.

Your screen should be similar to Figure 1.40

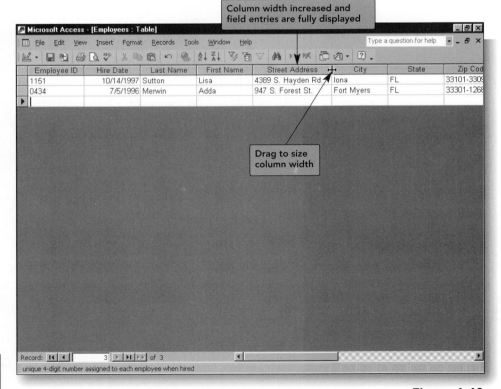

Figure 1.40

Using Best Fit

Rather than change the widths of all the other columns individually, you can select all columns and change their widths at the same time. To select multiple columns, point to the column heading in the field selector area of the first or last column you want to select. Then, when the mouse pointer changes to ↓, click, and without releasing the mouse button, drag in either direction across the column headings.

1 ● **Point to the Employee ID field name.**

● **When the mouse pointer is ↓, drag to the right across all column headings.**

Additional Information

The fields will scroll horizontally in the window as you drag to select the columns.

● **Use the horizontal scroll bar to bring the first field column back into view in the window.**

Another Method

Clicking the box to the left of the first field name will select the entire table contents, excluding the field names.

Your screen should be similar to Figure 1.41

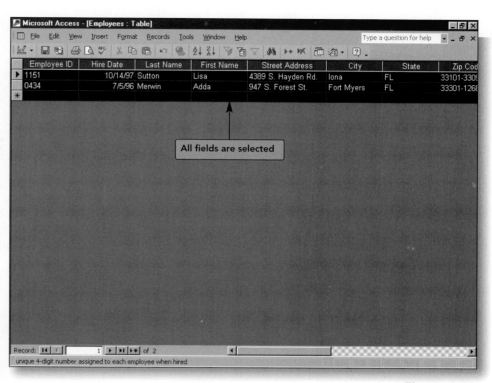

All fields are selected

Figure 1.41

Multiple columns are highlighted. Now, if you were to drag the column border of any selected column, all the selected columns would change to the same size. However, you want the column widths to be adjusted appropriately to fit the data in each column. To do this, you can double-click the column border to activate the Best Fit feature. The **Best Fit** feature automatically adjusts the column widths of all selected columns to accommodate the longest entry or column heading in each of the selected columns.

2 ● Double-click any column border line (in the
field selector) within
the selection when the
mouse pointer is ⊹.

● Click anywhere on the
table to deselect the
datasheet.

Another Method

You can also use the
Format/Column Width menu
equivalent and click [Best Fit]
in the Column Width dialog
box. The Column Width
command is also on the
shortcut menu when an
entire column is selected.

*Your screen should be
similar to Figure 1.42*

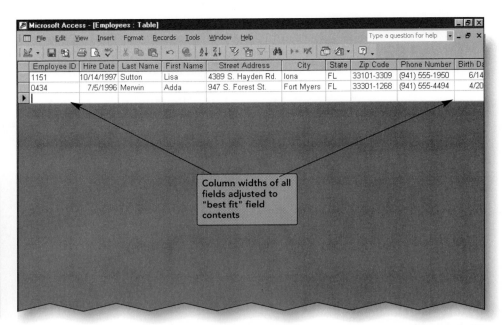

Figure 1.42

Now you can see the complete contents of each field. You are also no longer
in Navigation mode, because the insertion point is visible in the field.

3 ● Check each of the
records again and edit
any entries that are in-
correct.

● Add the record in the
table on the right as
record 3.

● Press ⏎Enter twice to
skip the Photo field
and complete the
record.

*Your screen should be
similar to Figure 1.43*

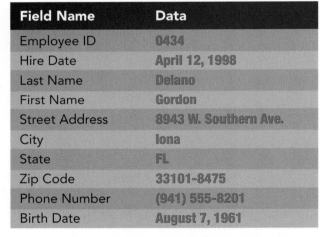

Field Name	Data
Employee ID	0434
Hire Date	April 12, 1998
Last Name	Delano
First Name	Gordon
Street Address	8943 W. Southern Ave.
City	Iona
State	FL
Zip Code	33101-8475
Phone Number	(941) 555-8201
Birth Date	August 7, 1961

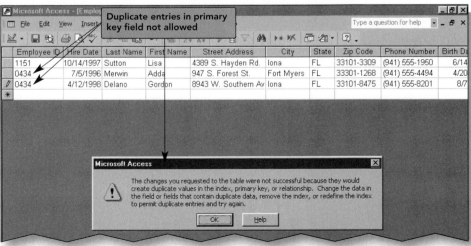

Figure 1.43

As soon as you complete the record, an error message dialog box appears indicating that Access has located a duplicate value in a key field. The key field is Employee ID. You realize you were looking at the employee number from the previous record when you entered the employee number for this record. You need to clear the message and enter the correct number.

4 ● Click [OK].

● Press [Home].

● **Change the Employee ID for record 3 to 0234.**

● Press [↓].

Your screen should be similar to Figure 1.44

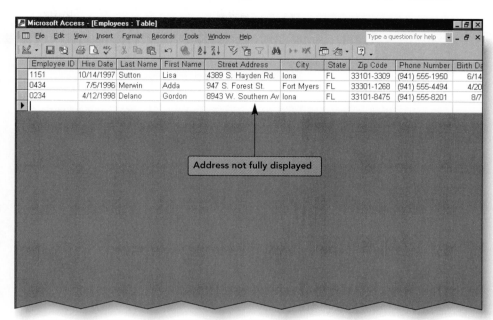

Figure 1.44

The record is accepted with the new employee number. However, you notice that the address for this record does not fully display in the Street Address field. It has a longer address than either of the other two records.

5 ● **Double-click the right border of the Street Address field to best fit the field column.**

Your screen should be similar to Figure 1.45

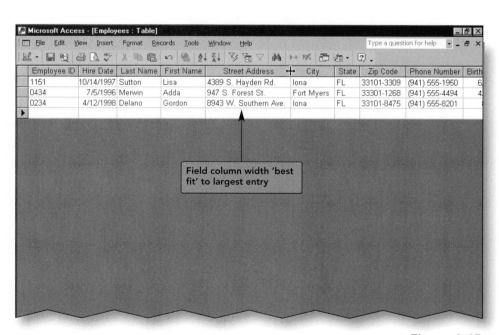

Figure 1.45

Displaying Records in Primary Key Order

When you add new records in a datasheet, the records are displayed in the order you enter them. However, they are stored on disk in order by the primary key field. You can change the display on the screen to reflect the correct order by using the ⇧Shift + F9 key combination.

6 ● Press ⇧Shift + F9.

Your screen should be similar to Figure 1.46

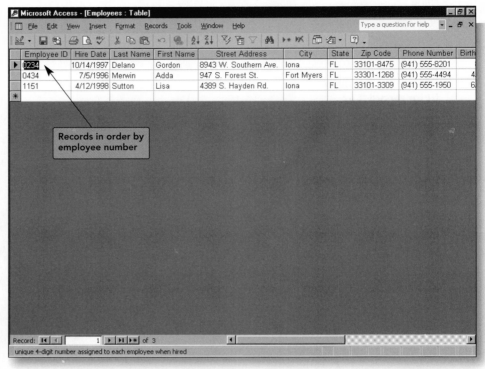

Records in order by employee number

Figure 1.46

Additional Information
The table order is also updated when you close and then reopen the table.

The records are now in order by employee number. This is the order determined by the primary key field.

Adding Records in Data Entry

Next you want to add several more employee records to the table. Another way to add records is to use the Data Entry command. Using this command hides all existing records in the datasheet and displays a blank datasheet area in which you can enter data. The advantage to using this command is that it prevents accidental changes to existing table data.

1 ● **Choose Records/Data Entry.**

Your screen should be similar to Figure 1.47

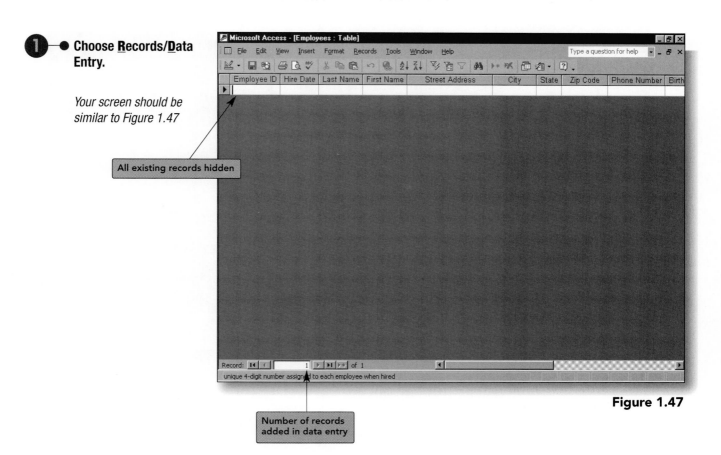

All existing records hidden

Number of records added in data entry

Figure 1.47

The existing records are hidden, and the only row displayed is a blank row where you can enter a new record. The status bar displays "1 of 1." This number reflects the number of new records as they are added in Data Entry rather than all records in the table.

You will add three more records to the table. If data for some fields, such as the City, State, or Zip Code, is the same from record to record, you can save yourself some typing by copying the data from one of the other records. Just select the field contents and click 📋 Copy. Then move to the field where you want the copy to appear and click 📋 Paste.

1 Enter the data for the two records shown in the table on the right.

• Enter a final record using your first and last names. Enter **9999** as your employee number and the current date as your date hired. The information you enter in all other fields can be fictitious.

• Best fit any columns that do not fully display the field contents.

• Check each of the records and correct any entry errors.

Your screen should be similar to Figure 1.48

Field	Record 1	Record 2
Employee ID	0839	0728
Hire Date	August 14, 1997	March 15, 1997
Last Name	Ruiz	Roman
First Name	Enrique	Anita
Street	358 Maple Dr.	2348 S. Bala Dr.
City	Cypress Lake	Fort Myers
State	FL	FL
Zip Code	33205-6911	33301-1268
Phone Number	(941) 555-0091	(941) 555-9870
Birth Date	December 10, 1963	March 15, 1961

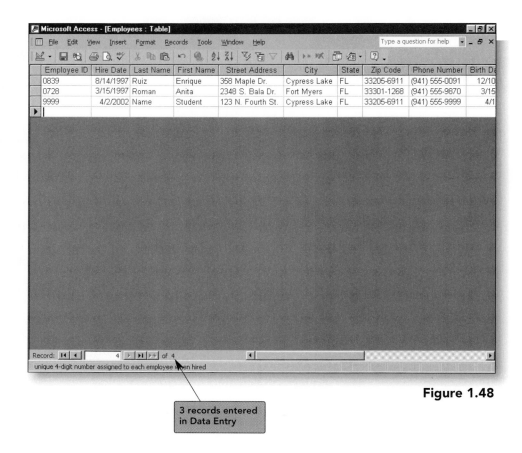

3 records entered in Data Entry

Figure 1.48

Now that you have entered the new records, you can redisplay all the records in the table.

2
● Choose **R**ecords/**R**emove Filter/Sort.

● Best fit any columns that do not fully display the field contents.

Your screen should be similar to Figure 1.49

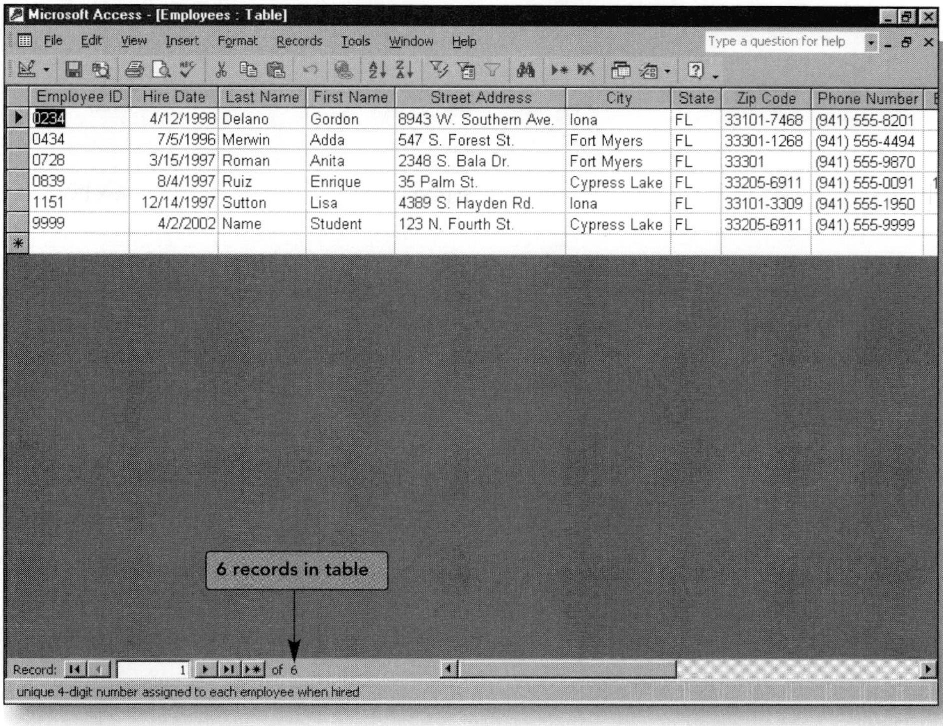

Figure 1.49

There is now a total of 6 records in the table. The records are displayed in the datasheet in sorted order by employee number. If you had added the new records in Datasheet view, they would not appear in primary key field order until you updated the table display. This is another advantage of using Data Entry.

Deleting Records

Additional Information

If you choose to select an entire record, you can do so by using **E**dit/Se**l**ect Record or clicking in the row selector when the mouse indicator shape is ➡. In Navigation mode, ⇧Shift + Spacebar also selects the current record.

While you are entering the employee records, you find a memo from one of your managers stating that Adda Merwin is no longer working at the club and asking you to remove her record from the employee files.

You can remove records from a table by selecting the entire record and pressing the Delete key. This method is useful when you have multiple records to be deleted that you can select and delete as a group. It is quicker, however, to use the 🞪 Delete Record button when you want to remove individual records. This is because the entire record is both selected and deleted at the same time.

Record deleted

Deletes selected record

1 ● Move to any field in record 2.

● Click ☒ Delete Record.

Another Method
The menu equivalent is Edit/Delete Record. You can also use Edit/Cut to delete a selected record.

Your screen should be similar to Figure 1.50

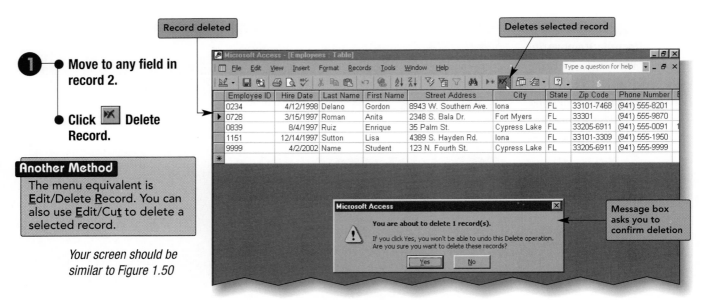

Message box asks you to confirm deletion

Figure 1.50

This message box asks you to confirm that you really want to delete the selected record. This is because this action cannot be reversed.

2 ● Click [Yes] to confirm that you want to delete the record.

Your screen should be similar to Figure 1.51

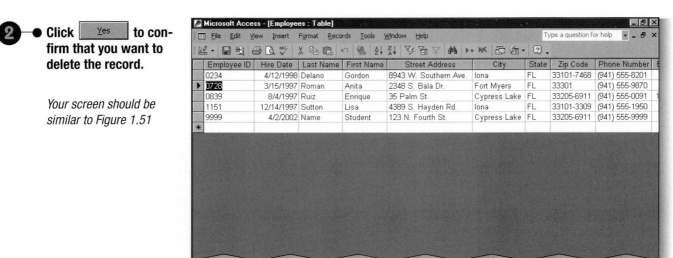

Figure 1.51

The table now consists of five employee records. You decide to print out the table as it stands now and get your managers' approval before you begin entering the rest of the employee records.

Previewing and Printing a Table

Now, you want to print a copy of the records in this table. Before printing the table, you will preview on screen how it will look when printed.

Previewing the Table

Previewing a table displays each page in a reduced size so you can see the layout. Then, if necessary, you can make changes to the layout before printing, to both save time and avoid wasting paper.

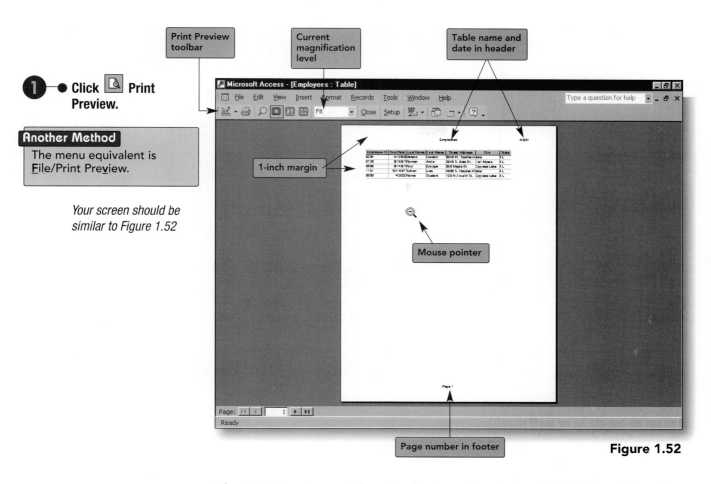

1 ● Click 🔍 **Print Preview.**

Another Method

The menu equivalent is File/Print Preview.

Your screen should be similar to Figure 1.52

Print Preview toolbar

Current magnification level

Table name and date in header

1-inch margin

Mouse pointer

Page number in footer

Figure 1.52

The Print Preview window displays a reduced view of how the table will appear when printed. The document will be printed using the default report and page layout settings, which include such items as 1-inch margins, the table name and date displayed in a header, and the page number in a footer.

To better see the information in the table, you can change the magnification level of the Preview window. The current magnification level, Fit, is displayed in the Fit button in the Print Preview toolbar. This setting adjusts the magnification of the page to best fit in the size of the window. Notice that the mouse pointer is a 🔍 Magnifying glass when it is positioned on the page. This indicates that you can click on the page to switch between the Fit magnification level and the last used level.

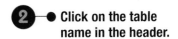

2 ● Click on the table name in the header.

Another Method

Clicking 🔍 Zoom will toggle between magnification levels.

Additional Information

The location where you click will determine the area that is displayed initially.

Your screen should be similar to Figure 1.53

Additional Information

You can also use View/Zoom or the Fit ▾ Zoom button on the Print Preview toolbar to increase the character size up to ten times the normal display (1000 percent) or reduce it to 10 percent.

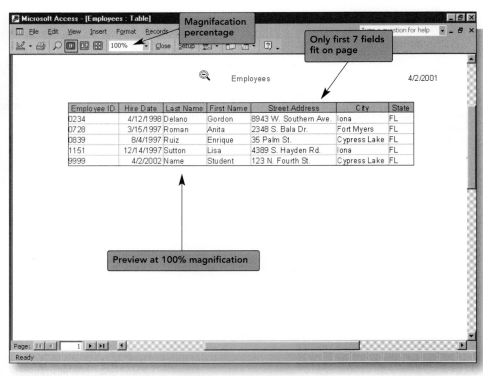

Figure 1.53

The table appears in 100 percent magnification. This is the size it will appear when printed. Notice, however, that because the table is too wide to fit across the width of a page, only the first seven fields are displayed on the page. Tables with multiple columns are typically wider than what can fit on an 8½ by 11 piece of paper. You would like to see both pages displayed onscreen.

3 ● Click 🔳 Two pages.

Your screen should be similar to Figure 1.54

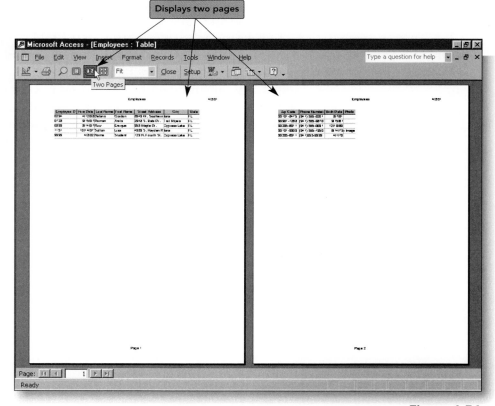

Figure 1.54

Changing the Page Orientation

Rather than print the table on two pages, you decide to see if changing the orientation of the table will allow you to print it on one page. **Orientation** refers to the direction that text prints on a page. Normal orientation is to print across the width of an 8½-inch page. This is called **portrait** orientation. You can change the orientation to print across the length of the paper. This is called **landscape** orientation.

You already know from seeing the table in Print Preview that it will not fit on one page in the default portrait orientation, so you need to change it to landscape.

1 ● Click .

Another Method
The menu equivalent is File/Page Setup.

Your screen should be similar to Figure 1.55

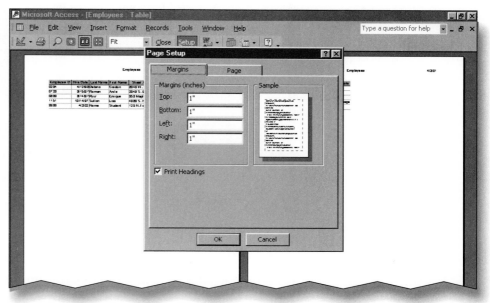

Figure 1.55

The Page Setup dialog box lets you specify the basic layout for your table. There are two types of layout changes that you can make, Margins and Page. The orientation setting is on the Page tab.

2 ● Click the Page tab to open it.

Your screen should be similar to Figure 1.56

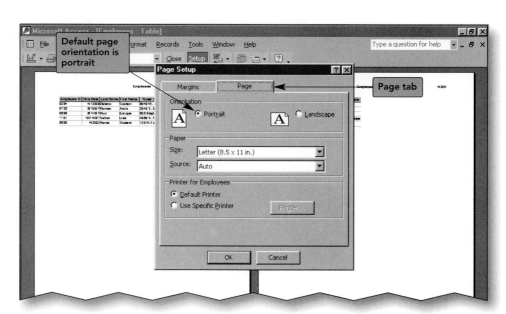

Figure 1.56

The Orientation panel shows how text will print in each orientation. You select the desired orientation by clicking on its radio button.

③ ● Select **L**andscape.

● Click [OK].

Your screen should be similar to Figure 1.57

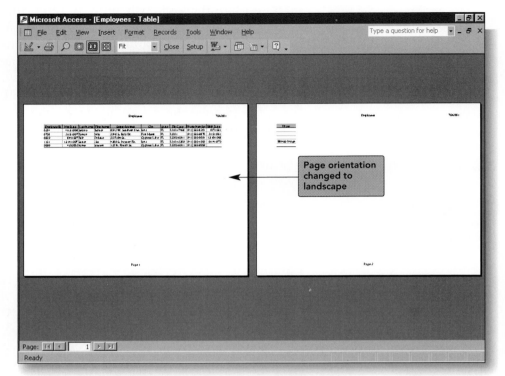

Page orientation changed to landscape

Figure 1.57

The Print Preview view now shows all but the Photo field of the table will print on one page. Because none of the employee photos have actually been inserted yet (and the photos would not actually print as part of the table — only the placeholders would), you decide that this is acceptable for now and will go ahead and print the table.

Printing a Table

The 🖨 Print button on the toolbar will immediately start printing the report using the default print settings. However, if you want to check the print settings first, you need to use the Print command.

1 ● If necessary, make sure your printer is on and ready to print.

● Choose **File/Print**.

Another Method

The keyboard shortcut is Ctrl + P.

Your screen should be similar to Figure 1.58

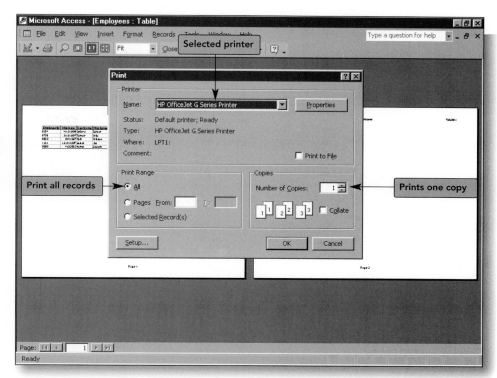

Selected printer

Print all records

Prints one copy

Figure 1.58

HAVING TROUBLE?

Please consult your instructor for printing procedures that may differ from the directions given here.

From the Print dialog box, you specify the printer you will be using and the document settings. The printer that is currently selected is displayed in the Name drop-down list box in the Printer section of the dialog box.

The Page Range area of the Print dialog box lets you specify how much of the document you want printed. The range options are described in the following table.

Option	Action
All	Prints the entire document.
Pages	Prints pages you specify by typing page numbers in the text box.
Selected Records	Prints selected records only.

Because the second page contains the Photo field, you decide to print only the first page of the table.

2 ● If you need to change the selected printer to another printer, open the Name drop-down list box and select the appropriate printer (your instructor will tell you which printer to select).

● Select **Pages**.

● Type **1** in both the **From** and **To** text boxes.

● Click ⬚ OK ⬚.

A status message box is displayed briefly, informing you that the table is being printed. Your printed copy should be similar to the printout shown here.

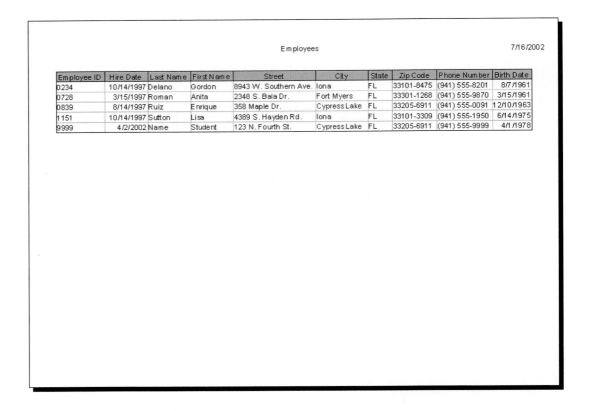

Employee ID	Hire Date	Last Name	First Name	Street	City	State	Zip Code	Phone Number	Birth Date
0234	10/14/1997	Delano	Gordon	8943 W. Southern Ave.	Iona	FL	33101-8475	(941) 555-8201	8/7/1961
0728	3/15/1997	Roman	Anita	2348 S. Bala Dr.	Fort Myers	FL	33301-1268	(941) 555-9870	3/15/1961
0839	8/14/1997	Ruiz	Enrique	358 Maple Dr.	Cypress Lake	FL	33205-6911	(941) 555-0091	12/10/1963
1151	10/14/1997	Sutton	Lisa	4389 S. Hayden Rd.	Iona	FL	33101-3309	(941) 555-1950	6/14/1975
9999	4/2/2002	Name	Student	123 N. Fourth St.	Cypress Lake	FL	33205-6911	(941) 555-9999	4/1/1978

Employees   7/16/2002

You can now close the Print Preview window and return to Datasheet view.

Your screen should look similar to Figure 1.59

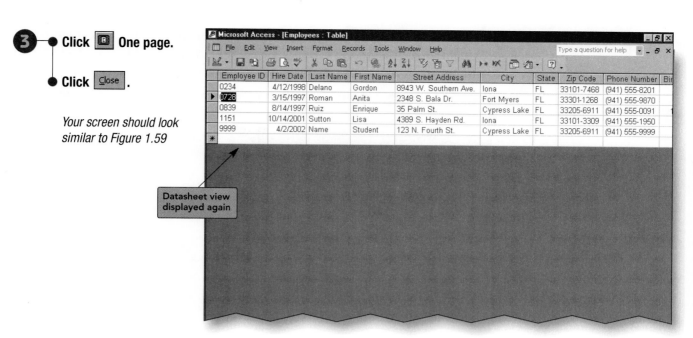

Datasheet view displayed again

Figure 1.59

Closing and Opening a Table and Database

You are ready to show your managers your printed table and get approval on how you set up the data. But first you need to close the table and database that you created.

Closing a Table and Database

You close a table by closing its window and saving any layout changes you have made since your last Access session.

1 ● Click ⊠ Close Window in the menu bar.

> **Another Method**
>
> The menu equivalent is File/Close.

Your screen should look similar to Figure 1.60

Closes table window

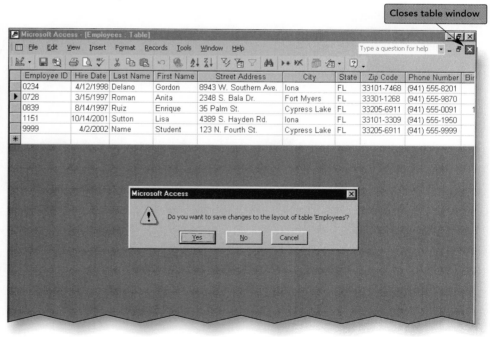

Figure 1.60

Because you changed the column widths of the table in Datasheet view, you are prompted to save the layout changes before the table is closed. If you do not save the table, your column width settings will be lost.

2 ● Click [Yes].

Your screen should be similar to Figure 1.61

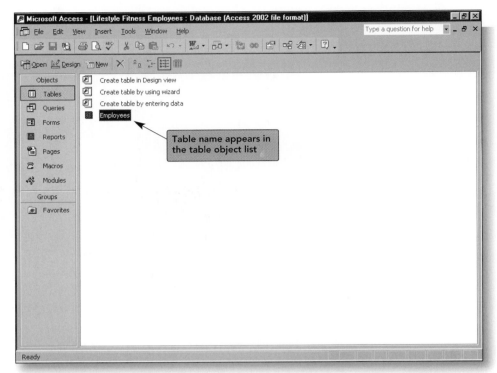

Figure 1.61

The Database window is displayed again. The name of the table you created appears in the Table object list. Next, you will close the database.

3 ● Click [X] **Close Window in the menu bar.**

Your screen should be similar to Figure 1.62

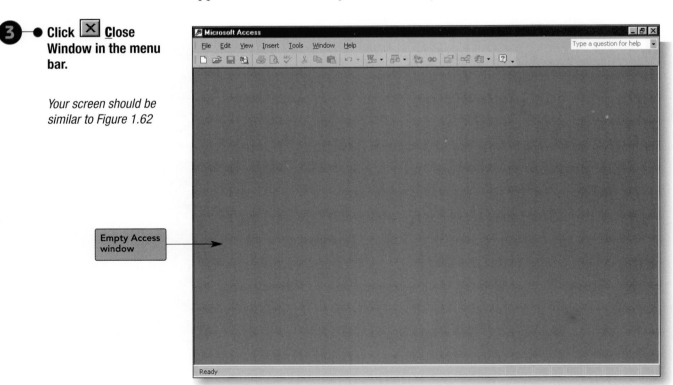

Figure 1.62

You are left with an empty Access application window. The main Access menu commands and buttons are still available, however, for you to create new and access existing database files.

Opening a Table and Database

You want to make sure you know how to access your table of employee records, so you will reopen it and then close it again.

 **1** ● Click  Open.

● **If necessary, open the Look In drop-down list and select the location of your data files.**

Your screen should be similar to Figure 1.63

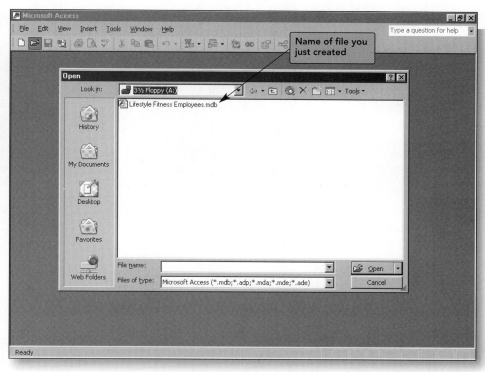

Figure 1.63

Now the name of the database file you just created is displayed in the list box. Your list box may display additional database file names.

2
• **Select** Lifestyle Fitness Employees.

• **Click** 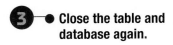.

Another Method

You can also double-click the database file name to open it.

• **If necessary, select "Employees."**

• **Click** Open.

Another Method

You can also double-click an object name to open it.

Your screen should be similar to Figure 1.64

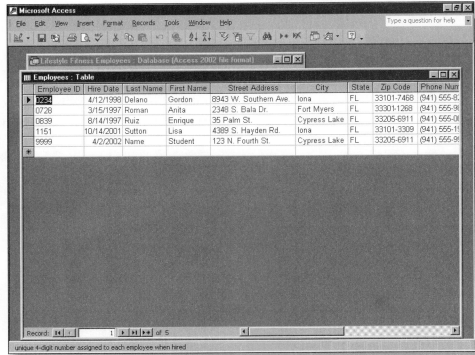

Figure 1.64

The table of employee records is displayed in Datasheet view again, just as it was before you saved and closed the table.

3
• **Close the table and database again.**

Your screen should be similar to Figure 1.65

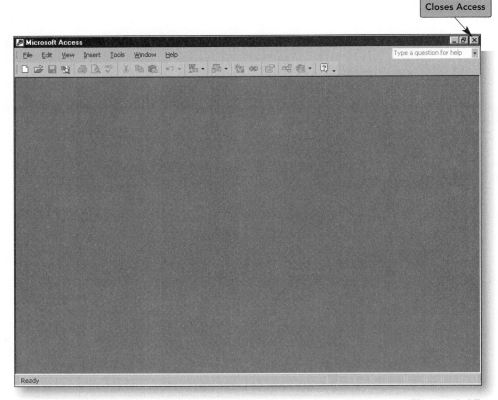

Figure 1.65

Notice that this time you were not prompted to save the table because you did not make any layout changes.

Exiting Access

You will continue to build and use the table of employee records in the next lab. Until then, you can exit Access and return to the Windows desktop.

 Click ☒ Close in the Access window title bar.

Another Method
The menu equivalent is File/Exit.

Warning: If you are using a floppy disk, do not remove it from the drive until you exit Access.

LAB 1
Creating a Database

Database (AC1.6)

A **database** is an organized collection of related information. Typically, the information in a database is stored in a table consisting of vertical columns and horizontal rows.

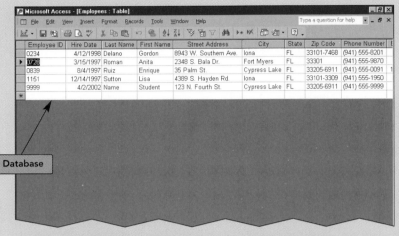

Database

Object (AC1.11)

An **object** is an item, such as a table or report, that can be created, selected, and manipulated as a unit.

Object

Field Name (AC1.13)

A **field name** is used to identify the data stored in the field.

Data Type (AC1.16)

The **data type** defines the type of data the field will contain.

Field Property (AC1.18)

A **field property** is a characteristic that helps define a field. A set of field properties is associated with each field.

Data type

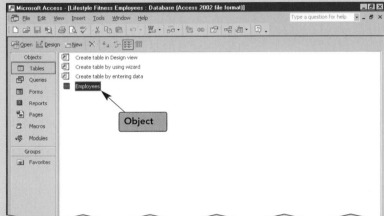

Field name

Field Property

Primary Key

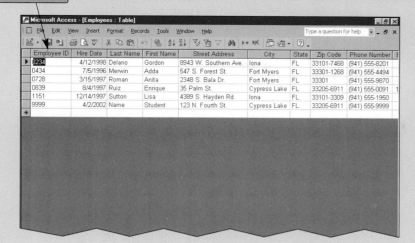

Primary Key (AC1.20)

A **primary key** is a field that uniquely identifies each record.

Graphics

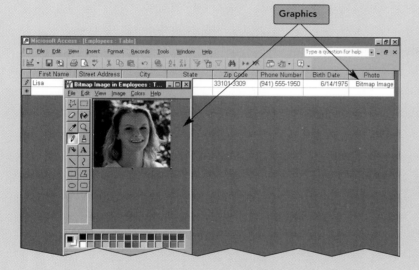

Graphics (AC1.31)

A **graphic** is a non-text element or object, such as a drawing or picture, which can be added to a table.

Column width

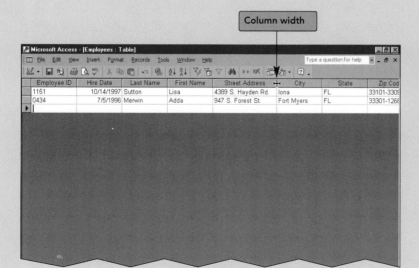

Column Width (AC1.40)

Column width refers to the size of a field column in Datasheet view. It controls the amount of data you can see on the screen.

lab review

key terms

Best Fit   AC1.41
bound object   AC1.31
clip art   AC1.31
column width   AC1.40
current record   AC1.26
database   AC1.6
Database toolbar   AC1.5
datasheet   AC1.26
data type   AC1.16
drawing object   AC1.31
field   AC1.6

field name   AC1.13
field property   AC1.18
field selector   AC1.26
field size   AC1.18
graphic   AC1.31
landscape   AC1.51
navigation buttons   AC1.26
Navigation mode   AC1.36
object   AC1.11
orientation   AC1.51
picture   AC1.31

portrait   AC1.51
primary key   AC1.20
record   AC1.6
record number indicator   AC1.26
record selector   AC1.26
relational database   AC1.6
table   AC1.6
unbound object   AC1.31
view   AC1.25
workspace   AC1.5

mous skills

The Microsoft Office User Specialist (MOUS) certification program is designed to measure your proficiency in performing basic tasks using the Office XP applications. Getting certified demonstrates that you have the skills and provides a valuable industry credential for employment. After completing this lab, you have learned the following Access 2002 Microsoft Office User Specialist skills:

Skill	Description	Page
Creating and Using Databases	Create Access databases	AC1.8
	Open database objects in different views	AC1.25
	Move among records	AC1.36
Creating and Modifying Tables	Create and modify tables	AC1.10, AC1.23
	Modify field properties	AC1.18
Viewing and Organizing Information	Enter, edit, and delete records	AC1.27, AC1.47

command summary

Command	Shortcut Keys	Button	Action
File/New	Ctrl + N		Opens New File task pane
File/Open	Ctrl + O		Opens an existing database
File/Close		X	Closes open window
File/Save	Ctrl + S		Saves database object
File/Page Setup		Setup	Setting page margins and page layout for printed output
File/Print Preview			Displays file as it will appear when printed
File/Print	Ctrl + P		Specifies print settings and prints current database object
File/Exit		X	Closes Access
Edit/Cut	Ctrl + X		Removes selected item and copies to the Clipboard
Edit/Copy	Ctrl + C		Duplictes selected item and copies to the Clipboard
Edit/Paste	Ctrl + V		Inserts copy of item in clipboard
Edit/Select Record			Selects current record
Edit/Delete Record			Deletes selected record
Edit/Delete Rows			Deletes selected field in Design view
Edit/Primary Key			Defines a field as a primary key field
View/Toolbars/Task Pane			Displays task pane
View/Datasheet View			Displays table in Datasheet view
View/Zoom/%		Fit	Displays previewed database object at specified percentage
Insert/Rows			Inserts new field in table in Design view
Insert/Object			Inserts an object into current field
Format/Column Width			Changes width of table columns in Datasheet view
Records/Remove Filter/Sort			Displays all records in table
Records/Data Entry			Hides existing records and displays Data Entry window

lab exercises

screen identification

In the following Access screen, several items are identified by letters. Enter the correct term for each item in the spaces provided.

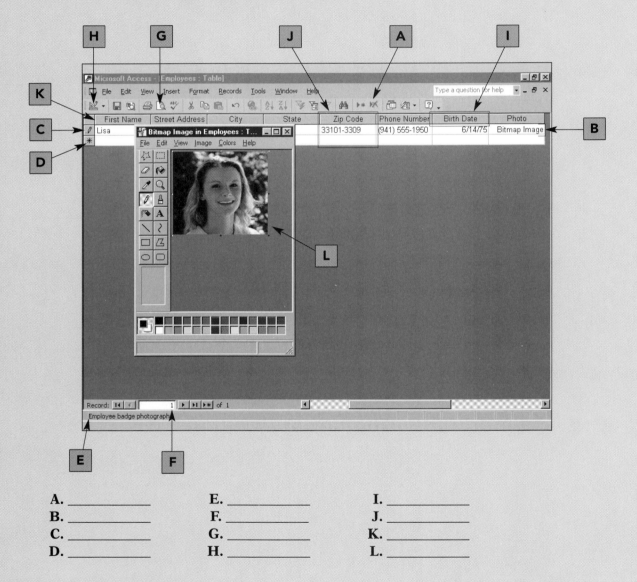

A. _____   E. _____   I. _____

B. _____   F. _____   J. _____

C. _____   G. _____   K. _____

D. _____   H. _____   L. _____

matching

Match the numbered item with the correct lettered description.

1. record   _____   a. an object associated with the table as a whole and not
2. view   connected to a specific field
3. relational database   _____   b. collection of related fields
4. primary key   _____   c. a way of looking at table data
5. Best Fit   _____   d. used to define the table structure
6. field size   _____   e. feature used to adjust column width to field contents
7. data type   _____   f. controls the type of data a field can contain
8. Design view   _____   g. field used to order records
9. Datasheet view   _____   h. displays table in row and column format
10. unbound object   _____   i. contains multiple tables linked by a common field
                             _____   j. controls the maximum number of characters that can be
                                          entered in a field

multiple choice

Circle the letter of the correct response.

1. The field property that limits a text data type to a certain size is called _____.
    a. label control
    b. operator
    c. field size
    d. field property

2. The steps of database development include planning, creating, and _____ data.
    a. entering
    b. graphing
    c. developing
    d. organizing

3. You can use the Objects _____ located at the left of the Database window to select the type
    of object you want to work with.
    a. bar
    b. buttons
    c. properties
    d. tabs

4. A field name is used to identify the _____ stored in a field.
    a. characters
    b. keys
    c. data
    d. graphics

5. The _____ type defines the type of data the field contains.
   a. property
   b. entry
   c. data
   d. specification

6. Field size, format, input mask, caption, and default value are _____.
   a. key elements
   b. field properties
   c. navigating modes
   d. data types

7. The record selector symbol indicates which record is the _____.
   a. bound control
   b. primary key
   c. destination file
   d. current record

8. The _____ mode is used to move from field to field and to delete an entire field entry.
   a. Edit
   b. Browser
   c. Entry
   d. Navigation

9. The _____ is a field that uniquely identifies each record.
   a. format
   b. table
   c. table definition
   d. primary key
   e. text property

10. You can examine the objects in your database using different window formats called _____.
    a. views
    b. masks
    c. tables
    d. dialog objects
    e. perspectives

true/false

Circle the correct answer to the following statements.

1. There is one specific view that is used to edit table data.		True	False
2. The first step in database development is planning.		True	False
3. Tables, forms, and reports are objects.		True	False
4. Field names are used to define properties for a database.		True	False
5. Text, memo, number, and date/time are data types.		True	False
6. Data properties are a set of characteristics that are associated with each field.		True	False
7. A person's first name is often used as the primary key.		True	False
8. You may lose data if your data and data type are incompatible.		True	False
9. Drawings and pictures can be added to a database.		True	False
10. While column width does not affect the amount of data that you can see on the screen, it does affect the amount of data that you can enter into a field.		True	False

Concepts

fill-in

Complete the following statements by filling in the blanks with the correct terms.

1. Database information is stored in _____.

2. Relational databases define _____ between tables by having common data in the tables.

3. The first step in developing a database is _____.

4. The _____ defines the type of data that can be entered in a field.

5. A(n) _____ is an item made up of different elements.

6. The set of characteristics associated with a field are the _____.

7. A descriptive label called a(n) _____ is used to identify the data stored in a field.

8. The _____ data type is used to format numbers with dollar signs and decimal places.

9. A(n) _____ is a field that uniquely identifies each record in a table.

10. _____ view allows the user to enter, edit, and delete records in a table.

discussion questions

Answer the following questions by preparing written responses.

1. Discuss several uses you may have for a relational database. Then explain the steps you would follow to create the first table.

2. Discuss why it is important to plan a database before creating it. How can proper planning save you time later?

3. Discuss the difference between a bound and an unbound object.

4. Design view and Datasheet view are two of the Access views. Discuss when it would be appropriate to use each of these views.

5. Discuss why it is important to choose the correct data type for a field. What may happen to the data if you change the data type?

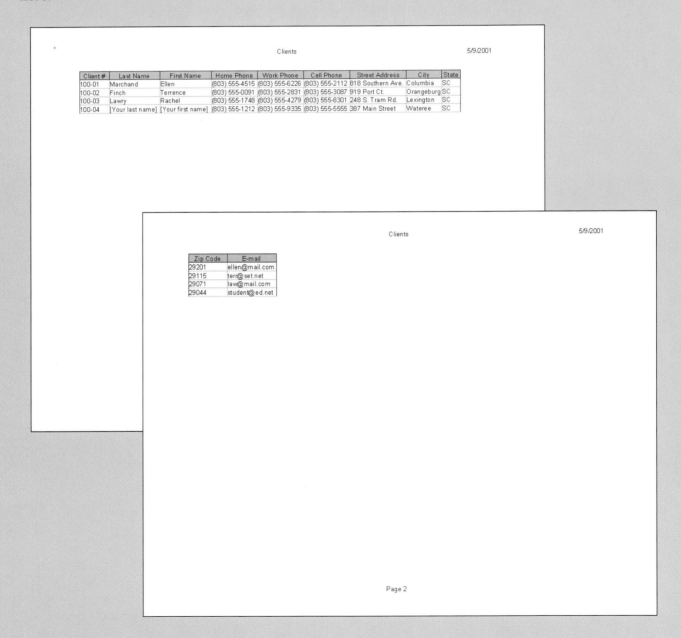

Hands-On Exercises

step-by-step

Creating a Client Database

★ **1.** Simply Beautiful is a day spa with several Tri-County locations. Up until now the spa's owner, Maria Dell, has kept separate records at each location. She is finding, however, that several of the spa's clients frequent more than one location. Therefore, Ms. Dell has asked you to build a database that will enable her to keep information about the spa's clients in one central location. When you are finished, a printout of your completed database table should look like that shown here.

To create the client database, follow these steps:

a. Create a database named Beautiful. Design a table using the following field information:

Field Data	Type	Description	Field Size
Client #	Text	A unique 5-digit number	6
Last Name	Text		25
First Name	Text		25
Home Phone	Text		15
Work Phone	Text		15
Cell Phone	Text		15
Street Address	Text		30
City	Text		25
State	Text	2-letter abbreviation	2
Zip Code	Text		10
E-mail	Text		30

b. Make the Client No. field the primary key field.
c. Save the table as Clients.
d. Switch to Datasheet view and enter the following records into the table:

Record 1	Record 2	Record 3	Record 4
100-01	100-02	100-03	100-04
Marchand	Finch	Lawry	[Your last name]
Ellen	Terrence	Rachel	[Your first name]
(803) 555-4515	(803) 555-0091	(803) 555-1748	(803) 555-1212
(803) 555-6226	(803) 555-2831	(803) 555-4279	(803) 555-9335
(803) 555-2112	(803) 555-3087	(803) 555-8301	(803) 555-5555
818 Southern Ave.	919 Port Ct.	248 S. Tram Rd.	387 Main Street
Columbia	Orangeburg	Lexington	Wateree
SC	SC	SC	SC
29201	29115	29071	29044
Ellen@mail.com	Terr@set.net	Law@mail.com	Student@ed.net

e. Adjust the column widths appropriately.
f. Change the page orientation to landscape.
g. Preview, print, save, and close the table.

Creating an Advertiser Database

★★ **2.** You are a member of the homeowner's association for your community. To keep the residents informed about issues and events, the association distributes a monthly newsletter, Happenings. In the past year, there has been a rapid growth in building, including more houses and small office complexes. There are also plans to bring a school, fire station, and shopping center to your community. Consequently, the newsletter is now the size of a small magazine, and the homeowners' dues are not covering the expense of publishing it. The editorial staff has already begun selling ad space in the newsletter to local businesses, and based on your background in database management, they have asked you to set up a database to keep track of the advertiser contact information. You agree to design such a database and tell them you will have something to show them at the next meeting. Your printed database table should look like that shown here.

Advertisers   5/9/2001

Billing #	Business Name	Business Type	Contact Name	Contact Phone	Billing Street	Billing City	Billing State	Billing Zip
01D01	Discount Drugs	Pharmacy	Linda Donaldson	(520) 555-2233	124 Desert Way	Benson	AZ	85602
02A01	Ace Auto	Auto Repair	Frank Mason	(520) 555-3903	595 Main St.	Benson	AZ	85602
03P01	Pen and Ink	Office Supplies	Lu Yung	(520) 555-5050	201 Main St.	Benson	AZ	85602
04W01	Walkwells	Shoe Store	Student Name	(520) 555-3589	101 A Street	Benson	AZ	85602

Page 1

To create the advertiser database, follow these steps:

a. Create a database named Happenings. Design a table using the following field information:

Field Data	Type	Description	Field Size
Billing #	Text	Unique 5-digit billing code and business ID	5
Business Name	Text		25
Business Type	Text		15
Contact Name	Text		30
Contact Phone	Text		15
Billing Street	Text		30
Billing City	Text		25
Billing State	Text		2
Billing Zip	Text		10

b. Make the Billing # field the primary key field.
c. Save the table as Advertisers.
d. Switch to Datasheet view and enter the following records into the table, using Copy and Paste for fields that have the same data (such as the city):

Record 1	Record 2	Record 3	Record 4
01D01	02A01	03P01	04W01
Discount Drugs	Ace Auto	Pen and Ink	Walkwells
Pharmacy	Auto Repair	Office Supplies	Shoe Store
Linda Donaldson	Frank Mason	Lu Yung	[Your Name]
(520) 555-2233	(520) 555-3903	(520) 555-5050	(520) 555-3589
124 Desert Way	595 Main St.	201 Main St.	101 A Street
Benson	Benson	Benson	Benson
AZ	AZ	AZ	AZ
85602	85602	85602	85602

e. Switch back to Design view and change the field sizes for Business Name and Business Type to 30 and 20, respectively. Save the changes.
f. Switch back to Datasheet view and best fit the column widths.
g. Display the records in primary key order.
h. Change the page orientation to landscape.
i. Print, save, and close the table.

Creating a Product Vendor Database

★ ★ **3.** The Downtown Internet Cafe, which you helped the owner, Evan, get off the ground, is an
★   overwhelming success. The clientele is growing every day, as is the demand for the beverages you
serve. Up until now, the information about the vendors has been kept in an alphabetical card file.
This has become quite unwieldy, however, and Evan would like a more sophisticated tracking
system. For starters, he would like you to create a database containing each supply item and the
contact information for the vendor that sells that item. When you are finished, your printed
database table should look like that shown here.

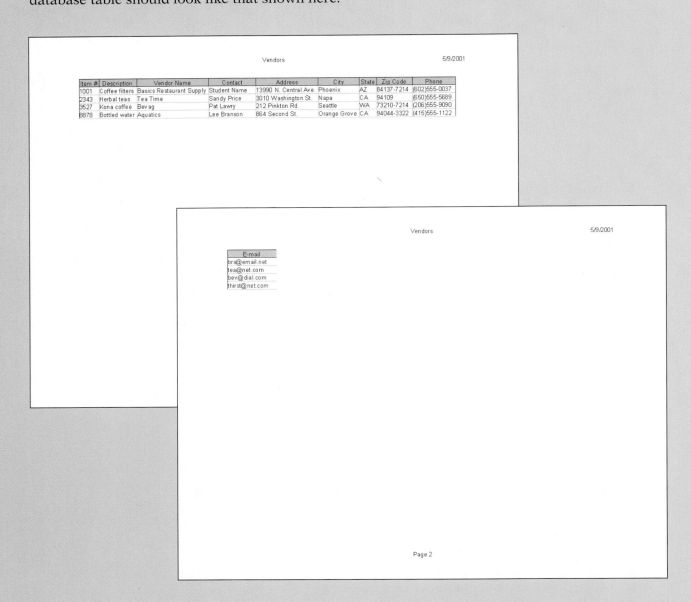

To create the database, follow these steps:

a. Create a database named Supplies. Design a table using the following field information:

Field Data	Type	Description	Field Size
Item #	Text	Unique 4-digit product number	4
Description	Text	Name of product	50
Vendor Name	Text	Name of supplier	50
Contact	Text	First & last name of contact person	50
Address	Text		50
City	Text		50
State	Text	2-letter abbreviation	2
Zip Code	Text	Include the 4-digit extension number if possible	10
Phone	Text	Include the area code in parentheses: (999) 123-4567	15
E-mail	Text	E-mail address of contact person	30

b. Make the Item # field the primary key field.

c. Save the table as Vendors.

d. Enter the following records into the table in Datasheet view:

Record 1	Record 2	Record 3
3527	2343	5721
Kona coffee	Herbal teas	Juice
Bevag	Tea Time	Natural Nectors
Pat Lawry	Sandy Price	Roberta White
212 Pinkton Rd.	3010 Washington St.	747 Manson Ave.
Seattle	Napa	Seattle
WA	CA	WA
73210-7214	94019	73210
(206) 555-9090	(650) 555-5689	(206) 555-0616
bev@dial.com	tea@net.com	nector@dial.com

e. Add the following records into the table in Data Entry:

Record 1	Record 2
8878	1001
Bottled water	Coffee filters
Aquatics	Basics Restaurant Supply
Lee Branson	Mandy Swanson
864 Second St.	13990 N. Central Ave.
Orange Grove	Phoenix
CA	AZ
94044-3213	84137-7214
(415) 555-1122	(602) 555-0037
thirst@net.com	brs@email.net

f. Return to Datasheet view and display the records in primary key order.

g. Adjust the column widths appropriately.

h. Edit the record for Item # 8878 to change the four-digit zip code extension from 3213 to **3322**.

i. Delete the record for Natural Nectors.

j. Edit the record for Item # 1001 to replace the current Contact name with your name.

k. Change to landscape orientation.

l. Preview the table.

m. Print, save, and close the table.

Creating an Informational Database

★ ★ ★ **4.** You have just been hired by Adventure Travel to create and maintain a database containing information about the tours they offer and the accommodations that are part of each tour package. When you are finished, your printed database table should look like that shown here.

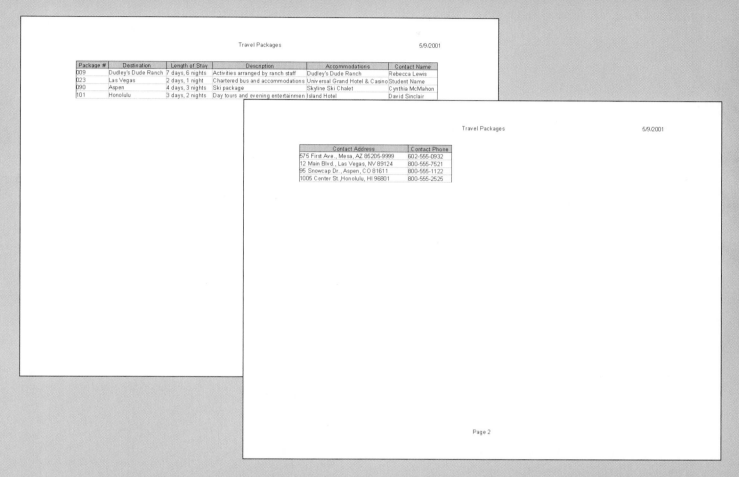

To create the database, follow these steps:

a. Create a database named Adventure Travel. Design a table using the following field information and copy repetitive text where possible:

Field Data	Type	Description	Field Size
Package #	Text	Unique 3-digit number	3
Destination	Text		20
Length of Stay	Text	Enter as # days, # nights	20
Description	Text	Package details (20 words or less)	20
Accommodations	Text	Name of hotel, motel, or other lodging	20
Contact Name	Text		20
Contact Address	Text	Street address, city, state, and zip code	20
Contact Phone	Text	Enter as ###-###-#### (e.g., 800-555-5555)	15

b. Make the Package # field the primary key field.

c. Change the Contact Name and Accomodations field sizes to **30** and the Contact Address field size to **50**.

d. Change the size of the Description field to **50** and its description to **10 words or less**.

e. Save the table as **Travel Packages**.

f. Enter the following records into the table in Table Datasheet view:

Record 1	**Record 2**	**Record 3**
101	009	212
Honolulu	Dudley's Dude Ranch	Washington, DC
3 days, 2 nights	7 days, 6 nights	7 days, 6 nights
Day tours and evening entertainment	Activities arranged by ranch staff	Tour of capital sites
Island Hotel	Dudley's Dude Ranch	Capitol Motel
David Sinclair	Rebecca Lewis	Lawrence Hallins
1005 Center St., Honolulu, HI 96801	575 First Ave., Mesa, AZ 85205	1000 Capitol Way, Washington, DC 20235
800-555-2525	602-555-0932	202-555-0048

g. Add the following records into the table in Data Entry:

Record 1	**Record 2**
023	090
Las Vegas	Aspen
2 days, 1 night	4 days, 3 nights
Chartered bus and accommodations	Ski package
Universal Grand Hotel & Casino	Skyline Ski Chalet
Barry Frazier	Cynthia McMahon
12 Main Blvd., Las Vegas, NV 89124	95 Snowcap Dr., Aspen, CO 81611
800-555-7521	800-555-1122

h. Return to Datasheet view and display the records in primary key order.

i. Adjust the column widths appropriately.

j. Edit the record for Package # 023 to replace Barry Frazier's name with your name.

k. Add a four-digit zip code extension of **9999** to the dude ranch address.

l. Delete record 212.

m. Change the orientation to landscape.

n. Preview and print the table, then save and close it.

Creating a Tracking Database

★ ★ 5. As a volunteer at the Animal Rescue Foundation, you offer to create an Access database for them, to
★ help them keep track of the animals that are picked up from local shelters. It needs to show when
and which animals were boarded at the foundation, placed in foster homes, and placed in adoptive
homes. When you are finished, your printed database table should look like that shown here.
To create the database, follow these steps:

Tracking							5/9/2001
ID #	Type	Gender	Name	Boarded Date	Foster Date	Adoption Date	Photo
012	Dog	F	Erin	3/2/1998	4/1/1998		Bitmap Image
062	Cat	M	Max	12/9/1998			
123	Cat	M	Puddy	3/23/1998	4/15/1998		
199	Cat	F		1/15/1999		2/1/1999	
752	Horse	F	Student pet	2/7/1999			

Page 1

a. Create a database named Animal Rescue. Design a table using the following field information:

Field Data	Type	Description	Field Size/Format
ID #	Text	Unique 3-digit number given to animal when picked up from shelter	3
Type	Text	Type of animal (cat, dog, horse, etc.)	50
Gender	Text	Enter M (male) or F (female)	1
Name	Text	Name of animal, if any	50
Boarded Date	Date/Time	Date animal was boarded	Short Date
Foster Date	Date/Time	Date animal was placed in foster home	Short Date
Adoption Date	Date/Time	Date animal was adopted	Short Date
Photo	OLE object		

b. Change the field size of Type to 10 and Name to 30.
c. Make the ID # field the primary key field, and save the table as Tracking.

d. Enter six records: two for animals that are still being boarded (make one of these a dog), another two for animals in foster homes, and another two for animals that have been adopted. Enter [your name]'s Pet in the Name field of the last new record you add.

e. In Datasheet view, select the Photo field in a record you entered for a dog that is still being boarded. Insert the Whitedog.bmp picture file as an object in the selected field. View the inserted picture.

f. Display the records in primary key order. Adjust the column widths appropriately and change to landscape orientation.

g. Preview and print the table, then save and close the table.

on your own

Music Collection Database

★ 1. You have just purchased a 200-disk CD carousel and now you would like to organize and catalogue your CDs. You realize that without an updateable list, it will be difficult to maintain an accurate list of what is in the changer. To get the most out of your new purchase you decide a database is in order. Create a new database called Music Collection, and a table called CD Catalogue. The table you create should include the Artist's Name, Album title, Genre, and Position Number. Make the Position field the primary key (because you may have multiple CDs by a given artist). Add an entry that includes your name as the artist. Enter at least 15 records. Preview and print the table when you are finished.

Employee Phone List

★★ 2. When you first started working at Lewis & Lewis, Inc., as an administrative assistant, you knew everyone by name and had no problems taking and transferring calls. However, the company has grown quite a bit and you no longer have everyone's phone extension memorized. Since you are on the computer most of the day, you decide that having this information online would be quite helpful, not only when you receive calls, but also to print out and distribute phone lists within the office. Create a database called Lewis Personnel and a table named Phone List that contains the employees' last and first names, position, and extension number, with the extension field as the primary key (because each employee should have a unique phone extension). Enter at least ten records, including one with your name as the employee and a phone extension of 0. Preview and print the table when you are finished.

Patient Database

★★ 3. You have been hired to create a patient database by a dentist who just opened his own office. Create a database called Patient Information and a table named Patient Data. The database table you set up should contain patient identification numbers, last and first names, addresses, phone numbers, "referred by" information, "patient since" dates, and insurance company information. Use appropriate field sizes and make the ID number field the primary key. Enter at least ten records, using both Data Entry and Datasheet view, adjusting the column widths as necessary. Display the table in primary key order. To practice editing data, change two of the records. Add a record that contains your name as the patient. Preview and print the table.

Expenses Database

★★ 4. You work in the accounting department at a start-up company called JK Enterprises. One of your ★ duties is to process expense reports, which up until now was a simple task of having the employees fill out a form and submit it to you for payment. You would then cut a check for them and charge it to the general expense fund of the company. However, the company has grown tremendously in the last year, adding employees and departments at a rapid rate, and the executive team has decided that it is time to start managing the income and expenses on a much more detailed level. To this end, you need to create a database that includes the employee ID, submission date, expense type, and expense amount for each expense report that is turned in. Name the database JK Enterprises and the table **Expenses**. Use the Currency data type for the amount field, and appropriate data types for the remaining fields. Make the employee ID the primary key. Use both Data Entry and Datasheet views to enter at least 15 records, copying and pasting some of the data to minimize your data entry efforts. Adjust the column widths as necessary. Delete one of the records you just entered, and then edit one of the remaining records so it contains your name as the employee. Set the orientation to landscape, and then preview and print the table. You work for Golden Oldies, a small company that locates and sells record albums.

on the web

The current method used to keep track of on-hand inventory is a notebook taped to the storeroom wall with a typewritten list where employees check records in and out. The business and inventory has grown large enough now to warrant an online database. Create a database named Golden Oldies with a table named **Inventory** that contains stock identification numbers, record titles, artist, category (such as jazz, blues, classical, and rock) cost, and inventory on hand. Size the fields as appropriate and assign a primary key to one of them. To obtain title, category, and artist information for records you might sell in this type of company, search for "collectable record albums" on the Web and select an appropriate site. Use this information to enter records into your table, adjusting column widths as necessary. Display the table in primary key order, edit one of the records, delete one of the records, and change the artist's name in one of the records to your name. Set landscape orientation, and then preview and print the table.

Modifying a Table and Creating a Form

LAB 2

objectives

After completing this lab, you will know how to:

1.	Navigate a large table.
2.	Change field format properties.
3.	Set default field values.
4.	Insert a field.
5.	Add validity checks
6.	Hide and redisplay fields.
7.	Find and replace data.
8.	Use Undo.
9.	Sort records.
10.	Create and enter records into a form.
11.	Preview, print, close, and save a form.

**Field properties make a table easier
to use and more accurate.**

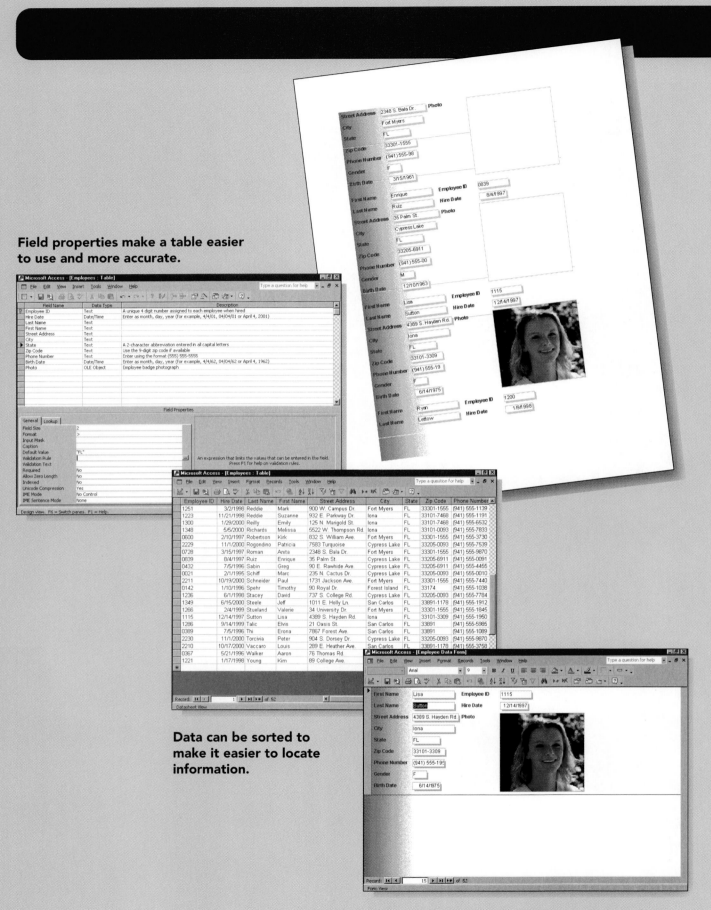

**Data can be sorted to
make it easier to locate
information.**

**Forms display information in an easy-to-read
manner and make data entry easier.**

Lifestyle Fitness Club

The Lifestyle Fitness Club owners, Brian and Tami, are very pleased with your plans for the organization of the database and with your progress in creating the first table of basic employee data. As you have seen, creating a database takes planning and a lot of time to set up the structure and enter the data. As you have continued to add more employee records to the table, you have noticed several errors. You also realize that you forgot to include a field for the employee's sex. Even with the best of planning and care, errors occur and the information may change. You will see how easy it is to modify the database structure and to customize field properties to provide more control over how and what data is entered in a field.

Even more impressive, as you will see in this lab, is the program's ability to locate information in the database. This is where all the hard work of entering data pays off. With a click of a button you can find data that might otherwise take hours to locate. The end result saves time and improves the accuracy of the output.

You will also see how you can make the data you are looking at onscreen more pleasing and easier to read by creating and using a form.

© Corbis

Navigating a Large Table

You have continued to add more records to the Lifestyle Fitness Employees database. As you entered the data, you know you made data entry errors that still need to be corrected. Additionally, you have found that with the addition of records, it is taking much longer to move around in the datasheet. Typical database tables are very large and consequently can be very inefficient to navigate. Learning how to move around in a large table will save time and help you get the job done faster. You want to open the expanded database which you saved using a new file name, and continue working on and refining the Employees table.

1
- Start Access.
- In the New File task pane, under Open a File, click [📂 More files...].

HAVING TROUBLE?
If your task pane is not displayed, choose View/Toolbars/Task Pane.

Another Method
You can also use the File/Open menu equivalent, or the Ctrl + O keyboard shortcut.

- From the Look In dropdown list box, change the location to the drive containing your data files.
- Double-click ac02_EmployeeRecords.

Your screen should be similar to Figure 2.1

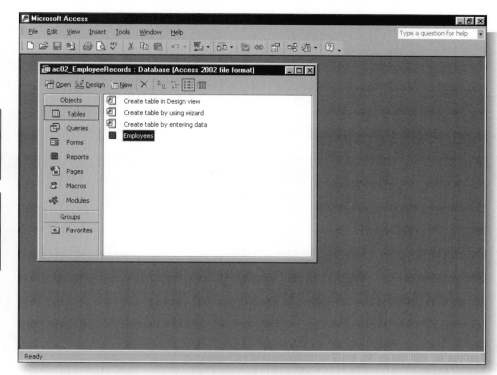

Figure 2.1

The Database window for the Employee Records file is displayed. You will open the "Employees" table containing the additional employee records.

2
- Double-click the "Employees" table.
- Maximize the Datasheet window.

Your screen should be similar to Figure 2.2

HAVING TROUBLE?
Your screen may display a different number of records depending on your monitor settings.

Records 1-26 displayed

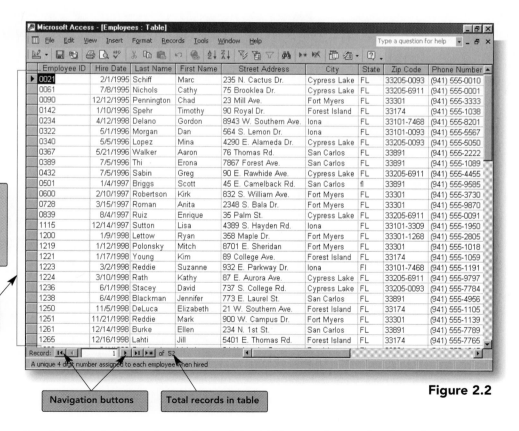

Navigation buttons   Total records in table

Figure 2.2

By default, the Datasheet view of the Table window is displayed. As you can see from the record number indicator, there are now 52 records in the table.

Navigating Using the Keyboard

In a large table, there are many methods you can use to quickly navigate through records in Datasheet view. You can always use the mouse to move from one field or record to another. However, if the information is not visible in the window, you must scroll the window first. The following table presents several keyboard methods that will help you move around in Navigation mode.

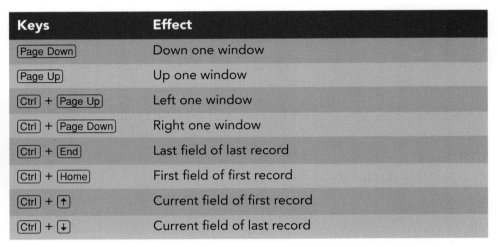

Keys	Effect
Page Down	Down one window
Page Up	Up one window
Ctrl + Page Up	Left one window
Ctrl + Page Down	Right one window
Ctrl + End	Last field of last record
Ctrl + Home	First field of first record
Ctrl + ↑	Current field of first record
Ctrl + ↓	Current field of last record

Another Method

You can also move to a specific record by typing its record number in the status bar's record indicator box.

Currently, records 1 through 26 are displayed in the window. You can easily move from one window of records to the next.

3 ● **Press** Page Down.

HAVING TROUBLE?

If your screen displays a different number of records, this is because your monitor size and system setup may be different than those used to create the figures in the text.

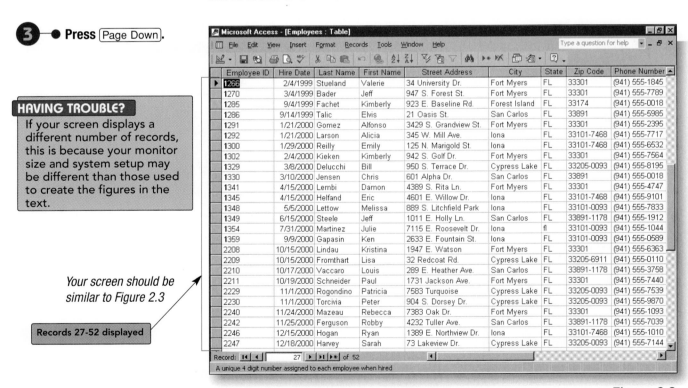

Your screen should be similar to Figure 2.3

Records 27-52 displayed

Figure 2.3

Now records 27 through 52 are displayed in the window. The first record in the window is now the current record.

Due to the number and width of the fields, not all fields can be displayed in the window at the same time. Rather than scrolling the window horizontally to see the additional fields, you can quickly move to the right a window at a time.

4 ● Press Ctrl + Page Down.

Your screen should be similar to Figure 2.4

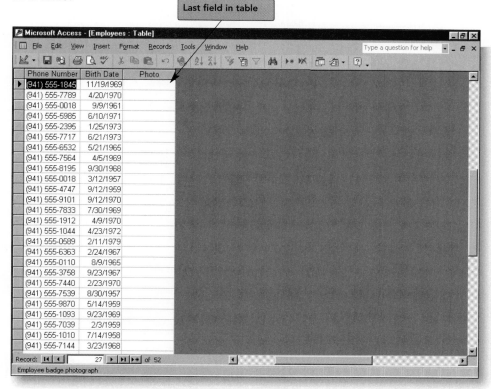

Figure 2.4

The last field in the table is now visible in the window.

Moving Using the Navigation Buttons

The navigation buttons in the status bar also provide navigation shortcuts. These buttons are described in the following table.

Button	Effect
◄	First record, same field
◄	Previous record, same field
►	Next record, same field
►|	Last record, same field
►*	New (blank) record

You will use the navigation buttons to move to the same field that is currently selected of the last record and then back to the same field of the first record then you will move to the first field of the first record.

5 ● Click 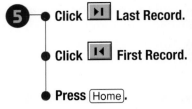 **Last Record.**

● Click **First Record.**

● Press Home.

*Your screen should be
similar to Figure 2.5*

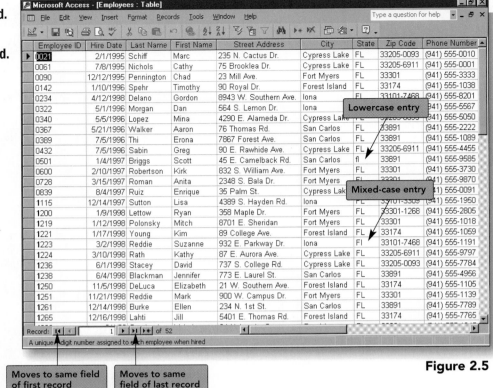

Employee ID	Hire Date	Last Name	First Name	Street Address	City	State	Zip Code	Phone Number
0021	2/1/1995	Schiff	Marc	235 N. Cactus Dr.	Cypress Lake	FL	33205-0093	(941) 555-0010
0061	7/8/1995	Nichols	Cathy	75 Brooklea Dr.	Cypress Lake	FL	33205-6911	(941) 555-0001
0090	12/12/1995	Pennington	Chad	23 Mill Ave.	Fort Myers	FL	33301	(941) 555-3333
0142	1/10/1996	Spehr	Timothy	90 Royal Dr.	Forest Island	FL	33174	(941) 555-1038
0234	4/12/1998	Delano	Gordon	8943 W. Southern Ave.	Iona	FL	33101-7468	(941) 555-8201
0322	5/1/1996	Morgan	Dan	564 S. Lemon Dr.	Iona			(941) 555-5567
0340	5/5/1996	Lopez	Mina	4290 E. Alameda Dr.	Cypress Lake	FL		(941) 555-5050
0367	5/21/1996	Walker	Aaron	76 Thomas Rd.	San Carlos	FL	33891	(941) 555-2222
0389	7/5/1996	Thi	Erona	7867 Forest Ave.	San Carlos	FL	33891	(941) 555-1089
0432	7/5/1996	Sabin	Greg	90 E. Rawhide Ave.	Cypress Lake	FL	33205-6911	(941) 555-4455
0501	1/4/1997	Briggs	Scott	45 E. Camelback Rd.	San Carlos	fl	33891	(941) 555-9585
0600	2/10/1997	Robertson	Kirk	832 S. William Ave.	Fort Myers	FL	33301	(941) 555-3730
0728	3/15/1997	Roman	Anita	2348 S. Bala Dr.	Fort Myers	FL	33301	(941) 555-9870
0839	8/4/1997	Ruiz	Enrique	35 Palm St.	Cypress Lake			(941) 555-0091
1115	12/14/1997	Sutton	Lisa	4389 S. Hayden Rd.	Iona	FL	33101-3309	(941) 555-1950
1200	1/9/1998	Lettow	Ryan	358 Maple Dr.	Fort Myers	FL	33301-1268	(941) 555-2805
1219	1/12/1998	Polonsky	Mitch	8701 E. Sheridan	Fort Myers	FL	33301	(941) 555-1018
1221	1/17/1998	Young	Kim	89 College Ave.	Forest Island	FL	33174	(941) 555-1059
1223	3/2/1998	Reddie	Suzanne	932 E. Parkway Dr.	Iona	Fl	33101-7468	(941) 555-1191
1224	3/10/1998	Rath	Kathy	87 E. Aurora Ave.	Cypress Lake	FL	33205-6911	(941) 555-9797
1236	6/1/1998	Stacey	David	737 S. College Rd.	Cypress Lake	FL	33205-0093	(941) 555-7784
1238	6/4/1998	Blackman	Jennifer	773 E. Laurel St.	San Carlos	FL	33891	(941) 555-4956
1250	11/5/1998	DeLuca	Elizabeth	21 W. Southern Ave.	Forest Island	FL	33174	(941) 555-1105
1251	11/21/1998	Reddie	Mark	900 W. Campus Dr.	Fort Myers	FL	33301	(941) 555-1139
1261	12/14/1998	Burke	Ellen	234 N. 1st St.	San Carlos	FL	33891	(941) 555-7789
1265	12/16/1998	Lahti	Jill	5401 E. Thomas Rd.	Forest Island	FL	33174	(941) 555-7765

Lowercase entry

Mixed-case entry

Record: 1 of 52

A unique 4-digit number assigned to each employee when hired

Moves to same field
of first record

Moves to same
field of last record

Figure 2.5

Customizing and Inserting Fields

As you looked through the records, you noticed that records 11 and 41 have
lowercase entries in the State field, and record 19 has a mixed-case entry.
You would like all the State field entries to be consistently entered in all uppercase letters. Additionally, you realize that you forgot to include a field
for each employee's gender. While developing a table, you can modify and
refine how the table operates. You can easily add and delete fields and add
restrictions on the data that can be entered in a field as well as define how
the data entered in a field will be displayed.

Setting Display Formats

You will begin by fixing the display of the entries in the State field. You do
this by setting a display format for the field in Design view.

1 Click 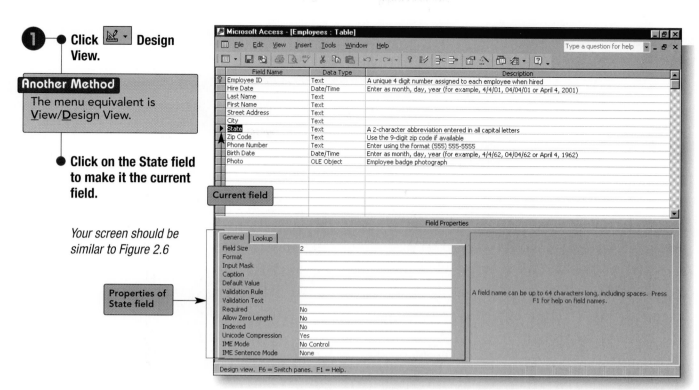 Design View.

Another Method

The menu equivalent is View/Design View.

● Click on the State field to make it the current field.

Your screen should be similar to Figure 2.6

Properties of State field

Figure 2.6

The properties associated with the State field are displayed in the General tab. The Format property is used to customize the way an entry is displayed.

concept 1

Format Property

1 You can change the way numbers, dates, times, and text display and print by defining the fields' **Format property**. Format properties do not change the way Access stores data, only how the data is displayed. To change the format of a field, you can select from predefined formats or create a custom format by entering different symbols in the Format text box. Text and Memo Data Types can use any of the four symbols shown in the following table.

Symbol	Meaning	Example
@	A required text character or space	@@@-@@-@@@@ would display 123456789 as 123–45–6789. Nine characters or spaces are required.
>	Forces all characters to uppercase	> would display SMITH whether you entered SMITH, smith, or Smith.
<	Forces all characters to lowercase	< would display smith whether you entered SMITH, smith, or Smith.
&	An optional text character	@@-@@& would display 12345 as 12–345 and 12.34 as 12–34. Four out of five characters are required, and a fifth is optional.

So, to change the State field's display format to all uppercase, you just have to enter the appropriate symbol.

2 ● **Move to the Format field property text box.**

● **Type >.**

Your screen should be similar to Figure 2.7

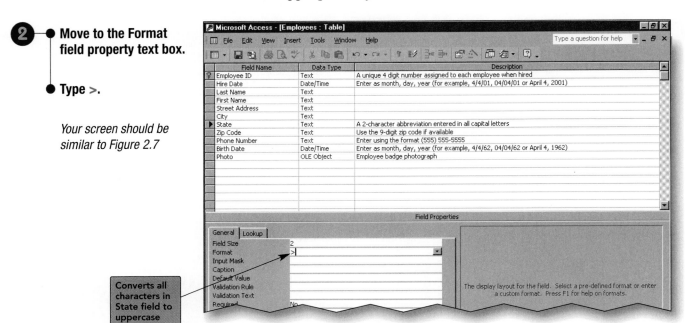

Converts all characters in State field to uppercase

Figure 2.7

Next, you'll see what effect your display format change has made on the existing records.

3 ● **Click** ▦ ▾ **Datasheet view.**

● **Click** Yes **to save the table.**

Your screen should be similar to Figure 2.8

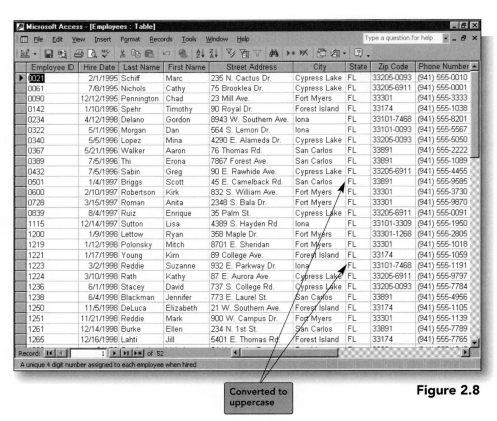

Converted to uppercase

Figure 2.8

In this window, you can see that records 11 (Scott Briggs) and 19 (Suzanne Reddie) now correctly display the state in capital letters.

Setting Default Values

Because all the club locations are in Florida, it is unlikely that any club employees will live in another state. So, rather than having to enter the same state for each record, you can have the State field automatically display FL. This is done by setting the field's Default Value property.

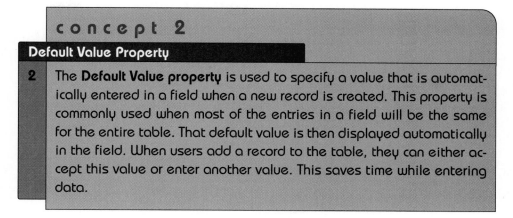

concept 2

Default Value Property

2   The **Default Value property** is used to specify a value that is automatically entered in a field when a new record is created. This property is commonly used when most of the entries in a field will be the same for the entire table. That default value is then displayed automatically in the field. When users add a record to the table, they can either accept this value or enter another value. This saves time while entering data.

You will set the State field's default value to display FL.

- Click 🖳 ▾ **Design View.**

- **Make the State field the current field.**

- **Click in the Default Value property text box.**

- **Type FL.**

- **Press** ⏎Enter.

Your screen should be similar to Figure 2.9

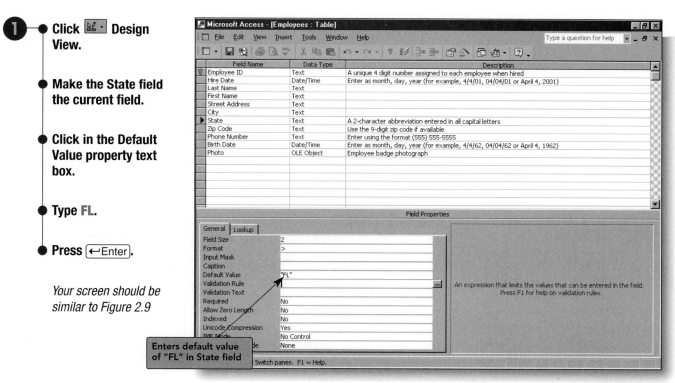

Enters default value of "FL" in State field

Figure 2.9

The default value is automatically enclosed in quotes to identify the entry as a group of characters called a **character string**. To see how setting a default value affects your table, you will return to Datasheet view and look at a new blank record.

● Click 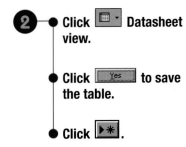 **Datasheet view.**

● Click [Yes] **to save the table.**

● Click [▶*].

Your screen should be similar to Figure 2.10

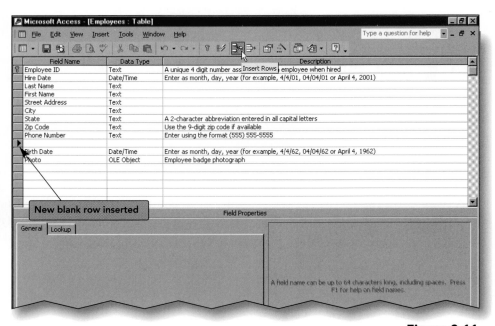

Default value displayed in State field of new record

Figure 2.10

Another Method

You can also add a field in Datasheet view by using Insert/Column to insert a column where you want the new field to be located, and giving the new column the desired field name. However, you still need to switch to Design view to set the new field's properties.

The new blank record at the end of the table displays FL as the default value for the State field.

Inserting a Field

Now you want to add the new field to hold each employee's gender. Although it is better to include all the necessary fields when creating the table structure, it is possible to add or remove fields from a table at a later time. After looking at the order of the fields, you decide to add the Gender field between the Phone Number and Birth Date fields. To do so, you will switch to Design view to insert the new field in the table.

1

● Click 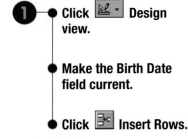 **Design view.**

● **Make the Birth Date field current.**

● Click [▦] **Insert Rows.**

Another Method

The menu equivalent is Insert/Rows. You can also use the Insert Row command on the shortcut menu.

Your screen should be similar to Figure 2.11

New blank row inserted

Figure 2.11

A new blank row is inserted into the table. Next, you'll name the field and set its properties.

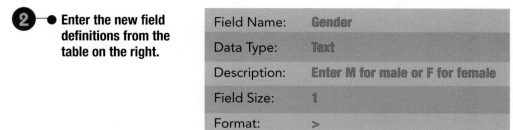

2 ● Enter the new field definitions from the table on the right.

Field Name:	Gender
Data Type:	Text
Description:	Enter M for male or F for female
Field Size:	1
Format:	>

Your screen should be similar to Figure 2.12

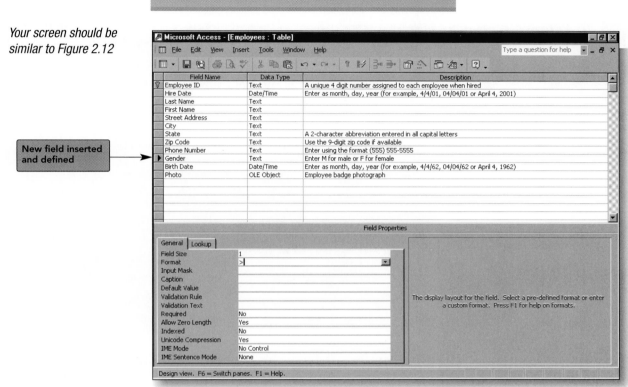

New field inserted and defined

Figure 2.12

Adding Validity Checks

The only two characters you want the Gender field to accept are M for male and F for female. To specify that these two characters are the only entries acceptable in the Gender field, you will add a validity check to it.

concept 3

Validity Check

3 Access automatically performs certain checks, called **validity checks**, on values entered in a field to make sure that the values are valid for the field type. A Text field type has few restrictions, whereas a Number field type accepts only numeric entries. You can also create your own validity checks for a field, which Access will apply during data entry. A validity check is defined by entering a validation rule for the field's property. A **validation rule** consists of an expression that defines the acceptable values. An **ex-**pression is a formula consisting of a combination of symbols that evaluates to a single value. Expressions are used throughout Access to create validity checks, queries, forms, and reports.

You can also include a validation text message. **Validation text** is an explanatory message that appears if a user attempts to enter invalid information in a text field for which there is a validity check. If you do not specify a message, Access will display a default error message, which will not clearly describe the reason for the error.

For some examples of possible expressions, see the table below.

Expression	Result
=[Sales Amount] + [Sales Tax]	Sums values in two fields.
="M" OR "F"	Includes M or F entries only.
>=#1/1/95# AND <=#12/31/95#	Includes entries greater than or equal to 1/1/95, and less than or equal to 12/31/95.
="Tennis Rackets"	Includes the entry Tennis Rackets only.

You create an expression by combining identifiers, operators, and values to produce the desired result. An **identifier** is an element that refers to the value of a field, a graphical object, or property. In the expression =[Sales Amount] + [Sales Tax], [Sales Amount] and [Sales Tax] are identifiers that refer to the values in the Sales Amount and Sales Tax fields.

An **operator** is a symbol or word that indicates that an operation is to be performed. A **comparison operator** is a symbol that allows you to make comparisons between two items. The table below describes the comparison operators.

Operator	Meaning
=	Equal to
<>	Not equal to
<	Less than
>	Greater than
<=	Less than or equal to
>=	Greater than or equal to

In addition, the OR and AND operators allow you to enter additional criteria in the same field or different fields.

Values are numbers, dates, or character strings. Character strings such as "M", "F", or "Tennis Rackets" are enclosed in quotation marks. Dates are enclosed in pound signs (#), as in #1/1/95#.

You want to enter a validation check for the Gender field that will only accept M for male and F for female.

The expression is entered in the Validation Rule field of the field's property.

1 ● **Move to the Validation Rule field property text box.**

● **Type M or F.**

● **Press ←Enter.**

● **For the validation text, type The only valid entry is M or F.**

Your screen should be similar to Figure 2.13

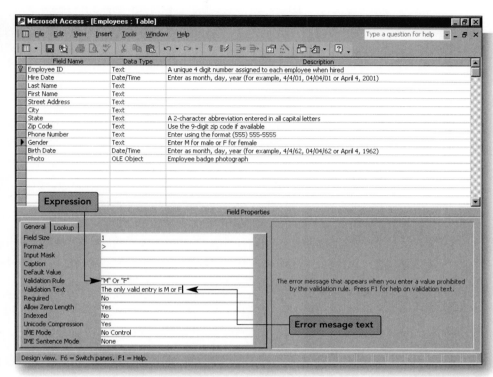

Figure 2.13

The expression states that the acceptable values can only be equal to an M or an F. Notice that Access automatically added quotation marks around the two character strings and changed the "o" in "or" to uppercase. Because the Format property has been set to convert all entries to uppercase, this means that an entry of m or f is as acceptable as M or F.

Next you want to add the data for the Gender field to the table, so you will switch back to Datasheet view.

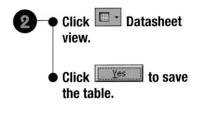

2 • Click [⊞ ▾] **Datasheet view.**

• Click [Yes] to save the table.

Your screen should be similar to Figure 2.14

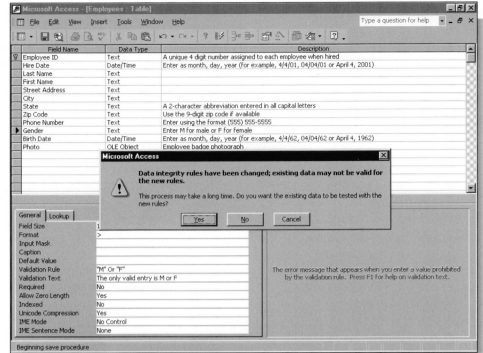

Figure 2.14

A message box advises you that data integrity rules have been changed. When you restructure a table, you often make changes that could result in a loss of data. Changes such as shortening field sizes, creating validity checks, or changing field types can cause existing data to become invalid. Because the field is new, there are no data values to verify, and a validation check is unnecessary at this time.

New field inserted

3 • Click [No].

• **Move to the Gender field for record 1.**

Your screen should be similar to Figure 2.15

Last Name	First Name	Street Address	City	State	Zip Code	Phone Number	Gender	Birth Dat ▲
▶ Schiff	Marc	235 N. Cactus Dr.	Cypress Lake	FL	33205-0093	(941) 555-0010		3/9/197
Nichols	Cathy	75 Brooklea Dr.	Cypress Lake	FL	33205-6911	(941) 555-0001		5/19/197
Pennington	Chad	23 Mill Ave.	Fort Myers	FL	33301	(941) 555-3333		7/7/196
Spehr	Timothy	90 Royal Dr.	Forest Island	FL	33174	(941) 555-1038		9/9/196
Delano	Gordon	8943 W. Southern Ave.	Iona	FL	33101-7468	(941) 555-8201		8/7/196
Morgan	Dan	564 S. Lemon Dr.	Iona	FL	33101-0093	(941) 555-5567		3/5/196
Lopez	Mina	4290 E. Alameda Dr.	Cypress Lake	FL	33205-0093	(941) 555-5050		2/25/196
Walker	Aaron	76 Thomas Rd.	San Carlos	FL	33891	(941) 555-2222		8/1/196
Thi	Erona	7867 Forest Ave.	San Carlos	FL	33891	(941) 555-1089		5/10/197
Sabin	Greg	90 E. Rawhide Ave.	Cypress Lake	FL	33205-6911	(941) 555-4455		9/30/197
Briggs	Scott	45 E. Camelback Rd.	San Carlos	FL	33891	(941) 555-9585		9/15/197
Robertson	Kirk	832 S. William Ave.	Fort Myers	FL	33301	(941) 555-3730		4/5/196
Roman	Anita	2348 S. Bala Dr.	Fort Myers	FL	33301	(941) 555-9870		3/15/196
Ruiz	Enrique	35 Palm St.	Cypress Lake	FL	33205-6911	(941) 555-0091		12/10/196
Sutton	Lisa	4389 S. Hayden Rd.	Iona	FL	33101-3309	(941) 555-1950		6/14/197
Lettow	Ryan	358 Maple Dr.	Fort Myers	FL	33301-1268	(941) 555-2805		11/15/197
Polonsky	Mitch	8701 E. Sheridan	Fort Myers	FL	33301	(941) 555-1018		3/13/197
Young	Kim	89 College Ave.	Forest Island	FL	33174	(941) 555-1059		4/12/197
Reddie	Suzanne	932 E. Parkway Dr.	Iona	FL	33101-7468	(941) 555-1191		7/14/195
Rath	Kathy	87 E. Aurora Ave.	Cypress Lake	FL	33205-6911	(941) 555-9797		5/30/196
Stacey	David	737 S. College Rd.	Cypress Lake	FL	33205-0093	(941) 555-7784		9/30/195
Blackman	Jennifer	773 E. Laurel St.	San Carlos	FL	33891	(941) 555-4956		1/22/197
DeLuca	Elizabeth	21 W. Southern Ave.	Forest Island	FL	33174	(941) 555-1105		8/21/196
Reddie	Mark	900 W. Campus Dr.	Fort Myers	FL	33301	(941) 555-1139		11/5/197
Burke	Ellen	234 N. 1st St.	San Carlos	FL	33891	(941) 555-7789		9/30/196
Lahti	Jill	5401 E. Thomas Rd.	Forest Island	FL	33174	(941) 555-7765		6/14/196

Record: ◄ ◄ [1] ► ►I ►* of 52

Enter M for male or F for female

Figure 2.15

The new field was added to the table between the Phone Number and Birth Date fields. To verify that the validity check works, you will enter an invalid field value in the Gender field for the first record.

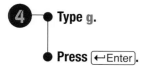

Type g.

Press ←Enter.

Your screen should be similar to Figure 2.16

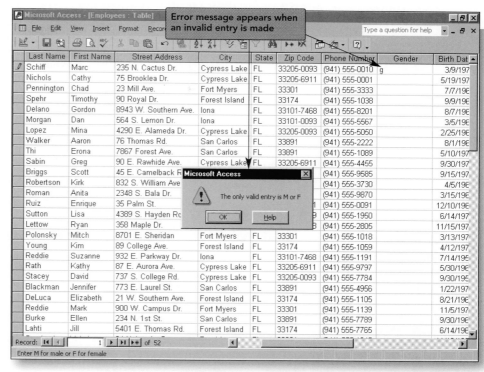

Figure 2.16

Access displays the error message you entered in the Validation Text box of Design view. To clear the error message and correct the entry,

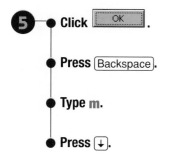

Click OK.

Press Backspace.

Type m.

Press ↓.

Your screen should be similar to Figure 2.17

Figure 2.17

The entry for the first record is accepted and displayed as an uppercase M.

Hiding and Redisplaying Fields

To enter the gender data for the rest of the fields, you want to use the First Name field as a guide. Unfortunately, the First Name and Gender fields are currently on opposite sides of the screen and will require you to scan your eyes back and forth across each record. You can avoid this by hiding the fields you do not need to see, and then redisplaying them when you are through entering the gender data.

Hiding Fields

A quick way to view two fields side by side (in this case, the First Name and Gender fields) is to hide the fields that are in between (the Street Address through Phone Number fields).

1 ● **Select the Street Address field through the Phone Number field.**

Additional Information
Drag along the column heads when the mouse pointer is ↓ to select the fields.

● **Choose Format/Hide Columns.**

Your screen should be similar to Figure 2.18

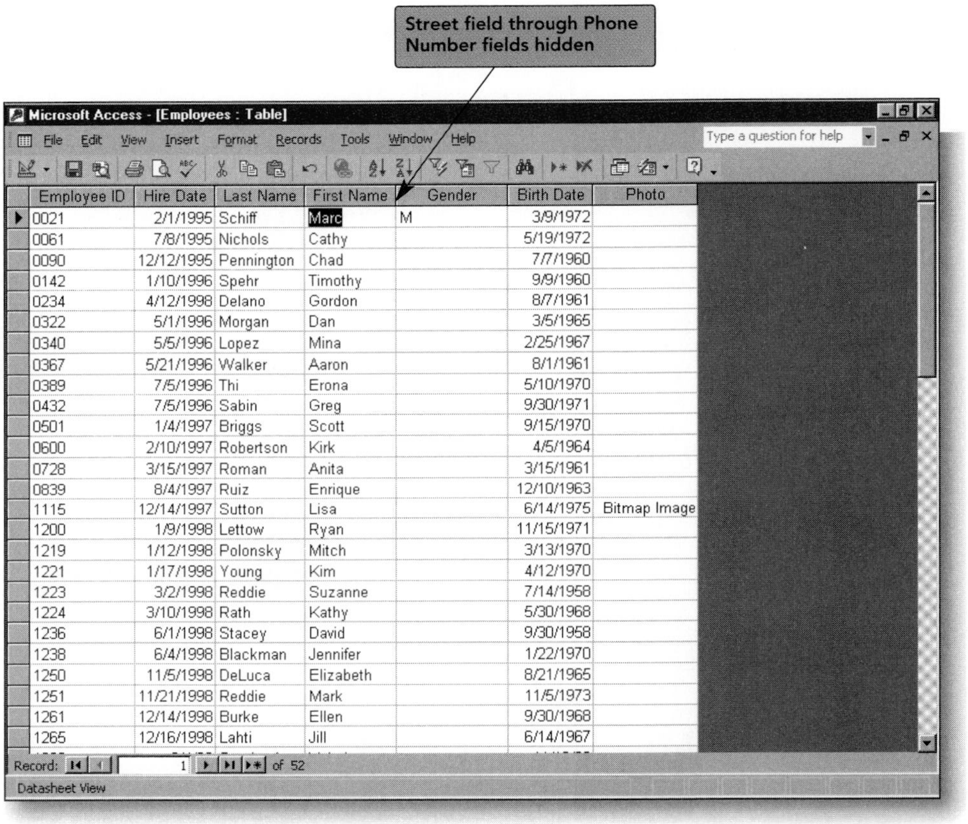

Street field through Phone Number fields hidden

Figure 2.18

Now the First Name and Gender columns are next to each other. You can now refer to the first name in each record to enter the correct gender data.

2 ● Enter the Gender field values for the remaining records by looking at the First Name field to determine whether the employee is male or female.

● Reduce the size of the Gender column using the Best Fit command.

HAVING TROUBLE?
Remember, to best fit data in a column, you double-click on its right border.

Your screen should be similar to Figure 2.19

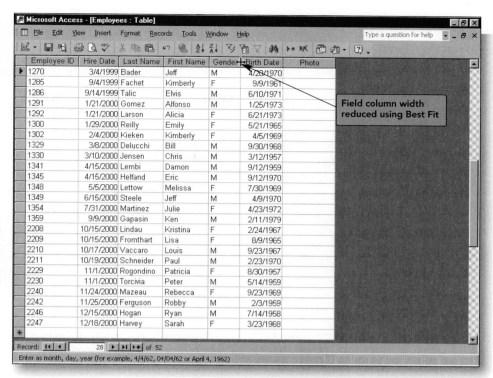

Figure 2.19

Redisplaying Hidden Fields

After you have entered the gender data for all of the records, you can redisplay the hidden fields.

1 ● Choose F**ormat**/**U**nhide Columns.

Your screen should be similar to Figure 2.20

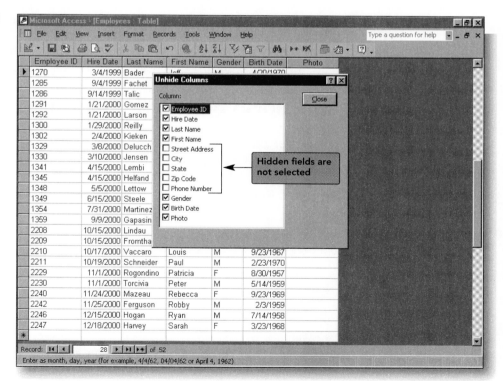

Figure 2.20

You use the Unhide Columns dialog box to select which currently hidden columns you want to redisplay. A checkmark in the box next to a column name indicates that the column is currently displayed; column names with no checkmarks indicate that they are currently hidden. You want to unhide all hidden columns in your table.

2 • Select the five column names that do not display checkmarks.

Additional Information
Notice that as you make each selection, the corresponding column reappears in the table datasheet behind the dialog box.

• Click **Close**.

Your screen should be similar to Figure 2.21

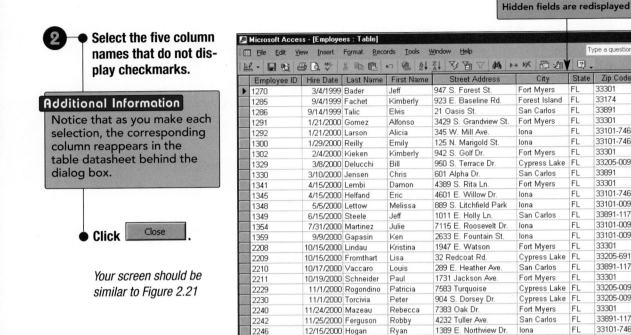

Hidden fields are redisplayed

Figure 2.21

All of the fields are now displayed again, and you can continue to refine your table data.

Finding and Replacing Data

Over the past few days you have received several change request forms to update the employee records. Rather than have to scroll through all the records to locate the ones that need to be modified, you can use the Find and Replace feature.

Find and Replace

4   The **Find and Replace** feature helps you quickly find specific information and automatically replace it with new information. The Find command will locate all specified values in a field, and the Replace command will both find a value and automatically replace it with another. For example, in a table containing supplier and item prices, you may need to increase the price of all items supplied by one manufacturer. To quickly locate these items, you would use the Find command to locate all records with the name of the manufacturer and then update the price appropriately. Alternatively, you could use the Replace command if you knew that all items priced at $9.95 were increasing to $11.89. This command would locate all values matching the original price and replace them with the new price. Finding and replacing data is fast and accurate, but you need to be careful when replacing not to replace unintended matches.

Finding Data

The first change request is for Melissa Lettow, who recently married and has both a name and address change. To quickly locate this record, you will use the Find command.

1 ● Move to the Last Name field of record 1.

● Click  Find.

Another Method

The menu equivalent is Edit/Find.

Your screen should be similar to Figure 2.22

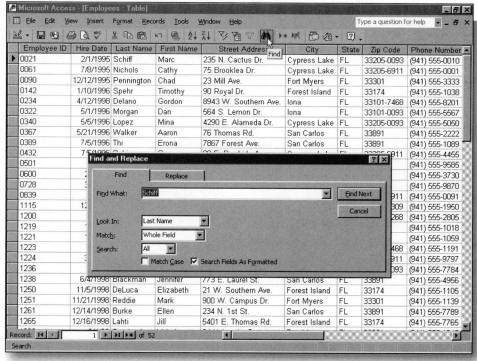

Figure 2.22

You use the Find and Replace dialog box to specify what you are looking for and how you want Access to search the table for it. In the Find What text box, you enter the text you want to locate. You can further refine your search by using the options described in the table on the next page.

Option	Effect
Look In	Searches the current field or the entire table for the specified text.
Match	Locates matches to the whole field, any part of the field, or the start of the field.
Search	Specifies the direction in which the table will be searched: All (search all records), Down (search down or up from the current insertion point location in the field), or Up (search up from the current insertion point location in the field).
Match Case	Finds words that have the same pattern of uppercase letters as entered in the Find What text box. Using this option makes the search case sensitive.
Search Fields as Formatted	Finds data based on its display format.

You are already in the field you want to search, and you want to find a specific last name, so you just need to enter the name in the Find What text box.

2 ● **Type lettow in the Find What text box.**

Additional Information

Because the Match Case option is not selected in the Find and Replace dialog box, it doesn't matter whether you enter the text to be located in uppercase, lowercase, or mixed case letters — Access will ignore the case and look for the specified text.

● Click [Find Next].

Your screen should be similar to Figure 2.23

HAVING TROUBLE?

If the Find command did not locate this record, try it again. Make sure that you enter the name "lettow" (upper- or lowercase) correctly and that Last Name is the selected field in the Look In box.

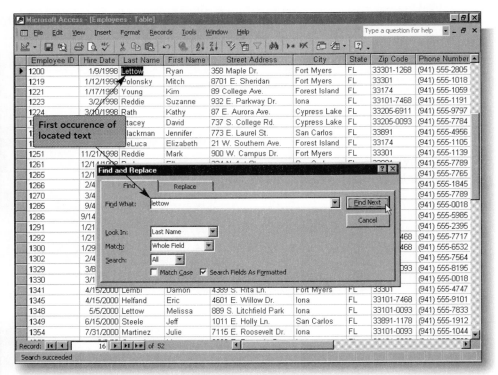

Figure 2.23

Access searches the table and moves to the first located occurrence of the entry you specified. The Last Name field is highlighted in record 16. You need to change the last name from Lettow to Richards.

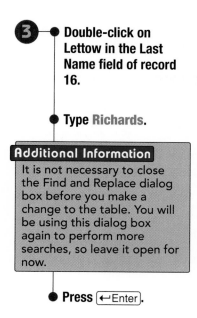

3 ● Double-click on Lettow in the Last Name field of record 16.

● Type **Richards**.

Additional Information

It is not necessary to close the Find and Replace dialog box before you make a change to the table. You will be using this dialog box again to perform more searches, so leave it open for now.

● Press ⏎Enter.

Your screen should be similar to Figure 2.24

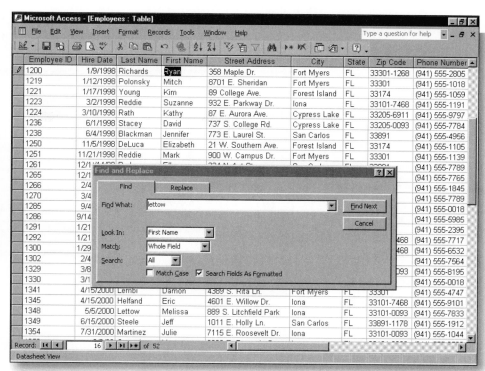

Figure 2.24

Now that the highlight is on the First Name field, you notice this is the record for Ryan Lettow, not Melissa. You changed the wrong record. You will use the Undo command next to quickly fix this error.

Using Undo

Undo will cancel your last action as long as you have not made any further changes to the table. Even if you save the record or the table, you can undo changes to the last edited record by using the Undo Saved Record command on the Edit menu or by clicking ↰ Undo. Once you have changed another record or moved to another window, however, the earlier change cannot be undone. You will use Undo to revert Ryan's record to how it was before you made the change.

1 ● Click ↰ Undo.

Another Method

The menu equivalent is **E**dit/**U**ndo Current Field/Record and the keyboard shortcut is Ctrl + Z.

Your screen should be similar to Figure 2.25

Figure 2.25

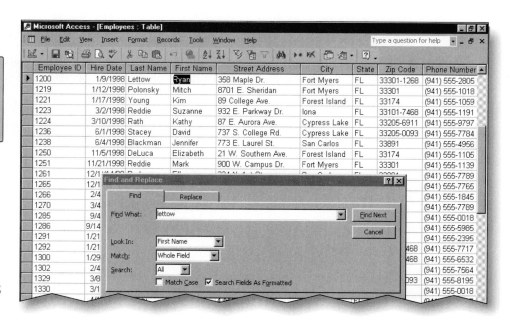

The original field value of Lettow is restored. Now you want to continue the search to locate the next record with the last name of Lettow.

2 ● **Move back to the Last Name field of record 16.**

● **Click** Find Next **in the Find and Replace dialog box.**

● **When Access locates the record for Melissa Lettow (record 39), change her last name to Richards and the street to 5522 W. Thompson Rd.**

Your screen should be similar to Figure 2.26

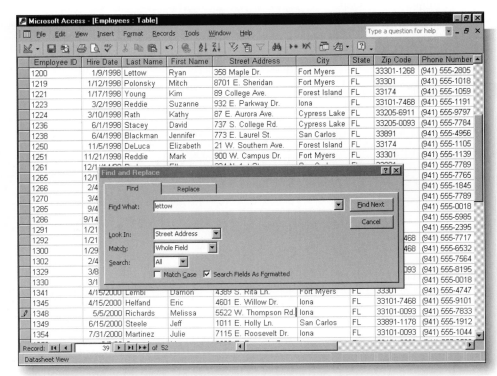

Figure 2.26

The Find method works well when you need to locate an individual field in order to view the data and/or modify it. However, when you need to make the same change to more than one record, the Replace command is the quicker method because it both finds and replaces the data.

Replacing Data

You have checked with the U.S. Postal Service and learned that all zip codes of 33301 have a four-digit extension of 1555. To locate all the records with this zip code, you could look at the Zip Code field for each record to find the match and then edit the field to add the extension. If the table is small, this method would be acceptable. For large tables, however, this method could be quite time consuming and more prone to errors. A more efficient way is to search the table to find specific values in records and then replace the entry with another.

1 • **Move to the Zip Code field of record 1.**

• **Open the Replace tab.**

Your screen should be similar to Figure 2.27

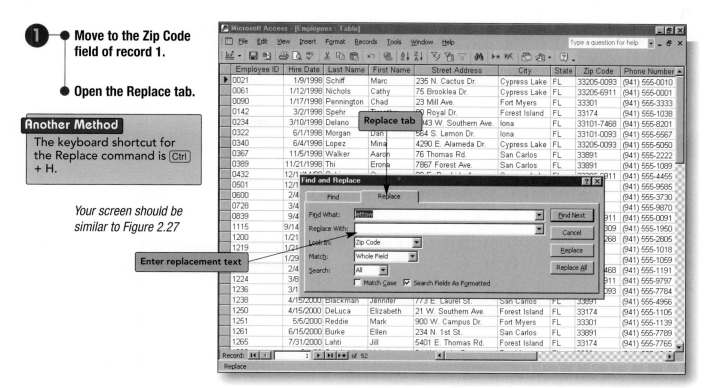

Figure 2.27

The options in the Replace tab are the same, with the addition of a Replace With text box, where you enter the replacement text exactly as you want it to appear in your table.

2 • **In the Find What text box, type 33301.**

• **Press Tab to move to the Replace With text box.**

• **Type 33301-1555.**

• **Click Find Next.**

Your screen should be similar to Figure 2.28

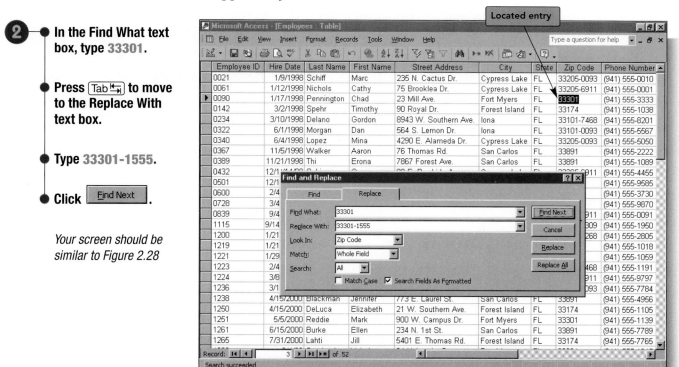

Figure 2.28

Immediately the highlight moves to the first occurrence of text in the document that matches the Find What text and highlights it. You can now replace this text with the click of a button.

3 • Click  **Replace** .

Your screen should be similar to Figure 2.29

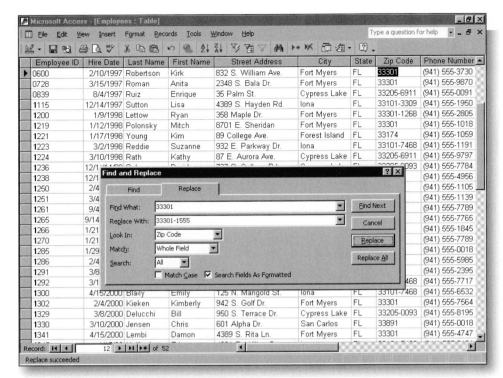

Figure 2.29

The original zip code entry is replaced with the new zip code. The program immediately continues searching and locates a second occurrence of the entry. You decide the program is locating the values accurately, and it will be safe to replace all finds with the replacement value.

Original zip code replaced with correction

4 • Click **Replace All** .

• Click **Yes** in response to the advisory message.

• Close the Find and Replace dialog box.

Your screen should be similar to Figure 2.30

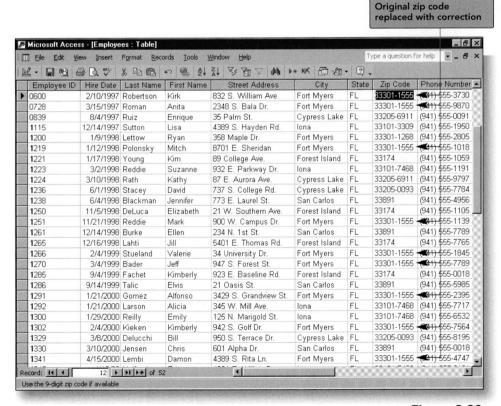

Figure 2.30

All matches are replaced with the replacement text. It is much faster to use Replace All than to confirm each match separately. However, exercise care when using Replace All, because the search text you specify might be part of another field and you may accidentally replace text you want to keep.

Sorting Records

As you may recall from Lab 1, the records are ordered by the primary key field, Employee ID. The Accounting department manager, however, has asked you for an alphabetical list of all employees. To do this, you can sort the records in the table.

concept 5

Sort

5 You can quickly rearrange a table's records by **sorting** the table data in a different order. Sorting data often helps you find specific information quickly. In Access you can sort data in ascending order (A to Z or 0 to 9) or descending order (Z to A or 9 to 0). You can sort all records in a table by a single field, such as State, or you can select adjacent columns and sort by more than one field, such as State and then City. When you select multiple columns to sort, Access sorts records starting with the column farthest left, then moves to the right across the columns. For example, if you want to quickly sort by State, then by City, the State field must be to the left of the City field. Access saves the new sort order with your table data and reapplies it automatically each time you open the table. To return to the primary key sort order, you must remove the temporary sort.

Sorting on a Single Field

You will sort the records on a single field, Last Name. To perform a sort on a single field, you move to the field you want to base the sort on and click the button that corresponds to the type of sort you want to do. In this case, you will sort the Last Name field in ascending alphabetical order.

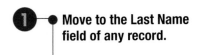

1 • **Move to the Last Name field of any record.**

• **Click** [↓] **Sort Ascending.**

Another Method

The menu equivalent is Records/**S**ort/Sort **A**scending.

Your screen should be similar to Figure 2.31

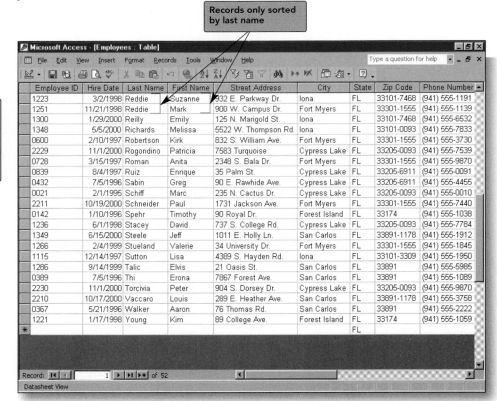

Records are in ascending alphabetical order | Ascending sort | Descending sort

Employee ID	Hire Date	Last Name	First Name	Street Address	City	State	Zip Code	Phone Number
1270	3/4/1999	Bader	Jeff	947 S. Forest St.	Fort Myers	FL	33301	(941) 555-7789
1238	6/4/1998	Blackman	Jennifer	773 E. Laurel St.	San Carlos	FL	33891	(941) 555-4956
0501	1/4/1997	Briggs	Scott	45 E. Camelback Rd.	San Carlos	fl	33891	(941) 555-9585
1261	12/14/1998	Burke	Ellen	234 N. 1st St.	San Carlos	FL	33891	(941) 555-7789
0234	4/12/1998	Delano	Gordon	8943 W. Southern Ave.	Iona	FL	33101-7468	(941) 555-8201
1250	11/5/1998	DeLuca	Elizabeth	21 W. Southern Ave.	Forest Island	FL	33174	(941) 555-1105
1329	3/8/2000	Delucchi	Bill	950 S. Terrace Dr.	Cypress Lake	FL	33205-0093	(941) 555-8195
1285	9/4/1999	Fachet	Kimberly	923 E. Baseline Rd.	Forest Island	FL	33174	(941) 555-0018
2242	11/25/2000	Ferguson	Robby	4232 Tuller Ave.	San Carlos	FL	33891-1178	(941) 555-7039
2209	10/15/2000	Fromthart	Lisa	32 Redcoat Rd.	Cypress Lake	FL	33205-6911	(941) 555-0110
1359	9/9/2000	Gapasin	Ken	2633 E. Fountain St.	Iona	FL	33101-0093	(941) 555-0589
1291	1/21/2000	Gomez	Alfonso	3429 S. Grandview St.	Fort Myers	FL	33301	(941) 555-2395
2247	12/18/2000	Harvey	Sarah	73 Lakeview Dr.	Cypress Lake	FL	33205-0093	(941) 555-7144
1345	4/15/2000	Helfand	Eric	4601 E. Willow Dr.	Iona	FL	33101-7468	(941) 555-9101
2246	12/15/2000	Hogan	Ryan	1389 E. Northview Dr.	Iona	FL	33101-7468	(941) 555-1010
1330	3/10/2000	Jensen	Chris	601 Alpha Dr.	San Carlos	FL	33891	(941) 555-0018
1302	2/4/2000	Kieken	Kimberly	942 S. Golf Dr.	Fort Myers	FL	33301	(941) 555-7564
1265	12/16/1998	Lahti	Jill	5401 E. Thomas Rd.	Forest Island	FL	33174	(941) 555-7765
1292	1/21/2000	Larson	Alicia	345 W. Mill Ave.	Iona	FL	33101-7468	(941) 555-7717
1341	4/15/2000	Lembi	Damon	4389 S. Rita Ln.	Fort Myers	FL	33301	(941) 555-4747
1200	1/9/1998	Lettow	Ryan	358 Maple Dr.	Fort Myers	FL	33301-1268	(941) 555-2805
2208	10/15/2000	Lindau	Kristina	1947 E. Watson	Fort Myers	FL	33301	(941) 555-6363
0340	5/5/1996	Lopez	Mina	4290 E. Alameda Dr.	Cypress Lake	FL	33205-0093	(941) 555-5050
1354	7/31/2000	Martinez	Julie	7115 E. Roosevelt Dr.	Iona	fl	33101-0093	(941) 555-1044
2240	11/24/2000	Mazeau	Rebecca	7383 Oak Dr.	Fort Myers	FL	33301	(941) 555-1093
0322	5/1/1996	Morgan	Dan	564 S. Lemon Dr.	Iona	FL	33101-0093	(941) 555-5567

Record: ⏮ ◀ 20 ▶ ⏭ ▶* of 51

Datasheet View

Figure 2.31

The employee records are displayed in alphabetical order by last name.
Next you want to check the rest of the table to see if there is anything else you need to do.

2 • **Use the scroll box to scroll down to record 31.**

Additional Information

As you drag the scroll box, the record location is displayed on top of it (for example, "Record 31 of 52").

Your screen should be similar to Figure 2.32

Records only sorted by last name

Employee ID	Hire Date	Last Name	First Name	Street Address	City	State	Zip Code	Phone Number
1223	3/2/1998	Reddie	Suzanne	932 E. Parkway Dr.	Iona	FL	33101-7468	(941) 555-1191
1251	11/21/1998	Reddie	Mark	900 W. Campus Dr.	Fort Myers	FL	33301-1555	(941) 555-1139
1300	1/29/2000	Reilly	Emily	125 N. Marigold St.	Iona	FL	33101-7468	(941) 555-6532
1348	5/5/2000	Richards	Melissa	5522 W. Thompson Rd.	Iona	FL	33101-0093	(941) 555-7833
0600	2/10/1997	Robertson	Kirk	832 S. William Ave.	Fort Myers	FL	33301-1555	(941) 555-3730
2229	11/1/2000	Rogondino	Patricia	7583 Turquoise	Cypress Lake	FL	33205-0093	(941) 555-7539
0728	3/15/1997	Roman	Anita	2348 S. Bala Dr.	Fort Myers	FL	33301-1555	(941) 555-9870
0839	8/4/1997	Ruiz	Enrique	35 Palm St.	Cypress Lake	FL	33205-6911	(941) 555-0091
0432	7/5/1996	Sabin	Greg	90 E. Rawhide Ave.	Cypress Lake	FL	33205-6911	(941) 555-4455
0021	2/1/1995	Schiff	Marc	235 N. Cactus Dr.	Cypress Lake	FL	33205-0093	(941) 555-0010
2211	10/19/2000	Schneider	Paul	1731 Jackson Ave.	Fort Myers	FL	33301-1555	(941) 555-7440
0142	1/10/1996	Spehr	Timothy	90 Royal Dr.	Forest Island	FL	33174	(941) 555-1038
1236	6/1/1998	Stacey	David	737 S. College Rd.	Cypress Lake	FL	33205-0093	(941) 555-7784
1349	6/15/2000	Steele	Jeff	1011 E. Holly Ln.	San Carlos	FL	33891-1178	(941) 555-1912
1266	2/4/1999	Stueland	Valerie	34 University Dr.	Fort Myers	FL	33301-1555	(941) 555-1845
1115	12/14/1997	Sutton	Lisa	4389 S. Hayden Rd.	Iona	FL	33101-3309	(941) 555-1950
1286	9/14/1999	Talic	Elvis	21 Oasis St.	San Carlos	FL	33891	(941) 555-5985
0389	7/5/1996	Thi	Erona	7867 Forest Ave.	San Carlos	FL	33891	(941) 555-1089
2230	11/1/2000	Torcivia	Peter	904 S. Dorsey Dr.	Cypress Lake	FL	33205-0093	(941) 555-9870
2210	10/17/2000	Vaccaro	Louis	289 E. Heather Ave.	San Carlos	FL	33891-1178	(941) 555-3758
0367	5/21/1996	Walker	Aaron	76 Thomas Rd.	San Carlos	FL	33891	(941) 555-2222
1221	1/17/1998	Young	Kim	89 College Ave.	Forest Island	FL	33174	(941) 555-1059
*						FL		

Record: ⏮ ◀ 1 ▶ ⏭ ▶* of 52

Datasheet View

Figure 2.32

Now you can see that the records for Suzanne and Mark Reddie are sorted by last name but not by first name. You want all records that have the same last name to be further sorted by first name. To do this, you need to sort using multiple sort fields.

Sorting on Multiple Fields

When sorting on multiple fields, the fields must be adjacent to each other, and the most important field in the sort must be to the left of the secondary field. The Last Name and First Name fields are already in the correct locations for the sort you want to perform. To specify the fields to sort on, both columns must be selected.

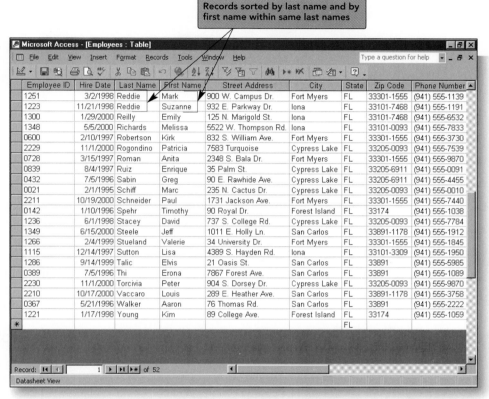

Records sorted by last name and by first name within same last names

Figure 2.33

Additional Information

If the columns to sort were not already adjacent, you would hide the columns that are in between. If the columns were not in the correct order, you would move the columns. You will learn how to do this in Lab 3.

1 ● **Select the Last Name and First Name field columns.**

● **Click** 🔼 **Sort Ascending.**

● **Scroll down to record 31 again.**

Your screen should be similar to Figure 2.33

The record for Mark Reddie is now before the record for Suzanne. As you can see, sorting is a fast, useful tool. The sort order remains in effect until you remove the sort or replace it with a new sort order. Although Access remembers your sort order even when you exit the program, it does not actually change the table records. You can remove the sort at any time to restore the records to the primary key sort order. You decide to do this now and re-sort the table alphabetically for the Accounting department later, after you have finished making changes to it.

Records sorted
by primary key

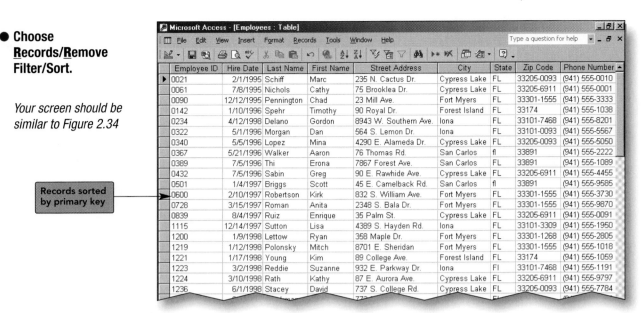

Figure 2.34

The table is back to primary key order.

Formatting the Datasheet

Finally, you want to **format** or enhance the appearance of the datasheet on the screen to make it more readable or attractive by applying different effects. Datasheet formats include settings that change the appearance of the cell, gridlines, background and gridline colors, and border and line styles. In addition, you can change the text color and add text effects, such as bold and italics to the datasheet. Datasheet formats affect the entire datasheet appearance and cannot be applied to separate areas of the datasheet.

Changing Background and Gridline Color

You first want to see how changing the color of the datasheet background will look.

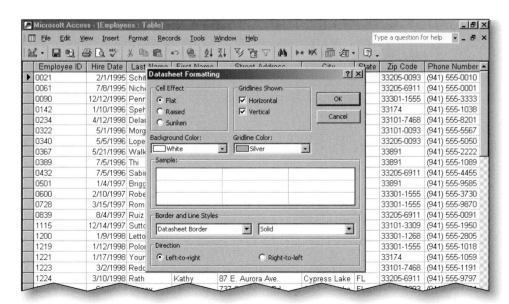

Figure 2.35

The Datasheet Formatting dialog box allows you to make changes to the format and preview how the changes will appear in the sample area. The default datasheet settings are selected. You want to change the background color from the default of white and the gridline color from the default of silver to different colors.

2 ● **Open the Background Color drop-down list.**

● **Select Yellow.**

● **Open the Gridline Color drop-down list.**

● **Select Blue.**

Your screen should be similar to Figure 2.36

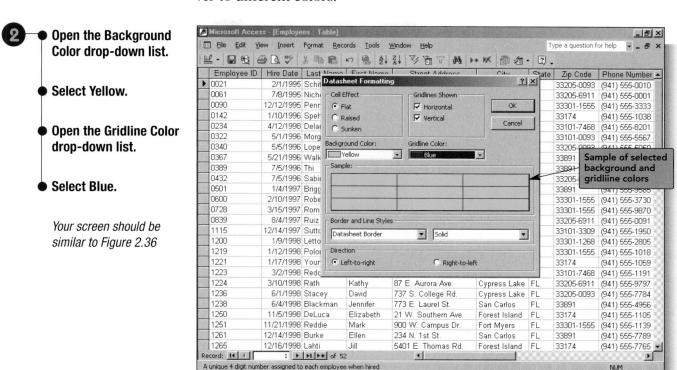

Figure 2.36

The sample area shows how your selections will appear. You will see how the datasheet looks with these new settings next.

3 ● **Click** OK **.**

Your screen should be similar to Figure 2.37

Datasheet displays in selected background and gridline colors

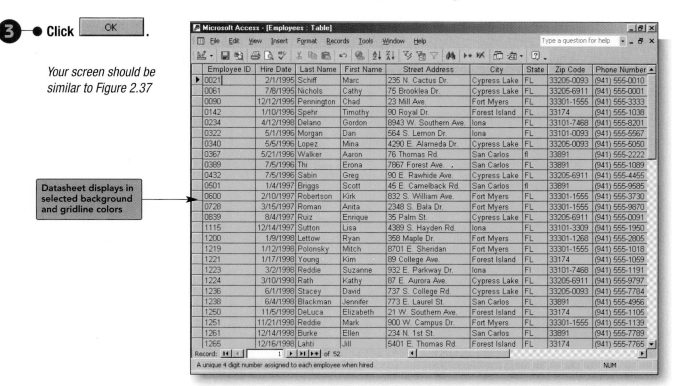

Figure 2.37

Changing the Font Color

The datasheet background and gridline colors brighten the screen appearance, but you think the text is a little difficult to read. You will change the text color to blue and bold. Many of the formatting features can also be applied using the Formatting toolbar. Using the Formatting toolbar to make changes to the datasheet, applies changes instantly.

1 ● **Display the Formatting toolbar.**

● **Open the [A ▾] Font/ Fore Color drop-down menu.**

● **Select Blue from the color palette.**

● **Click [B] Bold.**

Your screen should be similar to Figure 2.38

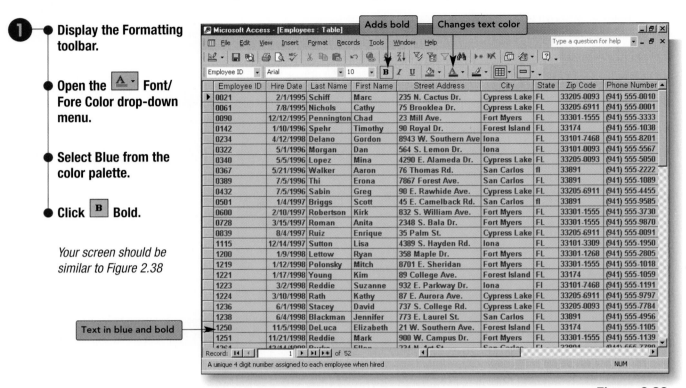

Figure 2.38

The text is now easier to read.

2 ● **Close the Formatting toolbar.**

● **Close the table saving your design changes.**

You're now back at the Database window for the Employee Records file. Next you will learn how to create and use a form in Access.

NOTE: If you are ending your session now, close the database file and exit Access. When you begin again, load Access and open the Database window for the Employees Records.

Creating and Using Forms

One of your objectives is to make the database easy to use. You know from experience that long hours of viewing large tables can be tiring. Therefore, you want to create an onscreen form to make this table easier to view and use.

concept 6

Forms

6 A **form** is a database object used primarily to display records on-screen to make it easier to enter new records and to make changes to existing records. Forms are based on an underlying table, and include design control elements such as descriptive text, titles, labels, lines, boxes, and pictures. Forms often use calculations as well, to summarize data that is not listed on the actual table, such as a sales total. Forms make working with long lists of data easier. They enable people to use the data in the tables without having to sift through many lines of data to find the exact record.

You want the onscreen form to be similar to the paper form that is completed by each new employee when hired (shown below). The information from that form is used as the source of input for the new record that will be added to the table for the new employee.

EMPLOYEE DATA

First Name _____   Last Name _____
Street _____
City _____   State _____   Zip Code _____
Phone Number _____
Gender _____   Birth Date _____
For Personnel Use Only:
Employee ID _____
Hire Date _____

Using the Form Wizard

The Form Wizard guides you through the steps required to create a form. This is only one of the methods available for form creation — as with tables, you can create a form in Design view instead. In order to become familiar with all the parts of a form, you will use the Form Wizard to create a form for the "Employees" table.

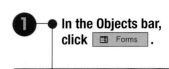

1 ● **In the Objects bar, click** [▦ Forms].

HAVING TROUBLE?
The Objects bar is on the left side of the Database window.

● **Double-click the "Create form by using wizard" option.**

Another Method
You can also click the [🗅New] button and select the Form Wizard in the New Form dialog box.

Your screen should be similar to Figure 2.39

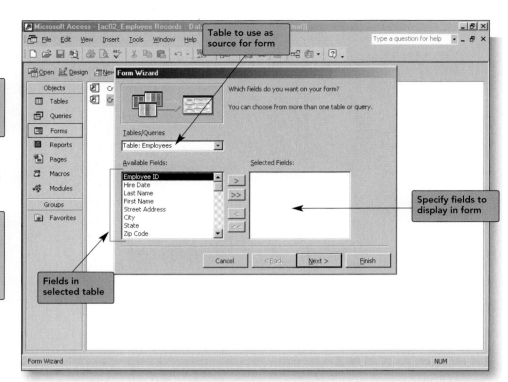

Figure 2.39

Additional Information
If your database contained multiple tables, you could open the Tables/Queries drop-down list to select the appropriate underlying table to use for the form.

The Form Wizard dialog box displays the name of the current table, Employees, in the Tables/Queries list box. This is the underlying table that Access will be use to create the form. The fields from the selected table are displayed in the Available Fields list box. You use this box to select the fields you want included on the form, in the order that you want them to appear. This is called the **tab order** because it is the order that the highlight will move through the fields on the form when you press the [Tab⇄] key during data entry. You decide that you want the fields to be in the same order as they are on the paper form shown in the illustration above.

2 ● **Select First Name.**

● **Click** [>].

Another Method
You can also double-click on each field name in the Available Fields list box to move the field name to the Selected Fields list box.

Additional Information
The [>>] button adds all available fields to the Selected Fields list, in the same order that they appear in the Available Fields list.

Your screen should be similar to Figure 2.40

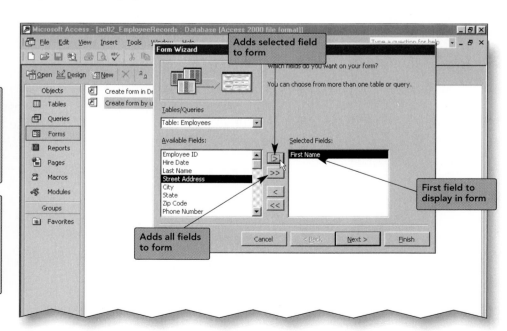

Figure 2.40

The First Name field is removed from the Available Fields list and added to the top of the Selected Fields list box.

3 ● **In the same manner, add the following fields to the Selected Fields list in the order shown here:**

Last Name

Street Address

City

State

Zip Code

Phone Number

Gender

Birth Date

Employee ID

Hire Date

Photo

Your screen should be similar to Figure 2.41

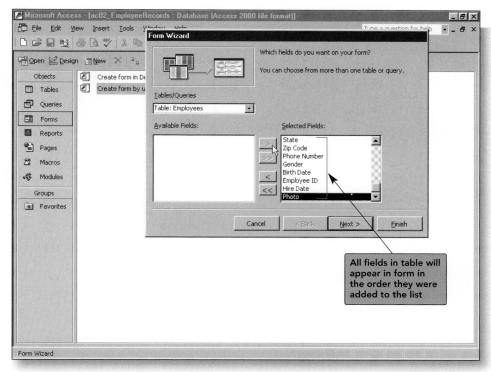

Figure 2.41

When you are done, the Available Fields list box is empty, and the Selected Fields list box lists the fields in the selected order. You are now ready to move on to the next Form Wizard screen.

4 ● **Click**  **.**

Your screen should be similar to Figure 2.42

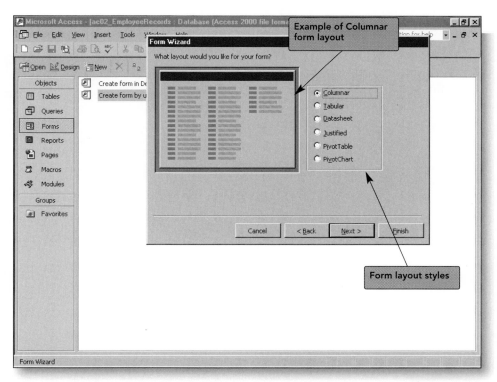

Figure 2.42

In this Form Wizard screen, you are asked to select the layout for the form. Six form layouts are available: The four basic form layouts are described in the following table.

Form	Layout Style	Description
Columnar	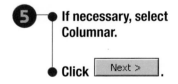	Presents data for the selected fields in columns. The field name labels display down the left side of the column, with the data for each field just to the right of its corresponding label. A single record is displayed in each Form window.
Tabular		Presents data in a table layout with field name labels across the top of the page and the corresponding data in rows and columns under each heading. Multiple records are displayed in the Form Window, each on a single row.
Datasheet		Displays data in rows and columns similar to the Table Datasheet view, but only selected fields display in the order chosen during form design. Displays multiple records, one per row, in the Form window.
Justified		Displays data in rows, with field name labels across the top of the row and the corresponding field data below it. A single record may appear in multiple rows in the Form window in order to fully display the field name label and data.

The columnar layout appears most similar to the paper form currently in use by the Club, so you decide to select that layout for your form.

5 ● **If necessary, select Columnar.**

● **Click** Next >.

Your screen should be similar to Figure 2.43

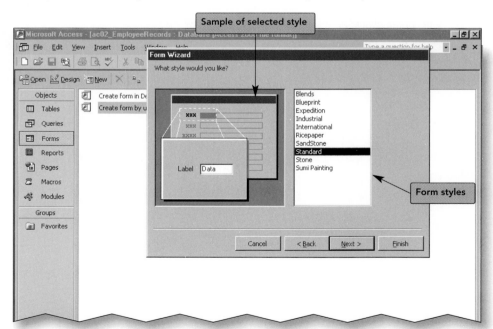

Figure 2.43

In this Form Wizard dialog box, you select from ten different styles for your form. A sample of each style as it is selected is displayed on the left side of the dialog box. Standard is the default selection. You will create the form using the Blends style.

6 ● **Select Blends.**

Additional Information
The last selected form style is the currently selected style.

● **Click** Next > .

Your screen should be similar to Figure 2.44

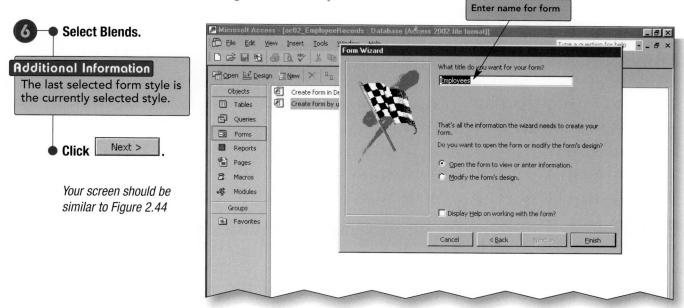

Figure 2.44

In this final Form Wizard dialog box, you need to enter a form title to be used as the name of the form, and you need to specify whether the form should open with data displayed in it. The Form Wizard uses the name of the table as the default form title. You want to change the form's title, and you want to keep the default of displaying the form when you are through creating it.

7 ● **Type** Employee Data Form.

● **Click** Finish .

● **If necessary, maximize the Form window.**

Your screen should be similar to Figure 2.45

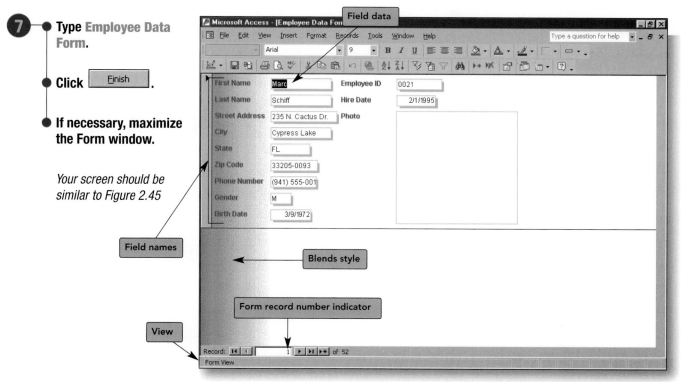

Figure 2.45

The completed form is displayed in the Form view window. The form displays the selected fields in columnar layout using the Blends style. The field name labels are in two columns with the field data text boxes in adjacent columns to the right. The employee information for Marc Schiff, the current record in the table, is displayed in the text boxes.

Navigating in Form View

You use the same navigation keys in Form view that you used in Datasheet view. You can move between fields in the form by using the Tab⇆, ←Enter, ⇧Shift + Tab⇆, and the directional arrow keys on the keyboard. You can use Page Up and Page Down, as well as the navigation buttons at the bottom of the form, to move between records.

You can also use the Find command to locate and display specific records. The Find command works the same way in a form as in a table. To try this out, you will find and display the record for Lisa Sutton.

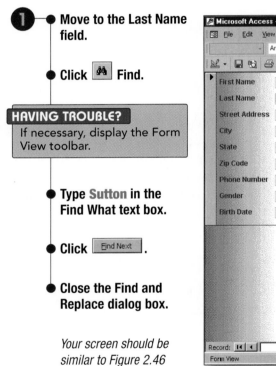

1 ● **Move to the Last Name field.**

● **Click** 🔍 **Find.**

HAVING TROUBLE?
If necessary, display the Form View toolbar.

● **Type Sutton in the Find What text box.**

● **Click** Find Next .

● **Close the Find and Replace dialog box.**

Your screen should be similar to Figure 2.46

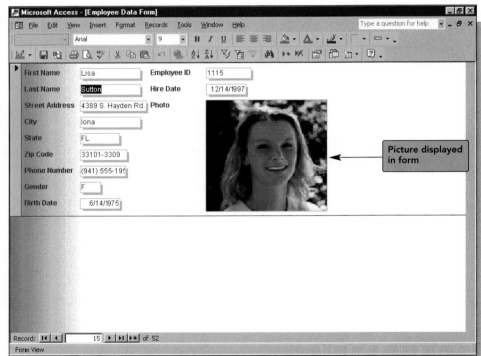

Figure 2.46

Additional Information
You can adjust the size of the panes by dragging the bar that separates them.

Lisa Sutton's record is displayed in the form. Because this record contains the inserted picture in the Photo field, the photo is displayed.

Adding Records in a Form

You need to add a new employee record to the database, whose paper employee record form is shown below. You will add the record in Form view using the information on the paper form for the field entry data.

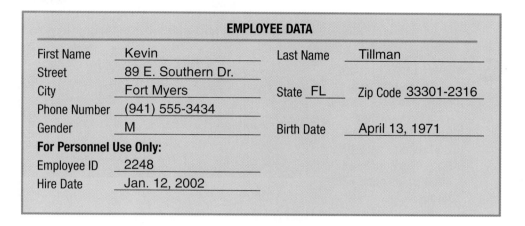

EMPLOYEE DATA

First Name   Kevin   Last Name   Tillman
Street   89 E. Southern Dr.
City   Fort Myers   State FL   Zip Code 33301-2316
Phone Number (941) 555-3434
Gender   M   Birth Date   April 13, 1971

For Personnel Use Only:
Employee ID 2248
Hire Date   Jan. 12, 2002

• Click **▶*** New Record to display a new blank entry form.

• Enter the data shown in the employee's paper form for the new record.

Additional Information

Press Tab⇆ to move from field to field.

Your screen should be similar to Figure 2.47

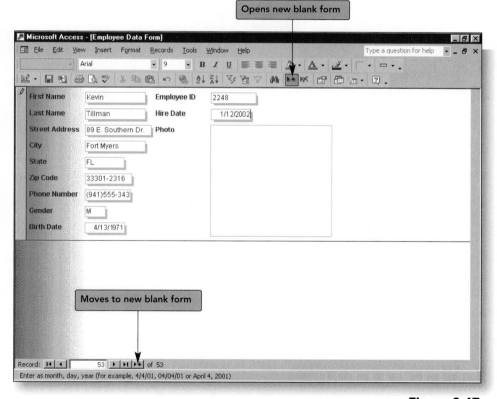

Figure 2.47

Using the form makes entering the new employee data much faster because the fields are in the same order as the information in the paper Employee Data form used by the personnel department. When you use the Form Wizard to create a form, most of the field text boxes are appropriately sized to display the data in the field. You probably noticed, however, that the Phone Number field is not quite large enough to display all the numbers. You will learn how to fix this problem in the next lab.

Before you end this lab, you will add a record for yourself.

2 • Enter another record using your special Employee ID **9999** and your first and last name. Enter the current date as your Hire Date. The data in all other fields can be fictitious.

• Open the ⌸ ▾ View button drop-down list and click ⊞ Datasheet View.

Another Method

The menu equivalent is View/Datasheet View.

• Scroll up a few rows to display both new records.

Your screen should be similar to Figure 2.48

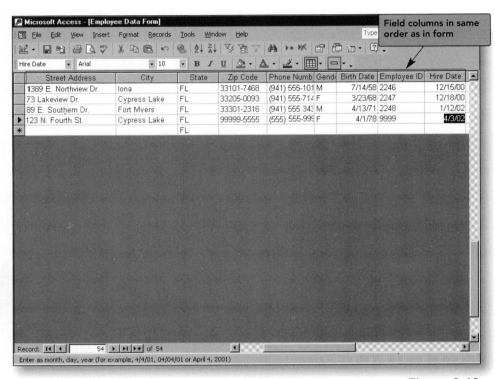

Figure 2.48

The Datasheet View of the form data is displayed. Notice that the field columns are now in the same order as in the form.

You will learn how to further manipulate and enhance forms in the next lab, but for now, you want to see how the form you designed looks printed out.

Previewing and Printing a Form

You want to preview and print only the form that displays your record.

1 ● **Switch back to Form view.**

● **Click** 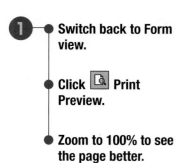 **Print Preview.**

● **Zoom to 100% to see the page better.**

Your screen should be similar to Figure 2.49

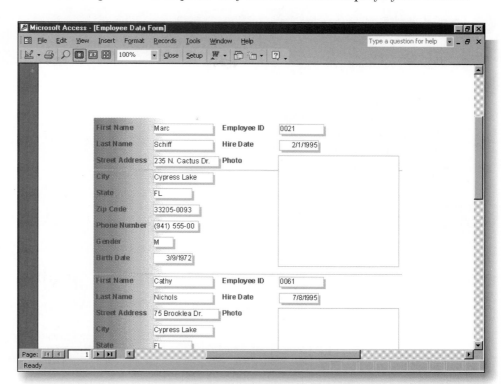

Figure 2.49

Print Preview displays whatever view you were last using. In this case, because you were last in Form view, the form is displayed in the Preview window. Access prints as many records as can be printed on a page in the Form layout. You want to print only the form displaying your record.

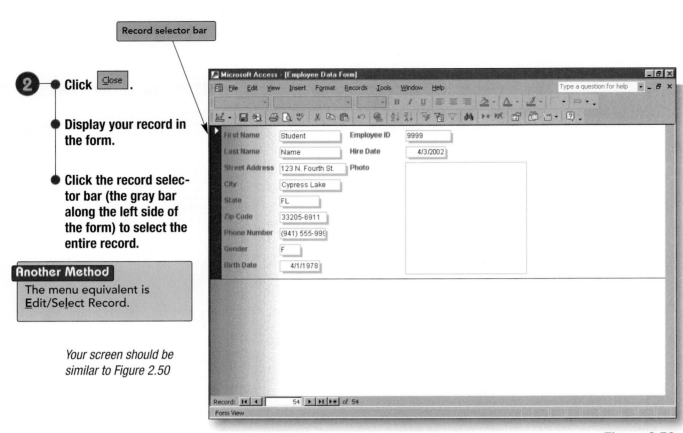

Record selector bar

2 ● Click Close .

● **Display your record in the form.**

● **Click the record selector bar (the gray bar along the left side of the form) to select the entire record.**

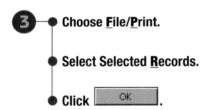

Another Method

The menu equivalent is Edit/Select Record.

Your screen should be similar to Figure 2.50

Figure 2.50

Now that the record is selected, you can print the record. The record will print using the current view, in this case Form View.

3 ● Choose File/Print.

● Select Selected Records.

● Click OK .

Closing and Saving a Form

Next you will close the form.

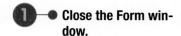

1 ● Close the Form window.

Your screen should be similar to Figure 2.51

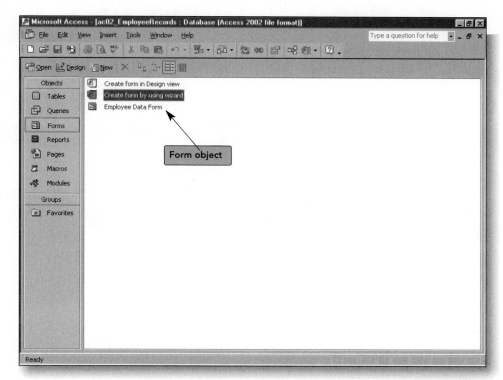

Figure 2.51

The Database window is displayed, showing the new form object name in the forms list box.

2 ● Exit Access.

LAB 2

Modifying a Table and Creating a Form

Format Property   (AC2.9)

You can use the Format property to create custom formats that change the way numbers, dates, times, and text display and print.

Format property

Default Value Property   (AC2.11)

The Default Value property is used to specify a value to be automatically entered in a field when a new record is created.

Default value property

Validity Check   (AC2.14)

Access automatically performs certain checks, called **validity checks**, on values entered in a field to make sure that the values are valid for the field type.

Validity check

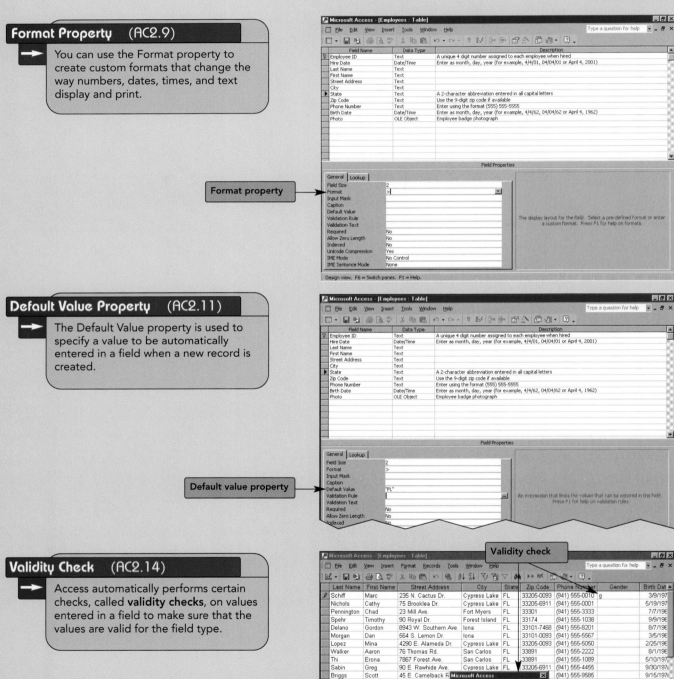

Find and Replace (AC2.21)

The Find and Replace feature helps you quickly find specific information and automatically replace it with new information.

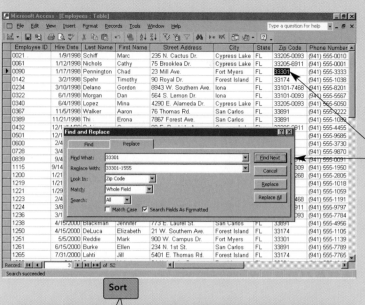

Find and Replace

Sort (AC2.27)

You can quickly rearrange a table's records by **sorting** the table data in a different order.

Sort

Form (AC2.33)

A **form** is a database object used primarily to display records onscreen to make it easier to enter new records and to make changes to existing records.

Form

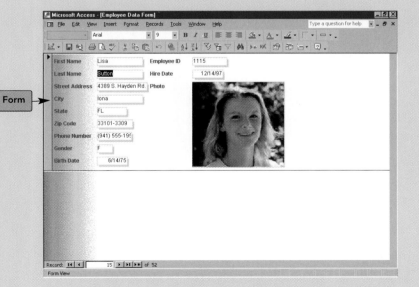

key terms

character string AC2.11	identifier AC2.14
comparison operator AC2.14	operator AC2.14
Default Value property AC2.11	sorting AC2.27
expression AC2.14	tab order AC2.34
Find and Replace AC2.21	validation rule AC2.14
form AC2.33	validation text AC2.14
format AC2.30	validity check AC2.14
Format property AC2.9	value AC2.15

mous skills

The Microsoft Office User Specialist (MOUS) certification program is designed to measure your proficiency in performing basic tasks using the Office XP applications. Getting certified demonstrates that you have the skills and provides a valuable industry credential for employment. After completing this lab, you have learned the following Access 2002 Microsoft Office User Specialist skills:

Skill	Description	Page
Creating and Using Databases	Open database objects in multiple views	AC2.40
	Move among records	AC2.6
	Format datasheets	AC2.30
Creating and Modifying Tables	Create and modify tables	AC2.8
	Modify field properties	AC2.8
Creating and Modifying Forms	Create and display forms	AC2.32
Viewing and Organizing Information	Enter and edit records	AC2.39
	Sort records	AC2.27

command summary

Command	Shortcut	Button	Action
Edit/Undo	Ctrl + Z	↰	Cancels last action
Edit/Find	Ctrl + F	🔍	Locates specified data
Edit/Replace	Ctrl + H		Locates and replaces specified data
View/Design View			Displays Design view
View/Form View			Displays a form in Form view
Insert/Column			Inserts a new field in a table in Datasheet view
Format/Hide Columns			Hides columns in Datasheet view
Format/Unhide Columns			Redisplays hidden columns
Records/Sort/Sort Ascending		↓	Reorders records in ascending alphabetical order

In the following Access screen, several items are identified by letters. Enter the correct term for each item in the spaces provided.

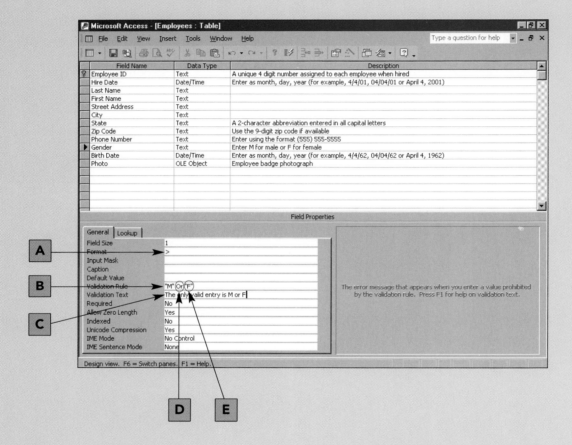

A. _____

B. _____

C. _____

D. _____

E. _____

matching

Match the numbered item with the correct lettered description.

1. match case   _____**a.** cancels your last action

2. Ctrl + Home   _____**b.** an expression

3. 🔙   _____**c.** database object used primarily for onscreen display

4. character string   _____**d.** moves to the first field of the first record

5. tab order   _____**e.** makes the search for specified data case sensitive

6. >   _____**f.** displays Design view

7. sort   _____**g.** order in which pressing Tab moves through fields in a form

8. ="Y" Or "N"   _____**h.** a group of characters

9. 📝 ▾   _____**i.** changes the display order of a table

10. form   _____**j.** format character that forces all data in a field to uppercase

multiple choice

Circle the letter of the correct response.

1. Format _____ is used to create custom formats that change the way numbers, dates, times, and text display and print.
   a. specification
   b. alignment
   c. range
   d. property

2. Values to be automatically entered into a field are specified in the _____ Value property.
   a. Auto
   b. Initial
   c. Default
   d. Assumed

3. _____ are automatically performed on values entered in a field to make sure that the values are valid for the field type.
   a. Object validations
   b. Security specifications
   c. Form searches
   d. Validity checks

4. You can quickly reorder _____ in a table by sorting the table.
   a. records
   b. columns
   c. fields
   d. objects

5. Forms are based on the underlying table by using design _____ elements.
   a. control
   b. default
   c. property
   d. object

6. To change the format of a field, different _____ are entered in the Format text box.
   a. symbols
   b. buttons
   c. objects
   d. graphics

7. When users add a record to a table, they can either accept the _____ value or enter another value.
   a. default
   b. initial
   c. last
   d. null

8. A(n) _____ is a sequence of characters (letters, numbers, or symbols) that must be handled as text, not as numeric data.
   a. identifier
   b. character string
   c. expression
   d. operator

9. Data sorted in _____ order is arranged alphabetically A to Z or numerically 0 to 9.
   a. increasing
   b. descending
   c. ascending
   d. decreasing

10. _____ are items made up of many elements that can be created, selected, and manipulated as a unit.
    a. Records
    b. Objects
    c. Tables
    d. Forms

true/false

Circle the correct answer to the following statements.

1.	Format properties do not change the way Access stores data.	True	False
2.	The Format property determines the value automatically entered into a field of a new record.	True	False
3.	An identifier is a symbol or word that indicates that an operation is to be performed.	True	False
4.	The Find command will locate specific values in a field and automatically replace them.	True	False

5. Format properties change the way data is displayed.	True	False
6. The Default Value property is commonly used when most of the entries in a field will be the same for the entire table.	True	False
7. Values are numbers, dates, or pictures.	True	False
8. The Replace command will automatically restore properties to an object.	True	False
9. Sorting reorders records in a table.	True	False
10. Forms are database objects used primarily for report generation.	True	False

Concepts

fill-in

Complete the following statements by filling in the blanks with the correct terms.

1. A(n) _____ is a combination of symbols that produces specific results.

2. The _____ property is used to specify a value that is automatically entered in a field when a new record is created.

3. When _____ are performed, Access makes sure that the entry is acceptable in the field.

4. Records can be temporarily displayed in a different order by using the _____ feature.

5. Forms are primarily used for _____ and making changes to existing records.

6. The _____ property changes the way data appears in a field.

7. The four form layouts are _____, _____, _____, and _____.

8. Use _____ to cancel your last action.

9. A(n) _____ is a symbol or word that indicates that an operation is to be performed.

10. To return to _____ order, you must remove the temporary sort.

discussion questions

Answer the following questions by preparing written responses.

1. Discuss several different Format properties and how they are used in a database.

2. Discuss the different types of form layouts and why you would use one layout type over another.

3. Discuss how validity checks work. What are some advantages of adding validity checks to a field? Include several examples.

4. Discuss the different ways records can be sorted. What are some advantages of sorting records?

Hands-On Exercises

step-by-step

Modifying the Client Database and Creating a Client Form

★ **1.** Maria Dell is very impressed with the work you have done on the database for the Simply
Beautiful Spa (Step-by-Step Exercise 1 of Lab 1). After an initial review of the database, Ms. Dell
realizes that the inclusion of additional data in the database can help her with other
administrative functions. For example, as part of her future advertising campaigns, she would like
to send birthday cards to each of her clients and wonders if it is possible to include birth date
information in the database. Also, she would like you to modify some client records, create a form
to ease data entry, and print a copy of the form. You have continued to add records to the
database and have saved the expanded database file as Simply Beautiful. You are now ready to make
the modifications to the Client table and to create a form. Your completed form is shown here.

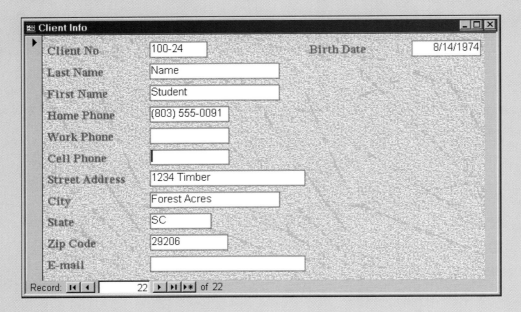

To make the requested changes to the database and create the form, follow these steps:

a. Open the expanded database named ac02_Simply Beautiful and the table named "Clients."

b. In Design view, add the following field to the end of the table:

    Field name: **Birth Date**

    Data type: **Date/Time**

    Description: **Identifies client's birthday**

    Field format: **Short date**

c. Make the First Name and Last Name required fields. (Hint: Set the Required property to Yes.)

d. Save the table design changes and return to Datasheet view. Update the table by filling in the new field for each record with appropriate data. Include several birth dates before 01/01/64.

e. Edit the appropriate records to reflect the client changes that Ms. Dell gave you:

- Sally Grimes has moved to **202 S. Jefferson**. The city, state, and zip code will remain the same.

- Mr. Fen Woo has a cell phone number. It is **(301) 555-9076**.

- Barbara Williams wrote down her e-mail address when she was last in. It is **Barbara@smart.com**.

f. Close the table.

g. Use the Form Wizard to create a form for the "Clients" table. Include all fields as listed. Use the columnar layout and Expedition style. Name it **Client Info**.

h. Use the new form to enter the following records:

Record 1	Record 2
100-23	100-24
Price	[Your last name]
Georgia	[Your first name]
(301) 555-5522	(301) 555-0091
(301) 555-6321	[no work phone]
(301) 555-3434	[no cell phone]
243 May Avenue	1234 Timber
Lexington	Forest Acres
SC	SC
29071	29206
gprice@mail.com	[no e-mail]
3/21/73	8/14/74

i. Preview and print the form for the second new record you added.

j. Exit Access, saving your changes as needed.

Modifying the Advertiser Database and Creating an Ad Rate Form

★★ 2. You have completed the advertiser contact portion of your homeowners' Happenings database (Step-by-Step Exercise 2 of Lab 1), and you are ready to expand it to include the ad size, rate, and frequency that the local merchants have contracted for. The ad rate is $50 for a 1/4-page ad, $100 for a 1/2-page ad, and $175 for a full-page ad. You also want to create a data-entry form when you're finished with the basic design. Your completed form is shown here.

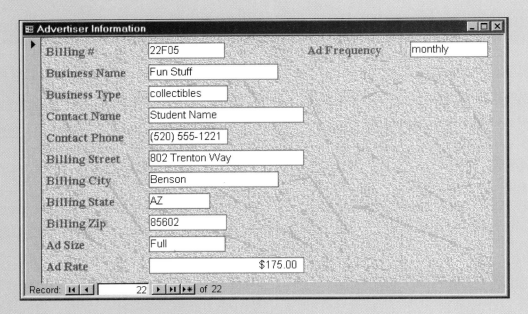

To add the new fields to the database and create the form, follow these steps:

a. Open the expanded database named ac02_Happening Ads and the table named "Advertisers."

b. In Design view, add the following three fields to the end of the table:

Field name: **Ad Size**

Data type: Text

Description: **Enter one of the following: ¼, ½, or Full**

Field size: **5**

Field name: **Ad Rate**

Data type: Currency

Description: **Contracted rate per ad**

Field name: **Ad Frequency**

Data type: Text

Description: **Enter one of the following: Single, Monthly, Bimonthly**

Field size: **10**

c. Save the table design changes and return to Datasheet view. Update the table by filling in the new fields for each record. Readjust the column widths as necessary.

d. Close and save the table.

e. Use the Form Wizard to create a form for the "Advertisers" table. Include all the table fields in their current order. Use the Columnar layout and Expedition style. Title the form **Advertiser Information**.

f. Use the new form to enter the following records:

Record 1	**Record 2**
21H03	**22F05**
Hearth & Home	**Fun Stuff**
Furniture Store	**Collectibles**
Doris Francis	**[Your Name]**
(912) 555-0022	**(912) 555-1221**
124 Desert Way	**802 Trenton Way**
Willcox	**Benson**
AZ	**AZ**
85643	**85602**
1/2	**Full**
100	**175**
Bimonthly	**Monthly**

g. Preview and print the form for the second new record you added.

h. Exit Access, saving your changes as needed.

Modifying the Product Vendor Database and Creating a Vendor Information Form

★ ★ ★ **3.** You and other employees of the Downtown Internet Cafe have been sharing the task of entering product and vendor information into the purchase items Supplies database (Step-by-Step Exercise 3 of Lab 1). You are now ready to add fields that show the inventory on hand and to indicate special orders so Evan, the cafe owner, knows when to place an order. However, when you open the database, you noticed that some of the information for the existing fields is missing, incorrect, or inconsistent. You realize that besides adding the new fields, you need to change some of the field properties, specify required fields, correct some errors, and create a form to make data entry easier. When you are finished, you will end up with an easy-to-use data entry form shown here.

To make the changes and create the form, follow these steps:

a. Open the expanded database named ac02_Cafe Supplies and the table named "Vendors."

b. Use the Replace command to replace item #2579 with the correct item number, 2575. Use the same command to replace Beverage with their new name, Better Beverages, Inc. Adjust the Vendor Name column to fit the new name.

c. In Design view, make the Item #, Description, and Vendor Name required fields. Add a Format property to the State field to force the data in that field to display in all capital letters.

d. Add a field before the Vendor Name to specify the inventory on hand for each item:

Field name: # On Hand

Data type: Number

Description: Number of individual units (bags, boxes, etc.) in stock

Field size: Integer

e. Add another field before the Vendor Name to specify whether the item is a special order (not regularly stocked):

Field name: Special Order?

Data type: Text

Description: Is this a special order item?

Field size: 1

Default value: N

Validation rule: Y or N

Validation text: The only valid entry is Y (yes) or N (no)

f. Return to Datasheet view and update the table by filling in the new fields for each record.

g. Use the Form Wizard to create a columnar form with the SandStone style and include all the table fields in their current order. Use the title **Vendor Info** for the table.

h. Use the new form to add the following purchase items to the table:

Record 1	Record 2
1102	2924
Napkins	Coffee mugs
50	12
N	Y
Basics Restaurant Supply	Central Ceramics
Mandy Swanson	[Your Name]
13990 N. Central Ave.	772 Hayden Road
Phoenix	Scottsdale
AZ	AZ
84137-7214	85254
(602) 555-0037	(602) 555-1924
brs@email.net	student@learn.com

i. Preview and print the form for the second new record you added.

Maintaining a Product Development Database

★ ★ ★ **4.** The EduSoft Company, which develops computer curriculums for grades K–8, has just hired you to update and maintain their software database. Some of the tasks your manager asks you to accomplish involve correcting some known errors and applying some validation rules. She would also like you to create a form, shown here, which will make it easier to enter new software titles.

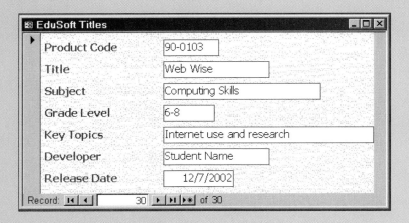

To update the database and create the form, follow these steps:

a. Open the database file named ac02_Learning and the table named "Software."

b. The corrections you need to make to the table are related to the software titles. Sort the table in ascending order by Title so it will be easier to see the names you need to correct.

c. You have a note that the name of the Figure It series has been changed to Solve It. Use the Replace command (match the Start of Field to retain the numbers) or navigate through the table to find the three records with this title and change them.

d. The program called Reading & Writing was never released and has been replaced by separate reading and writing programs. Find and delete this record.

e. Switch to Design view and add a validity rule and text to the Grade Level field so that it only allows an entry of K–2, 3–5, or 6–8 (all three valid entries must be in quotes).

f. Add a field above Release Date to specify the name of the lead program developer for each title.

Field name: **Developer**

Data type: Text

Description: **Name of lead program developer**

Field size: **20**

g. Return to Datasheet view and hide the Title through Key Topic columns. Next you need to update the table by filling in the new field for each record. Each lead programmer has a unique two-digit prefix on their product numbers. Using Teri O'Neill and other names of your choice, complete the Developer field for each record. For example, Teri O'Neill worked on products with the 36 prefix. Unhide the columns when you are done.

h. Create a columnar form using the Form Wizard. Use the Sumi Painting style and include all the fields in their current order. Use the name **EduSoft Titles** for the form.

i. Use the form to enter a new record for a software program called Web Wise, Product Code 90–0103, which is currently in development for grades 6–8 to help them learn to use the Internet and do research. Enter your name as the developer. Preview and print the form for this new record. Exit Access, saving changes as needed.

Maintaining a Tracking Database

★ ★ **5.** You have continued to add records to the database for tracking the animals that come into and go
★ out of the Animal Rescue Foundation (Step-by-Step Exercise 5 of Lab 1). Now you need to modify
the database structure and customize field properties to control the data entered by the Animal
Angels volunteers who are assigned this task. You also want to create a form to make it easier for
the volunteers to enter the necessary information, as shown here.

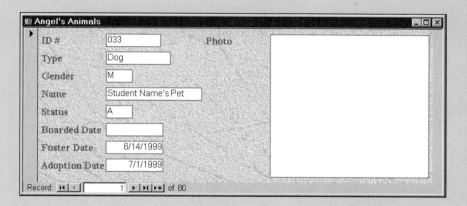

To enhance the Animal Rescue database and create the form, follow these steps:

a. Open the expanded database named ac02_AA and the table named "Animals."

b. In Design view, insert the following field above the Boarded Date field:

Field name: **Status**

Data type: Text

Description: **Enter B (boarded), F (in foster home), or A (adopted)**

Field size: **1**

Format: **>**

c. Make the following additional changes to the database structure:

- Add a validation rule and appropriate validation text to the Gender field to accept only M or F
  (male or female). Also format the field to display the information uppercase.

- Add a validation rule and appropriate validation text to the Status field to accept only B, F, or
  A (boarded, foster home, or adopted).

d. Return to Datasheet view and update the table by filling in the new Status field for each record
with data of your choice.

e. So you can easily see the current status of the animals to ascertain which still need homes,
sort the table in descending order by the Status, Boarded Date, Foster Date, and Adoption
Date fields (hold down the [Shift] key and click the Status column and then the Adoption Date
column). Change the status of Lemon to **A** and enter today's date as the Adoption Date.
Remove the sort filter.

f. Use the Form Wizard to create a columnar form. Use the Expedition style and include all the
fields in their current order. Title the form **Angel's Animals**.

g. Add two records using the new form. Enter **[your name]'s Pet** in the Name field of the second
record you add, and then select, preview, and print it.

h. Exit Access, saving changes as needed.

Adventure Travel Form

★ **1.** You have heard from the employees of Adventure Travel that the database table you created (Step-by-Step Exercise 4 of Lab 1) is a bit unwieldy for them to enter the necessary data, because it now contains so many fields that it requires scrolling across the screen to locate them. You decide to create a form that will make entering data not only easier, but more attractive as well. Open the Adventure Travel database and use the Form Wizard to create a form called **Packages** for the "Travel Packages" table. Use the form to enter one new record with a fictitious client name and another with your name as the client. Select and print the second new record.

Expense Account Tracking

★★ **2.** While creating the database table for JK Enterprises (On Your Own Exercise 4 of Lab 1), you learned that some employees have been receiving advances for anticipated expenses (such as for travel). You have also been informed that the executives want to start tracking the expenses by department. You need to add a currency field for the advance amount data and a field to enter the department name (or number, if you prefer). You also need to add a Yes/No field to record whether or not the expense has been paid, with a corresponding validation rule and message. Update the Expenses table to include appropriate values in the new fields in the existing records. Close the table, saving the changes. Then use the Form Wizard to create a data entry form called **JK Expenses** for this table. To test the form, enter a new record with your name as the contact and then select and print the record.

Dental Database Update

★★ **3.** The single-dentist office for which you created a patient database (On Your Own Exercise 3 of Lab 1) has now expanded to include a second dentist and receptionist, requiring you to identify required fields and to add more fields that identify which patient is assigned to which dentist. You also decide that creating a form for the database would make it easier for both you and the other receptionist to enter and locate patient information. Open the Patient Information database and "Patient Data" table and make the patient identification number, name, and phone number required fields. Add a Dentist Name field, with the two dentist's names in the field description and an appropriate validation rule and message. Update the table to "assign" some of the patients to one of the dentists and some patients to the other dentist. Sort the table by dentist name to see the results of your new assignments. "Reassign" one of the displayed patients and then remove the sort filter. Close the table, saving the changes. Create a form called **Administration** for the table using the Form Wizard. Enter two new records, one for each of the dentists. Use the Find command to locate the record form that has your name as the patient, and then select and print the displayed record.

Employee Database Update

★★ **4.** The management at Lewis & Lewis, Inc. is quite impressed with the employee database you
★ created (On Your Own Exercise 2 of Lab 1). However, they would like you to include home phone numbers and addresses so the database can be used to send mail (such as Christmas cards, 401k information, and tax forms) to employees. Also, you have been asked to create a form that will make it easier for other administrative assistants to enter employee data into the database as well. Open the Lewis Personnel database and "Phone List" table and add home address and phone number fields to it. Update the table to include information in the new fields for the existing records. Sort

the table by employee last name and use the Replace command or table navigation to locate and change the last name of a female employee who has gotten married since you first created the database. Use the same technique to locate and delete a record for an employee who has left the company. Remove the sort filter and close the table, saving the changes. Create a form called **Human Resources** for the table using the Form Wizard. Enter two new records. Use the Find command to locate the record form that has your name as the employee, and then select and print the displayed record.

on the web

You realize that you have left out some very important fields in the "Inventory" table you created in the Golden Oldies database (On the Web Exercise 1 of Lab 1)—fields that identify the sources where you can obtain the vintage records your customers are looking for. Repeat your Web search for collectible record albums and note the resources (for example, online shopping services, specialty stores, or individual collectors who are offering these items at online auctions) for the titles you have included in your table. Add source name and address fields to the table and update it to include this information in the existing records. Sort the records according to the source name field and adjust the column widths to accommodate the new information. Remove the sort filter and close the table, saving the changes. Now, to make data entry easier for the company's employees, create a data entry form called **Collectibles** using the Form Wizard. Use the form to enter a new record with your name as the source, and then print it.

Analyzing Data and Creating Reports

LAB **3**

objectives

After completing this lab, you will know how to:

1.	Filter table records.
2.	Create and modify a query.
3.	Move columns.
4.	Query two tables.
5.	Create reports from tables and queries.
6.	Modify a report design.
7.	Change page margins.
8.	Print a selected page.
9.	Compact a database.

Iona to Fort Myers Car Pool Report

First Name	Last Name	Street Address	City	Phone Number
Bill	Delucchi	950 S. Terrace Dr.	Cypress Lake	(941) 555-8195
Lisa	Fromthart	32 Redcoat Rd.	Cypress Lake	(941) 555-0110
Nichol	Lawrence	433 S. Gaucho Dr.	Cypress Lake	(941) 555-7656
Mina	Lopez	4290 E. Alameda Dr.	Cypress Lake	(941) 555-5050
Cathy	Nichols	75 Brooklea Dr.	Cypress Lake	(941) 555-0001
Marc	Schiff	235 N. Cactus Dr.	Cypress Lake	(941) 555-0010
Eric	Helfand	4601 E. Willow Dr.	Iona	(941) 555-9101
Suzanne	Reddie	932 E. Parkway Dr.	Iona	(941) 555-1191
Name	Student	89 Any St.	Iona	(941) 555-3333
Lisa	Sutton	4389 S. Hayden Rd.	Iona	(941) 555-1950

Employee Address Report

First Name	Last Name	Street Address	City	State	Zip Code	Phone Number
Jeff	Bader	947 S. Forest St.	Fort Myers	FL	33301-1555	(941) 555-7789
Andrew	Beinbrink	45 Burr Rd.	Fort Myers	FL	33301-1555	(941) 555-5322
Brian	Birch	742 W. Lemon Dr.	Fort Myers	FL	33301-1555	(941) 555-4321
Tamara	Birch	742 W. Lemon Dr.	Forest Island	FL	33301-1555	(941) 555-4321
William	Bloomquist	43 Kings Rd.	Fort Myers	FL	33174	(941) 555-6432
Anna	Brett	23 Suffolk Ln.	Fort Myers	FL	33301-1555	(941) 555-4543
Scott	Briggs	45 E. Camelback Rd.	San Carlos	FL	33891-1605	(941) 555-9585
Ellen	Burke	234 N. 1st St.	San Carlos	FL	33891-1605	(941) 555-7789
Gordon	Delano	8943 W. Southern Ave.	Iona	FL	33101-7468	(941) 555-8201
Elizabeth	DeLuca	21 W. Southern Ave.	Forest Island	FL	33174	(941) 555-1105
Bill	Delucchi	950 S. Terrace Dr.	Cypress Lake	FL	33205-0093	(941) 555-8195
Barbara	Ernster	1153 S. Wilson	San Carlos	FL	33891-1605	(941) 555-3211
Kimberly	Fachet	923 E. Baseline Rd.	Forest Island	FL	33174	(941) 555-0018
Darnel	Facqur	5832 Fremont St	Forest Island	FL	33174	(941) 555-4563
Nancy	Falk	9483 W. Island Dr.	San Carlos	FL	33891-1605	(941) 555-8665
Robby	Ferguson	4232 Teller Ave.	San Carlos	FL	33891-1178	(941) 555-7039
Lisa	Fromthart	32 Redcoat Rd.	Cypress Lake	FL	33205-6911	(941) 555-0110
Ken	Gapasin	2633 E. Fountain St.	Iona	FL	33101-0093	(941) 555-0589
Alfonso	Gomez	3429 S. Grandview Dr.	Fort Myers	FL	33301-1555	(941) 555-2395
Sarah	Harvey	73 Lakeview Dr.	Cypress Lake	FL	33205-6911	(941) 555-7144
Eric	Helfand	4601 E. Willow Dr.	Iona	FL	33101-7468	(941) 555-9101
Karen	Hemstreet	999 Solano Dr.	San Carlos	FL	33891-1605	(941) 555-6325
Ryan	Hogan	1389 E. Northview Dr.	Iona	FL	33101-7468	(941) 555-1010
Karen	Howard	9423 S. Forest Ave.	Fort Myers	FL	33301-1555	(941) 555-5326
Raya	Ingles	8432 N. Cimarron	Iona	FL	33101-7468	(941) 555-6433
Chris	Jensen	601 Alpha Dr.	San Carlos	FL	33891-1605	(941) 555-0018

Page 1 of 3

Thursday, April 05, 2001

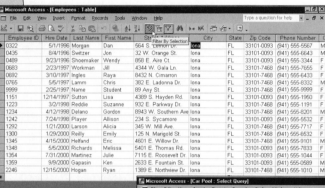

Filtering a datasheet displays only those records meeting the specified conditions.

Using a query helps you analyze the information in your database.

Custom reports can be generated to display database information in an attractive and meaningful manner.

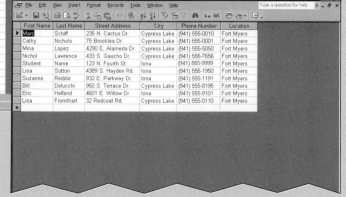

A multitable query is the power behind relational databases.

1
2
3
4
5

Lifestyle Fitness Club

After modifying the structure of the table of employee records, you have continued to enter many more records. You have also created a second table in the database that contains employee information about location and job titles. Again, the owners are very impressed with the database. They are anxious to see next how the information in the database can be used.

As you have seen, compiling, storing, and updating information in your database is very useful. The real strength of a database program, however, is how it can be used to find the information you need quickly, and manipulate and analyze it to answer specific questions. You will use the information in the tables to provide the answers to several inquiries about the Club employees. As you learn about the analytical features, think what it would be like to do the same task by hand. How long would it take? Would it be as accurate or as well presented? In addition, you will create several reports that present the information from the database attractively.

© Corbis

Filtering Records

Julie Martinez, an employee at the Fort Myers location, is interested in forming a car pool. She recently approached you about finding others who may also be interested. You decide this would be a great opportunity to see how you can use the employee table to find this information. To find the employees, you could sort the table and then write down the needed information. This could be time consuming, however, if you had hundreds of employees in the table. A faster way is to apply a filter to the table records to locate this information.

concept 1

Filter

1 A **filter** is a restriction placed on records in the open datasheet or form to quickly isolate and display a subset of records. A filter is created by specifying a set of limiting conditions, or **criteria**, which you want records to meet in order to be displayed. A filter is ideal when you want to display the subset for only a brief time and then return immediately to the full set of records. You can print the filtered records as you would any form or table. A filter is only temporary, and all records are redisplayed when you remove the filter or close and reopen the table or form. The filter results cannot be saved. However, the last filter criteria you specify are saved with the table, and the results can be quickly redisplayed.

You have continued to enter employee records into the "Employees" table. The updated table has been saved for you as Employees in the Personnel Records database. Before you begin filtering records, you need to open the current database.

1

● Start Access.

● Open the
ac03_Personnel Records
database file.

*Your screen should be
similar to Figure 3.1*

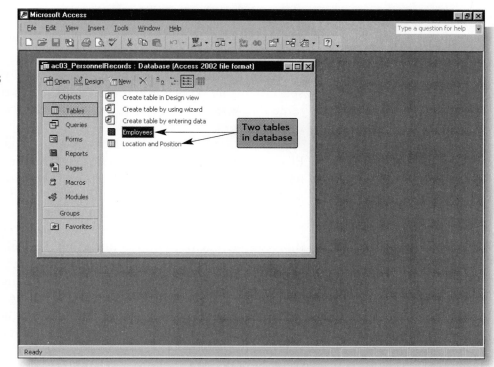

Figure 3.1

The tables list box of the Database window displays the names of two tables
in this database: Employees, and Location and Position. These tables will
be used throughout the lab.

2

● Open the "Employees"
table.

● Maximize the
datasheet window.

● Add your information
as record number 80
using your special ID
number **9999** and your
name. Enter **2/25/97**
as your hire date, city
as **Iona**, and zip code
as **33101-7468**. Fill in
the remaining fields as
desired.

Additional Information

You can copy the zip code
from another record that has
Iona as the city.

● Return to the first field
of the first record.

*Your screen should be
similar to Figure 3.2*

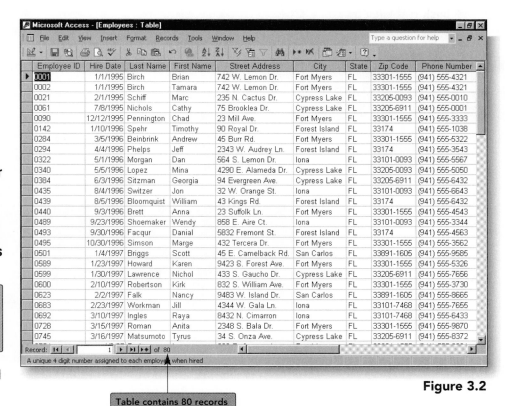

Figure 3.2

Table contains 80 records

Using Filter by Selection

Julie lives in Iona, and wants to find others who work at the same location and live in Iona. You can do this for her quite easily by using the Filter by Selection method. **Filter by Selection** displays only records containing a speccific value. This method is effective when there is only one value in the table that you want Access to use as the criterion for selecting and displaying records.

How the value is selected determines what results will be displayed. Placing the insertion point in a field selects the entire field contents. The filtered subset will include all records containing an exact match. Selecting part of a value in a field (by highlighting it) displays all records containing the selection. For example, in a table for a book collection, you could position the mouse pointer anywhere in a field containing the name of the author Stephen King, choose the Filter by Selection command, and only records for books whose author matches the selected name, "Stephen King," would be displayed. Selecting just "King" would include all records for authors Stephen King, Martin Luther King, and Barbara Kingsolver.

You want to filter the table to display only those records with a City field entry of Iona. To specify the city to locate, you need to select an example of the data in the table.

Additional Information

If the selected part of a value starts with the first character in the field, the subset displays all records with values that begin with the same selected characters.

1 ● **Move to the City field of record 9.**

● **Click** 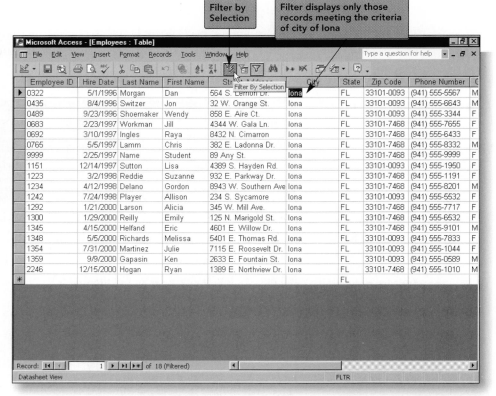 **Filter by Selection.**

Another Method

The menu equivalent is Records/Filter/Filter by Selection.

Your screen should be similar to Figure 3.3

Filter by Selection

Filter displays only those records meeting the criteria of city of Iona

Employee ID	Hire Date	Last Name	First Name	Street Address	City	State	Zip Code	Phone Number
0322	5/1/1996	Morgan	Dan	564 S. Lemon Dr.	Iona	FL	33101-0093	(941) 555-5567	M
0435	8/4/1996	Switzer	Jon	32 W. Orange St.	Iona	FL	33101-0093	(941) 555-6643	M
0489	9/23/1996	Shoemaker	Wendy	858 E. Aire Ct.	Iona	FL	33101-0093	(941) 555-3344	F
0683	2/23/1997	Workman	Jill	4344 W. Gala Ln.	Iona	FL	33101-7468	(941) 555-7655	F
0692	3/10/1997	Ingles	Raya	8432 N. Cimarron	Iona	FL	33101-7468	(941) 555-6433	F
0765	5/5/1997	Lamm	Chris	382 E. Ladonna Dr.	Iona	FL	33101-7468	(941) 555-8332	M
9999	2/25/1997	Name	Student	89 Any St.	Iona	FL	33101-7468	(941) 555-9999	F
1151	12/14/1997	Sutton	Lisa	4389 S. Hayden Rd.	Iona	FL	33101-0093	(941) 555-1950	F
1223	3/2/1998	Reddie	Suzanne	932 E. Parkway Dr.	Iona	FL	33101-7468	(941) 555-1191	F
1234	4/12/1998	Delano	Gordon	8943 W. Southern Ave	Iona	FL	33101-7468	(941) 555-8201	M
1242	7/24/1998	Player	Allison	234 S. Sycamore	Iona	FL	33101-0093	(941) 555-5532	F
1292	1/21/2000	Larson	Alicia	345 W. Mill Ave.	Iona	FL	33101-7468	(941) 555-7717	F
1300	1/29/2000	Reilly	Emily	125 N. Marigold St.	Iona	FL	33101-7468	(941) 555-6532	F
1345	4/15/2000	Helfand	Eric	4601 E. Willow Dr.	Iona	FL	33101-7468	(941) 555-9101	M
1348	5/5/2000	Richards	Melissa	5401 E. Thomas Rd.	Iona	FL	33101-0093	(941) 555-7833	F
1354	7/31/2000	Martinez	Julie	7115 E. Roosevelt Dr.	Iona	FL	33101-0093	(941) 555-1044	F
1359	9/9/2000	Gapasin	Ken	2633 E. Fountain St.	Iona	FL	33101-0093	(941) 555-0589	M
2246	12/15/2000	Hogan	Ryan	1389 E. Northview Dr.	Iona	FL	33101-7468	(941) 555-1010	M
*						FL		

Record: 1 ▶ ▶I ▶* of 18 (Filtered)

Datasheet View   FLTR

Figure 3.3

The datasheet displays only those records that contain the selected city. All other records are temporarily hidden. The status bar indicates the total number of filtered records (18) and shows that the datasheet is filtered.

After seeing how easy it was to locate this information, you want to locate employees who live in Cypress Lake. This information may help in setting up the car pool, because the people traveling from the city of Iona pass through Cypress Lake on the way to the Fort Myers location. Before creating the new filter, you will remove the current filter and return the table to its full display.

② ● Click 🔽 **Remove Filter.**

Your screen should be similar to Figure 3.4

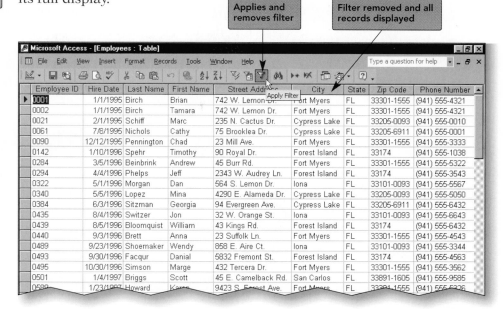

Figure 3.4

Using Filter by Form

The **Filter by Form** method allows you to perform filters on multiple criteria. In this case, you want to filter the employee data by two cities, Iona and Cypress Lake.

① ● Click 📋 **Filter by Form.**

Your screen should be similar to Figure 3.5

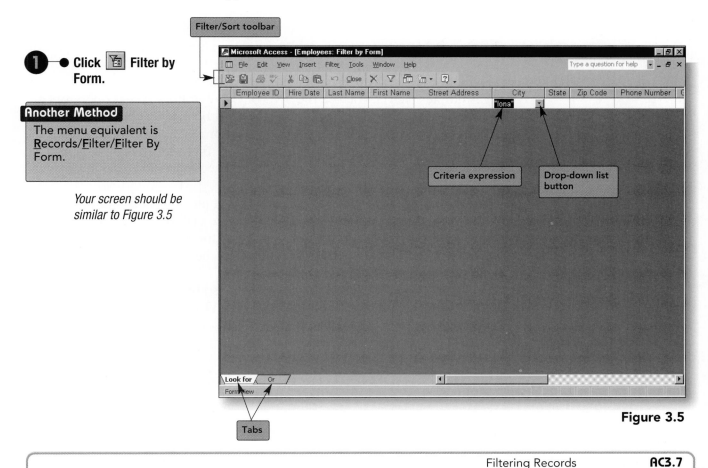

Figure 3.5

The Filter by Form window displays a blank version of the current datasheet with empty fields in which you specify the criteria. Notice that at the bottom of the Filter by Form window there are two tabs, Look For and Or. In the Look For tab, you enter the first filter criterion you want to use, and in the Or tab, you enter additional filter criteria. You want to filter the records on one field, City, with an initial criterion of Iona and a second criterion of Cypress Lake.

Also notice that the Filter/Sort toolbar displays several standard buttons as well as buttons specific to filtering records (identified in the following illustration).

To tell Access what specific data you want it to use for the filter criteria, you enter values in the blank field spaces of the record row as criteria expressions. A **criteria expression** is an expression that will select only the records that meet certain limiting criteria. You can create the criteria expression by either typing a value directly in its corresponding field or selecting a value from a drop-down list.

Currently the Look For tab is active and the City field displays "Iona," which is the criterion you specified when you did the Filter by Selection. Notice that the field displays a drop-down list button. Each field has a drop-down button when the field is selected. Clicking this button displays a list of values that are available in that field. You can use this list to select values and build a criteria expression, if necessary.

You do not need to select a different value for the initial criterion because the City field already contains the correct value (Iona). However, you do need to add the second criterion to the filter to include all records with a City field value of Cypress Lake. To instruct the filter to locate records meeting multiple criteria, you use the AND or OR operators. These operators are used to specify multiple conditions that must be met for the records to display in the filter datasheet. The **AND operator** narrows the search, because a record must meet both conditions to be included. The **OR operator** broadens the search, because any record meeting either condition is included in the output.

The AND operator is assumed when you enter criteria in multiple fields. Within a field, typing the word "and" between criteria in the same field establishes the AND condition. The OR operator is established by entering the criterion in the Or tab, or by typing "or" between criteria in the same field.

In this filter, you will use an OR operator so that records meeting either city criterion will be included in the output. To include the city as an OR criterion, you enter the criterion in the Or tab.

Additional Information

A value must be entered in the Look For tab before the Or tab is available (active). Then, each time you click the Or tab, another Or tab is added to the window to enable you to enter more filter criteria. Again, a value must be entered in each Or tab before the next Or tab is actually available for use (active).

Your screen should be similar to Figure 3.6

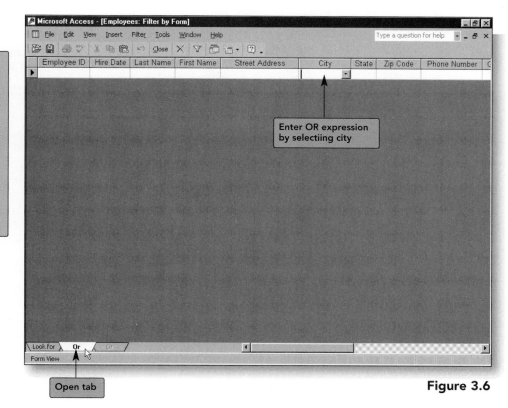

Enter OR expression by selectiing city

Open tab

Figure 3.6

The Or tab is opened, and a new blank row is displayed. You will enter this criteria expression by selecting the criterion from the City drop-down list.

③ ● **From the City field drop-down list, select Cypress Lake.**

Another Method

You could have typed "Cypress Lake" directly in the City field instead of selecting it from the drop-down list.

Your screen should be similar to Figure 3.7

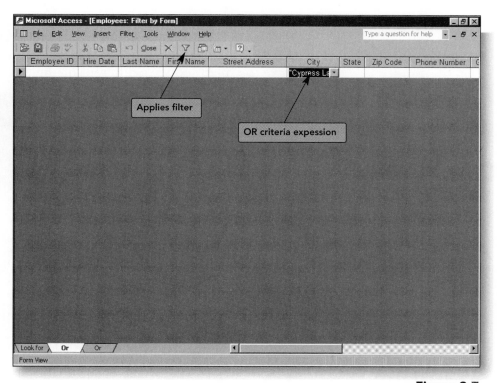

Applies filter

OR criteria expession

Figure 3.7

The selected criterion is displayed in the City field surrounded by quotes, as required of all text entries used in an expression, and the Look For tab still contains the criterion for the city of Iona. You can now apply the filter.

4 ● Click 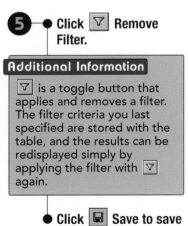 Apply Filter.

Another Method

The menu equivalent is Filter/Apply Filter/Sort.

Your screen should be similar to Figure 3.8

> Filtered database displays only records with a city of Iona or Cypress Lake

Employee ID	Hire Date	Last Name	First Name	Street Address	City	State	Zip Code	Phone Number
0021	2/1/1995	Schiff	Marc	235 N. Cactus Dr.	Cypress Lake	FL	33205-0093	(941) 555-0010
0061	7/8/1995	Nichols	Cathy	75 Brooklea Dr.	Cypress Lake	FL	33205-6911	(941) 555-0001
0322	5/1/1996	Morgan	Dan	564 S. Lemon Dr.	Iona	FL	33101-0093	(941) 555-5567
0340	5/5/1996	Lopez	Mina	4290 E. Alameda Dr.	Cypress Lake	FL	33205-0093	(941) 555-5050
0384	6/3/1996	Sitzman	Georgia	94 Evergreen Ave.	Cypress Lake	FL	33205-6911	(941) 555-6432
0435	8/4/1996	Switzer	Jon	32 W. Orange St.	Iona	FL	33101-0093	(941) 555-6643
0489	9/23/1996	Shoemaker	Wendy	858 E. Aire Ct.	Iona	FL	33101-0093	(941) 555-3344
0599	1/30/1997	Lawrence	Nichol	433 S. Gaucho Dr.	Cypress Lake	FL	33205-6911	(941) 555-7656
0683	2/23/1997	Workman	Jill	4344 W. Gala Ln.	Iona	FL	33101-7468	(941) 555-7655
0692	3/10/1997	Ingles	Raya	8432 N. Cimarron	Iona	FL	33101-0093	(941) 555-6433
0745	3/16/1997	Matsumoto	Tyrus	34 S. Onza Ave.	Cypress Lake	FL	33205-6911	(941) 555-8372
0765	5/5/1997	Lamm	Chris	382 E. Ladonna Dr.	Iona	FL	33101-7468	(941) 555-8332
9999	2/25/1997	Name	Student	123 N. Fourth St.	Iona	FL	33205-6911	(941) 555-9999
0839	8/4/1997	Ruiz	Enrique	35 Palm St.	Cypress Lake	FL	33205-6911	(941) 555-0091
1151	12/14/1997	Sutton	Lisa	4389 S. Hayden Rd.	Iona	FL	33101-0093	(941) 555-1950
1223	3/2/1998	Reddie	Suzanne	932 E. Parkway Dr.	Iona	FL	33101-7468	(941) 555-1191
1224	3/10/1998	Rath	Kathy	87 E. Aurora Ave.	Cypress Lake	FL	33205-0093	(941) 555-9797
1234	4/12/1998	Delano	Gordon	8943 W. Southern Ave	Iona	FL	33101-7468	(941) 555-8201
1236	6/1/1998	Stacey	David	737 S. College Rd.	Cypress Lake	FL	33205-0093	(941) 555-7784
1242	7/24/1998	Player	Allison	234 S. Sycamore	Iona	FL	33101-0093	(941) 555-5532
1273	5/25/1999	Sabin	Greg	90 E. Rawhide Ave.	Cypress Lake	FL	33205-6911	(941) 555-4458
1292	1/21/2000	Larson	Alicia	345 W. Mill Ave.	Iona	FL	33101-7468	(941) 555-7717
1300	1/29/2000	Reilly	Emily	125 N. Marigold St.	Iona	FL	33101-7468	(941) 555-6532
1329	3/8/2000	Delucchi	Bill	950 S. Terrace Dr.	Cypress Lake	FL	33205-0093	(941) 555-8195
1345	4/15/2000	Helfand	Eric	4601 E. Willow Dr.	Iona	FL	33101-7468	(941) 555-9101
1348	5/5/2000	Richards	Melissa	5401 E. Thomas Rd.	Iona	FL	33101-0093	(941) 555-7833

Record: ◄ ◄ | 1 | ► ►I ►* of 33 (Filtered)

A unique 4 digit number assigned to each employee when hired   FLTR

> Number of records meeting filter criteria

Figure 3.8

The filtered datasheet displays the records for all 33 employees who live in the city of Iona or Cypress Lake. After seeing this, you realize that it contains more information about each employee than someone would need (or should even have access to) in order to form a car pool. You decide to remove the filter and try a different method to gather only the necessary information.

5 ● Click Remove Filter.

Additional Information

 is a toggle button that applies and removes a filter. The filter criteria you last specified are stored with the table, and the results can be redisplayed simply by applying the filter with again.

● Click 💾 Save to save the changes you've made to the "Employees" table.

Your screen should be similar to Figure 3.9

> Filter removed and all records displayed

Employee ID	Hire Date	Last Name	First Name	Street Address	City	State	Zip Code	Phone Number
0001	1/1/1995	Birch	Brian	742 W. Lemon Dr.	Fort Myers	FL	33301-1555	(941) 555-4321
0002	1/1/1995	Birch	Tamara	742 W. Lemon Dr.	Fort Myers	FL	33301-1555	(941) 555-4321
0021	2/1/1995	Schiff	Marc	235 N. Cactus Dr.	Cypress Lake	FL	33205-0093	(941) 555-0010
0061	7/8/1995	Nichols	Cathy	75 Brooklea Dr.	Cypress Lake	FL	33205-6911	(941) 555-0001
0090	12/1/1995	Pennington	Chad	23 Mill Ave.	Fort Myers	FL	33301-1555	(941) 555-3333
0142	1/10/1996	Spehr	Timothy	90 Royal Dr.	Forest Island	FL	33174	(941) 555-1038
0284	3/5/1996	Beinbrink	Andrew	45 Burr Rd.	Fort Myers	FL	33301-1555	(941) 555-5322
0294	4/4/1996	Phelps	Jeff	2343 W. Audrey Ln.	Forest Island	FL	33174	(941) 555-3543
0322	5/1/1996	Morgan	Dan	564 S. Lemon Dr.	Iona	FL	33101-0093	(941) 555-5567
0340	5/5/1996	Lopez	Mina	4290 E. Alameda Dr.	Cypress Lake	FL	33205-0093	(941) 555-5050
0384	6/3/1996	Sitzman	Georgia	94 Evergreen Ave.	Cypress Lake	FL	33205-6911	(941) 555-6432
0435	8/4/1996	Switzer	Jon	32 W. Orange St.	Iona	FL	33101-0093	(941) 555-6643
0439	8/5/1996	Bloomquist	William	43 Kings Rd.	Forest Island	FL	33174	(941) 555-6432
0440	9/3/1996	Brett	Anna	23 Suffolk Ln.	Fort Myers	FL	33301-1555	(941) 555-4543
0489	9/23/1996	Shoemaker	Wendy	858 E. Aire Ct.	Iona	FL	33101-0093	(941) 555-3344
0493	9/30/1996	Facqur	Danial	5832 Fremont St.	Forest Island	FL	33174	(941) 555-4563
0495	10/30/1996	Simson	Marge	432 Tercera Dr.	Fort Myers	FL	33301-1555	(941) 555-3562
0501	1/4/1997	Briggs	Scott	45 E. Camelback Rd.	San Carlos	FL	33891-1605	(941) 555-9585
0589	1/23/1997	Howard	Karen	9423 S. Forest Ave.	Fort Myers	FL	33301-1555	(941) 555-5326
0599	1/30/1997	Lawrence	Nichol	433 S. Gaucho Dr.	Cypress Lake	FL	33205-6911	(941) 555-7656
0600	2/10/1997	Robertson	Kirk	832 S. William Ave.	Fort Myers	FL	33301-1555	(941) 555-3730
0623	2/2/1997	Falk	Nancy	9483 W. Island Dr.	San Carlos	FL	33891-1605	(941) 555-8665
0683	2/23/1997	Workman	Jill	4344 W. Gala Ln.	Iona	FL	33101-7468	(941) 555-7655

Figure 3.9

Querying a Database

To obtain exactly the information you need to give Julie for her car pool, you will use a query.

concept 2

Query

2 A **query** is a request for specific data contained in a database. Queries are used to view data in different ways, to analyze data, and even to change existing data. Because queries are based on tables, you can also use a query as the source for forms and reports. The five types of queries are described in the following table.

Query Type	Description
Select query	Retrieves the specific data you request from one or more tables, then displays the data in a query datasheet in the order you specify. This is the most common type of query.
Crosstab query	Summarizes large amounts of data in an easy-to-read, row-and-column format.
Parameter query	Displays a dialog box prompting you for information, such as criteria for locating data. For example, a parameter query might request the beginning and ending dates, then display all records matching dates between the two specified values.
Action query	Makes changes to many records in one operation. There are four types of action queries: a make-table query creates a new table from selected data in one or more tables; an update query makes update changes to records, such as when you need to raise salaries of all sales staff by 7 percent; an append query adds records from one or more tables to the end of other tables; and a delete query deletes records from a table or tables.
SQL query	Created using SQL (Structured Query Language), an advanced programming language used in Access.

Creating a query in Access is much the same as creating a table or a form. You can either create a new query from the Database window by selecting the Queries object and the creation method you want to use, or you can create a new query from within an open table. Because you already have the "Employees" table open, you will use the second method this time.

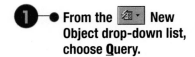

1 ● From the **New Object** drop-down list, choose **Query**.

Your screen should be similar to Figure 3.10

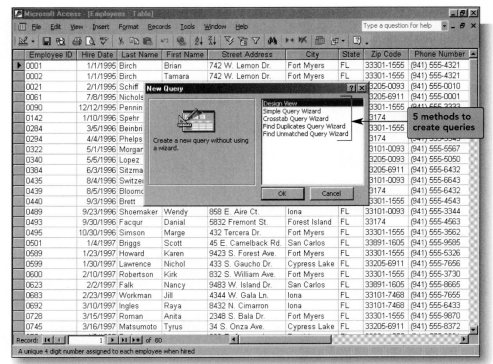

Figure 3.10

The New Query dialog box contains five options for creating queries. You can create a query from scratch in Query Design view or by using one of the four query Wizards. The following table explains the type of query that each of the Wizards creates.

Query Wizard	Type of Query Created
Simple	Select query
Crosstab	Crosstab query
Find Duplicates	Locates all records that contain duplicate values in one or more fields in the specified tables.
Find Unmatched	Locates records in one table that do not have records in another. For example, you could locate all employees in one table who have no hours worked in another table.

Using a Query Wizard

You decide that you want to try the Simple Query Wizard and create a select query to see if it gives you the results you want.

1 ● Select Simple Query Wizard.

● Click [OK].

Your screen should be similar to Figure 3.11

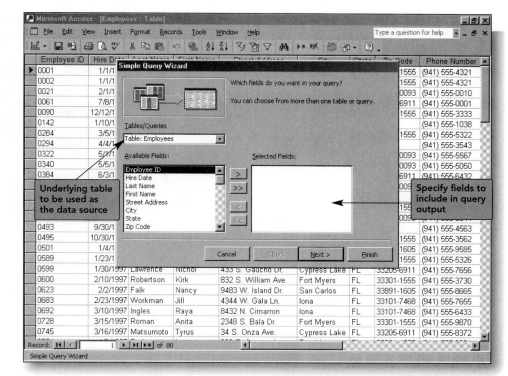

Figure 3.11

In the first Simple Query Wizard dialog box, you specify the underlying table and the fields from the table that will give you the desired query result, just as you did when creating a form. You will use data from the "Employees" table, which is already selected. You need to select the fields you want displayed in the query output.

2 ● Add the Last Name, First Name, Street Address, City, and Phone Number fields to the Selected Fields list.

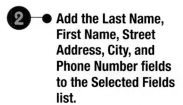
Additional Information
The quickest way to add a field to the Selected Fields list is to double-click its field name in the Available Fields list.

Your screen should be similar to Figure 3.12

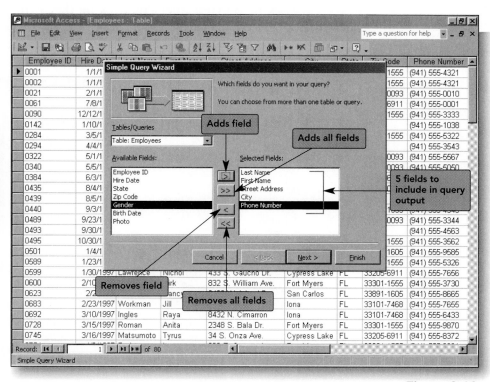

Figure 3.12

After you have selected all the fields that you want to include in your query, you can move on to the next step in the simple query creation.

3 ● **Click** [Next >].

Your screen should be similar to Figure 3.13

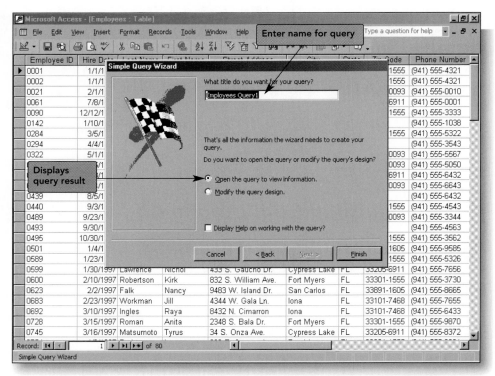

Figure 3.13

In the second Simple Query Wizard dialog box, you specify a name for your query, and whether you want to open it as is or in Design view so you can modify it. You can also have Access display Help messages while you are working on your query by clicking the corresponding box at the bottom of this Wizard screen. You decide that you just want to display the query results, and you want to give the query a name that will identify its purpose.

4 ● **Replace the suggested title in the text box with Car Pool.**

● **Click** [Finish].

Your screen should be similar to Figure 3.14

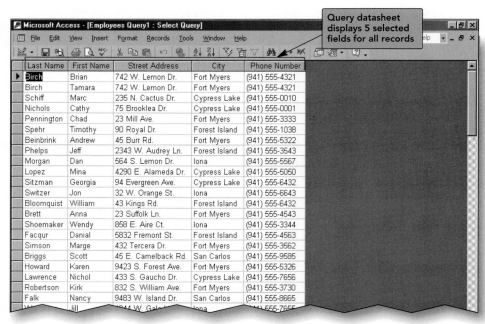

Figure 3.14

www.mhhe.com/oleary

The result of the query is displayed in a **query datasheet**. In this case, the query datasheet displays only the five specified fields for all records in the table. Query Datasheet view includes the same menus and toolbar buttons as in Table Datasheet view.

Moving Columns

The order of the fields in the query datasheet reflects the order they were placed in the Selected Fields list. You can still change the display order of the fields by moving the columns to where you want them. To move a column, you first select it and then drag it to its new location.

For the car pool list, there is no reason for the last name to be listed first, so you decide to move the Last Name column to follow the First Name column.

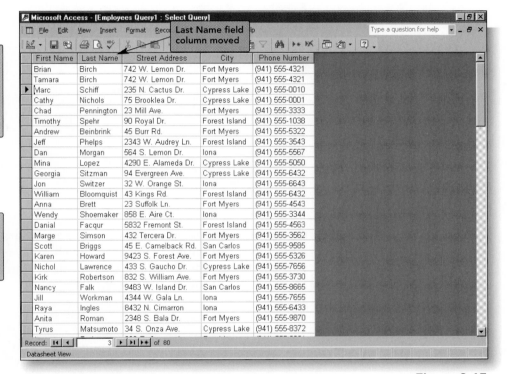

<table>
<tr><td>First Name</td><td>Last Name</td><td>Street Address</td><td>City</td><td>Phone Number</td></tr>
<tr><td>Brian</td><td>Birch</td><td>742 W. Lemon Dr.</td><td>Fort Myers</td><td>(941) 555-4321</td></tr>
<tr><td>Tamara</td><td>Birch</td><td>742 W. Lemon Dr.</td><td>Fort Myers</td><td>(941) 555-4321</td></tr>
<tr><td>Marc</td><td>Schiff</td><td>235 N. Cactus Dr.</td><td>Cypress Lake</td><td>(941) 555-0010</td></tr>
<tr><td>Cathy</td><td>Nichols</td><td>75 Brooklea Dr.</td><td>Cypress Lake</td><td>(941) 555-0001</td></tr>
<tr><td>Chad</td><td>Pennington</td><td>23 Mill Ave.</td><td>Fort Myers</td><td>(941) 555-3333</td></tr>
<tr><td>Timothy</td><td>Spehr</td><td>90 Royal Dr.</td><td>Forest Island</td><td>(941) 555-1038</td></tr>
<tr><td>Andrew</td><td>Beinbrink</td><td>45 Burr Rd.</td><td>Fort Myers</td><td>(941) 555-5322</td></tr>
<tr><td>Jeff</td><td>Phelps</td><td>2343 W. Audrey Ln.</td><td>Forest Island</td><td>(941) 555-3543</td></tr>
<tr><td>Dan</td><td>Morgan</td><td>564 S. Lemon Dr.</td><td>Iona</td><td>(941) 555-5567</td></tr>
<tr><td>Mina</td><td>Lopez</td><td>4290 E. Alameda Dr.</td><td>Cypress Lake</td><td>(941) 555-5050</td></tr>
<tr><td>Georgia</td><td>Sitzman</td><td>94 Evergreen Ave.</td><td>Cypress Lake</td><td>(941) 555-6432</td></tr>
<tr><td>Jon</td><td>Switzer</td><td>32 W. Orange St.</td><td>Iona</td><td>(941) 555-6643</td></tr>
<tr><td>William</td><td>Bloomquist</td><td>43 Kings Rd.</td><td>Forest Island</td><td>(941) 555-6432</td></tr>
<tr><td>Anna</td><td>Brett</td><td>23 Suffolk Ln.</td><td>Fort Myers</td><td>(941) 555-4543</td></tr>
<tr><td>Wendy</td><td>Shoemaker</td><td>858 E. Aire Ct.</td><td>Iona</td><td>(941) 555-3344</td></tr>
<tr><td>Danial</td><td>Facqur</td><td>5832 Fremont St.</td><td>Forest Island</td><td>(941) 555-4563</td></tr>
<tr><td>Marge</td><td>Simson</td><td>432 Tercera Dr.</td><td>Fort Myers</td><td>(941) 555-3562</td></tr>
<tr><td>Scott</td><td>Briggs</td><td>45 E. Camelback Rd.</td><td>San Carlos</td><td>(941) 555-9585</td></tr>
<tr><td>Karen</td><td>Howard</td><td>9423 S. Forest Ave.</td><td>Fort Myers</td><td>(941) 555-5326</td></tr>
<tr><td>Nichol</td><td>Lawrence</td><td>433 S. Gaucho Dr.</td><td>Cypress Lake</td><td>(941) 555-7656</td></tr>
<tr><td>Kirk</td><td>Robertson</td><td>832 S. William Ave.</td><td>Fort Myers</td><td>(941) 555-3730</td></tr>
<tr><td>Nancy</td><td>Falk</td><td>9483 W. Island Dr.</td><td>San Carlos</td><td>(941) 555-8665</td></tr>
<tr><td>Jill</td><td>Workman</td><td>4344 W. Gala Ln.</td><td>Iona</td><td>(941) 555-7655</td></tr>
<tr><td>Raya</td><td>Ingles</td><td>8432 N. Cimarron</td><td>Iona</td><td>(941) 555-6433</td></tr>
<tr><td>Anita</td><td>Roman</td><td>2348 S. Bala Dr.</td><td>Fort Myers</td><td>(941) 555-9870</td></tr>
<tr><td>Tyrus</td><td>Matsumoto</td><td>34 S. Onza Ave.</td><td>Cypress Lake</td><td>(941) 555-8372</td></tr>
</table>

Figure 3.15

 ● **Select the Last Name column.**

HAVING TROUBLE?
Remember, to select an entire column, you click on its column heading (which in this case, is Last Name) when the mouse pointer is a ↓.

● **Click and hold the mouse button on the Last Name column heading.**

Additional Information
When the mouse pointer is a ↳, it indicates you can drag to move the selection.

● **Drag the Last Name column to the right until a thick black line is displayed between the First Name and Street columns.**

● **Release the mouse button.**

● **Click anywhere in the table to clear the selection.**

Additional Information
You can move fields in Table Datasheet view in the same way.

Your screen should be similar to Figure 3.15

Additional Information
Changing the column order in the query datasheet does not affect the field order in the table, which is controlled by the table design.

Although the query result displays only the fields you want to see, it displays all the employee records in the database. You need to modify the query to include only the records for employees who live in Iona or Cypress Lake.

Modifying a Query

To modify a query to display only selected records, you specify the criteria in the Query Design view window.

1 ● Click 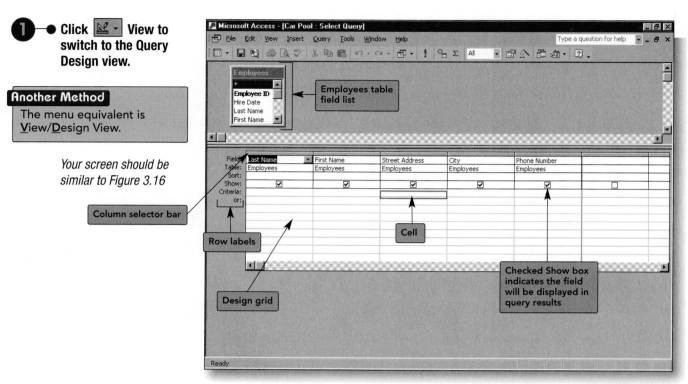 View to switch to the Query Design view.

Another Method

The menu equivalent is View/Design View.

Your screen should be similar to Figure 3.16

Figure 3.16

Query Design view is used to create and modify the structure of the query. This view automatically displays the Query Design toolbar, which contains the standard buttons as well as buttons (identified below) that are specific to the Query Design view window.

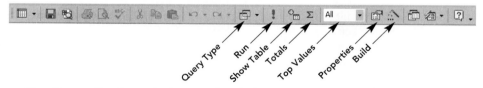

The Query Design window is divided into two areas. The upper area displays a list box of all the fields in the selected table. This is called the **field list**. The lower portion of the window displays the **design grid**. This is where you enter the settings that define the query. Each column in the grid holds the information about each field to be included in the query datasheet. The design grid automatically displays the fields that are specified when a query is created using a Query Wizard.

Above the field names is a narrow bar called the **column selector bar**. It is used to select an entire column. Each **row label** identifies the type of information that can be entered. The intersection of a column and row creates a **cell**. This is where you enter expressions to obtain the query results you need.

The boxes in the Show row are called **Show boxes**. The Show box for a field lets you specify whether you want that field displayed in the query result. A checked box indicates that the field will be displayed; no check means that it will not.

The Criteria row contains the criteria expression (field value or values) and a comparison operator.

The first thing you want to do in this query is locate and display only those records where the city is Iona. In the Criteria row of the City column, you first need to enter a criteria expression to select only those records.

2 ● Move to the City Criteria cell.

● Type **Iona**.

● Press (←Enter).

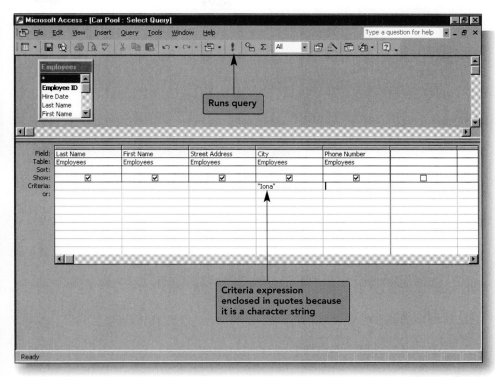

Runs query

Criteria expression enclosed in quotes because it is a character string

Figure 3.17

Your screen should be similar to Figure 3.17

The expression is enclosed in quotes because it is a character string. To display the query results, you run the query.

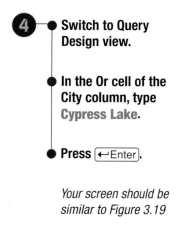

Another Method

The menu equivalent is Query/Run. You can also click [▦▾] Datasheet View to run the query and display the query datasheet.

Your screen should be similar to Figure 3.18

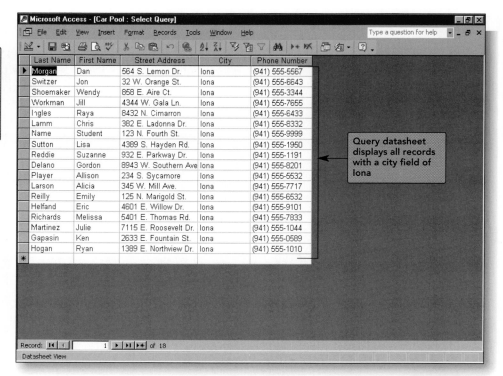

Query datasheet displays all records with a city field of Iona

Figure 3.18

The query datasheet displays only those records meeting the city criterion. This is the same result as the first simple-query filter you used, except that it displays only the specified fields.

Next, you will add a second criterion to include Cypress Lake in the result. As with filters, the AND and OR operators are used to combine criteria. If the results must meet both of the specified criteria for a field, this condition is established by typing the word "and" in a field's Criteria cell as part of its criteria expression. If the results can meet either of the specified criteria, this is established by entering the first criteria expression in the first Criteria cell for the field, and the second expression in the Or cell for the same field.

Because you want to display the records for employees who live in either city, you will enter this as an Or condition.

4 ● **Switch to Query Design view.**

● **In the Or cell of the City column, type Cypress Lake.**

● **Press** ⏎Enter.

Your screen should be similar to Figure 3.19

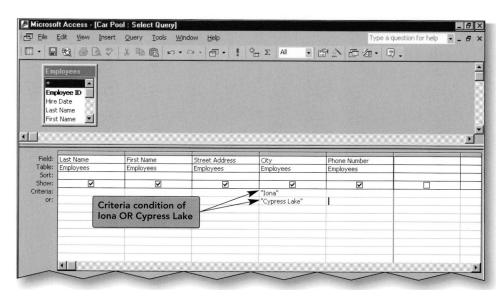

Criteria condition of Iona OR Cypress Lake

Figure 3.19

"Cypress Lake" is now set as the Or condition, and you are ready to run the query.

5 Click [!] Run.

Your screen should be similar to Figure 3.20

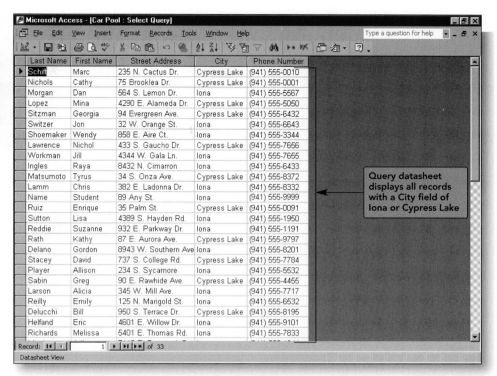

Figure 3.20

The query located 33 records in which the employee met the specified criteria. Notice that the fields are again in the order in which they appear in the design grid, which is not the most convenient way to look at them for your purposes. You will switch the Last Name and First Name columns again.

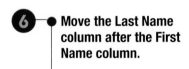

6 Move the Last Name column after the First Name column.

● Deselect the column.

Your screen should be similar to Figure 3.21

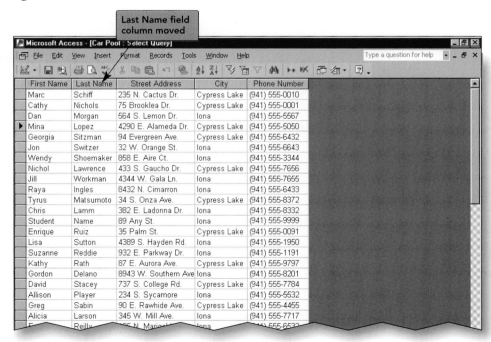

Figure 3.21

While you are working on the car pool query, Brian, the Club owner, stops in and asks if you can find some information quickly for him. Because you plan to continue working on the car pool query later, you will save the query so you do not have to recreate it. This is another advantage of queries over filters. Filters are temporary, whereas queries can be permanently saved with the database.

Click  **Save.**

Close the Query Datasheet window.

Your screen should be similar to Figure 3.22

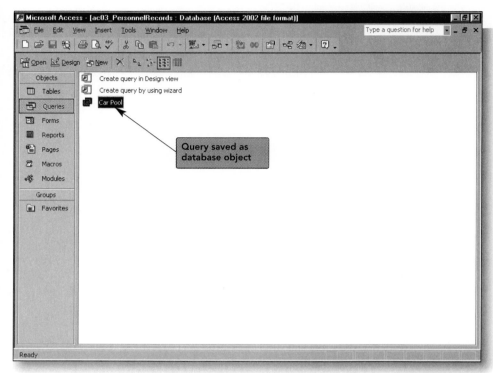

Query saved as database object

Figure 3.22

The query name, "Car Pool," is displayed in the queries list.

Creating a Query in Design View

In January, 2002, the Club celebrates its 10-year anniversary. Brian is planning an anniversary celebration party that month and wants to use the occasion to presnt 3-year and 5-year service awards. He needs to know how many employees are in each category so that he can order the correct number of awards. To help Brian locate these employees, you will create a new query. You decide to create the query directly in Query Design view this time, rather than using a Query Wizard.

1 ● Double-click Create
query in Design view.

● If necessary, open the
tables tab.

*Your screen should be
similar to Figure 3.23*

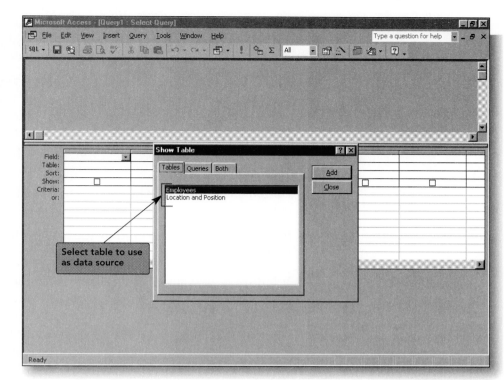

Figure 3.23

The Query Design window is open with the Show Table dialog box open on
top of it. The dialog box is used to specify the underlying table or query to
use to create the new query. The three tabs—Tables, Queries, and Both—
contain the names of the existing tables and queries that can be used as the
information source for the query. You need to add the "Employees" table to
the query design.

2 ● In the Tables tab,
select the "Employees"
table (if it is not
already selected).

● Click [Add] .

Another Method

You can also double-click the
table name to add it to the
query design.

● Click [Close] .

● If necessary, maximize
the Query Design
window.

*Your screen should be
similar to Figure 3.24*

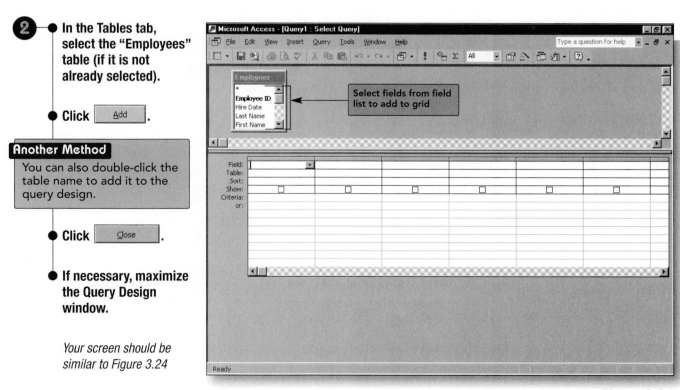

Figure 3.24

A field list for the selected table appears above the design grid. From the field list, you need to add the fields to the grid that you want to use in the query. You can use the following methods to add fields to the design grid:

- Select the field name and drag it from the field list to the grid. To select several adjacent fields, press ⇧Shift while you click the field names. To select nonadjacent fields, pressing Ctrl while clicking the field names. To select all fields, double-click the field list title bar. You can then drag all the selected fields into the grid, and Access will place each field in a separate column.

- Double-click on the field name. The field is added to the next available column in the grid.

- Select the Field cell drop-down arrow in the grid, then choose the field name.

In addition, if you select the asterisk in the field list and add it to the grid, Access displays the table or query name in the field row followed by a period and asterisk. This indicates that all fields in the table will be included in the query results. Using this feature also will automatically include any new fields that may later be added to the table, and will exclude deleted fields. You cannot sort records or specify criteria for fields, however, unless you also add those fields individually to the design grid.

The fields you want to add to the grid for this query are Hire Date, First Name, and Last Name.

3 ● **Double-click Hire Date in the field list to add it to the grid.**

● **Add the First Name field and the Last Name field to the grid, in that order.**

Your screen should be similar to Figure 3.25

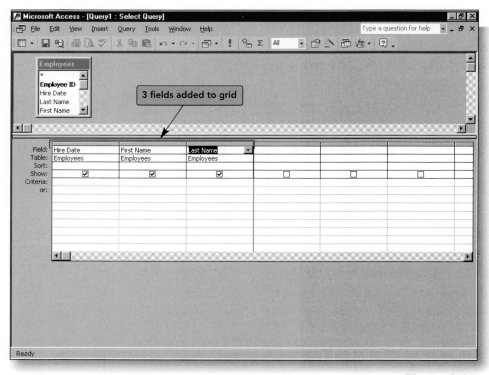

Figure 3.25

Now that you have set up the fields you want to include in this query, you can start entering the criteria that each field must meet to be included in the query results. First, you want to locate all employees who have at least 3 years with the Club. To do this you will use the < and = operators to include all records with a hire of 1/1/99 or earlier.

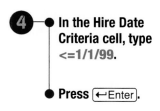

4 • In the Hire Date Criteria cell, type <=1/1/99.

• Press ⏎Enter.

Your screen should be similar to Figure 3.26

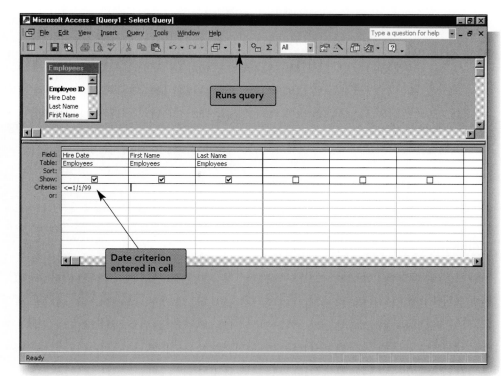

Runs query

Date criterion entered in cell

Figure 3.26

The expression appears in the cell as <=#1/1/1999#. Access adds # signs around the date to identify the values in the expression as a date. You decide to run the query to see the results.

5 • Click  Run.

Your screen should be similar to Figure 3.27

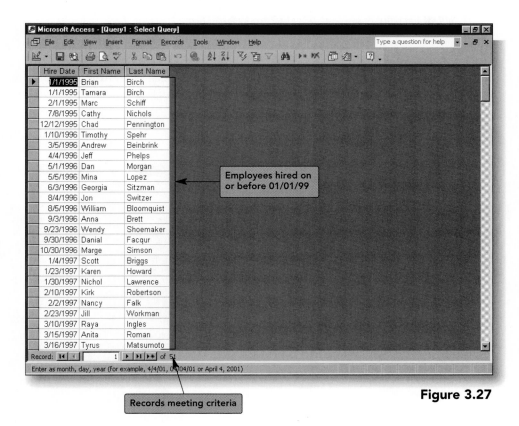

Employees hired on or before 01/01/99

Records meeting criteria

Figure 3.27

The query datasheet displays only those records meeting the date criterion. The record number indicator of the query datasheet shows that 50 employees were hired by January 1999. However, what you really want to find out are those employees who have 3 or more years of service, but less than 5 years. You will refine the search to locate just these employees.

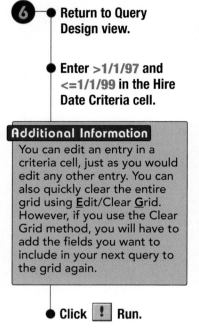

6 ● **Return to Query Design view.**

● **Enter >1/1/97 and <=1/1/99 in the Hire Date Criteria cell.**

Additional Information

You can edit an entry in a criteria cell, just as you would edit any other entry. You can also quickly clear the entire grid using Edit/Clear Grid. However, if you use the Clear Grid method, you will have to add the fields you want to include in your next query to the grid again.

● **Click ! Run.**

Your screen should be similar to Figure 3.28

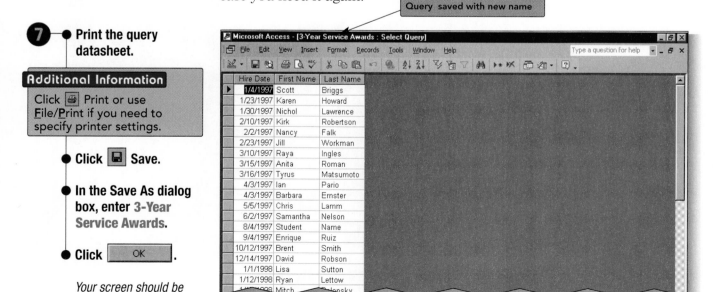

Figure 3.28

The number of employees with at least 3 but less than 5 years with the club is 33. These are the employees who are eligible for the 3-year service awards. You will print out this datasheet for Brian and save the query in case you need it again.

7 ● **Print the query datasheet.**

Additional Information

Click 🖨 Print or use File/Print if you need to specify printer settings.

● **Click 🖫 Save.**

● **In the Save As dialog box, enter 3-Year Service Awards.**

● **Click OK.**

Your screen should be similar to Figure 3.29

Figure 3.29

For the next level of awards that Brian wants to give out, you need to find the employees with more than 5 years of service.

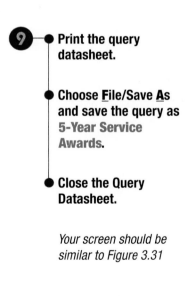

Return to Query Design view and enter <=1/1/97 in the Hire Date Criteria cell.

Run the query.

Your screen should be similar to Figure 3.30

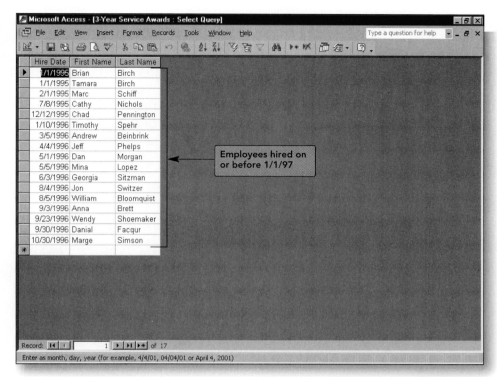

Figure 3.30

The query results show that there are 17 employees who have been with the club for at least 5 years and are eligible for the 5-year service award. You can now print and save this query.

Print the query datasheet.

Choose File/Save As and save the query as 5-Year Service Awards.

Close the Query Datasheet.

Your screen should be similar to Figure 3.31

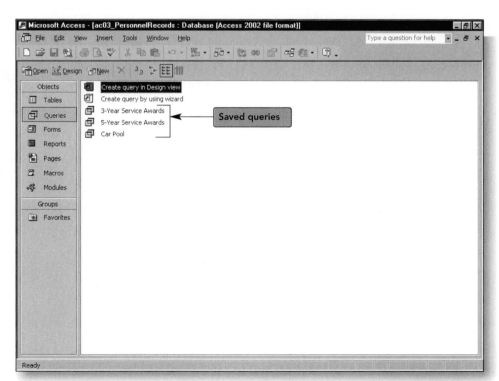

Figure 3.31

The two new queries you saved are listed in the queries object list box. Having provided Brian with the answers he needed, you are ready to get back to work on the car pool query.

Querying Two Tables

The car pool list would be more helpful if it had only the people that work at the Fort Myers location. Because the "Employees" table does not contain this information, you will need to create a query using the information from two tables to get these results. A query that uses more than one table is called a **multitable query**. To bring together two tables in a query, you create a join between the tables.

concept 3

Join

3   A **join** is an association between a field in one table or query and a field of the same data type in another table or query. Joining tables enables you to bring information from different tables in your database together or to perform the same action on data from more than one table. The capability to join tables is what makes relational databases so powerful.

In order to be joined, the tables must have at least one common field. **Common fields** are of the same data type and contain the same kind of information, but they can have different field names.

The following diagram shows an example of how, when the Employee ID fields of two tables are joined, a query can be created using data from both tables to provide the requested information.

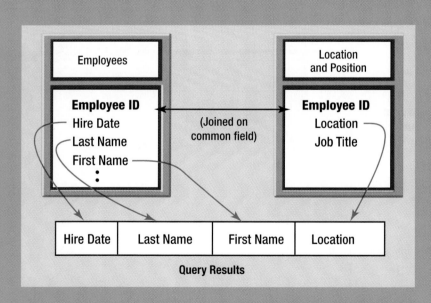

The location information for each employee is in a table named "Location and Position."

1 Click [⊞ Tables] and open the "Location and Position" table.

Your screen should be similar to Figure 3.32

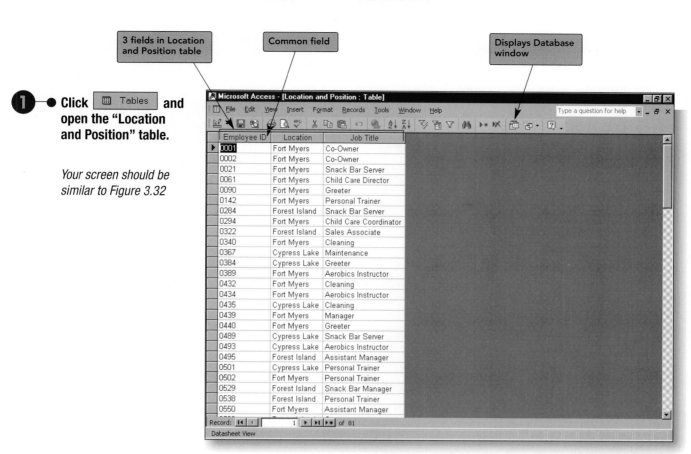

3 fields in Location and Position table

Common field

Displays Database window

Figure 3.32

The "Location and Position" table contains three fields of data for each employee: Employee ID, Club Location, and Job Title. The Employee ID field is the primary key field and is the common field between the two tables. To display the information on the Fort Myers employees, you need to create a query using information from this table and from the Employees table.

As a starting point, you will open the "Car Pool" query you already created and saved.

2 ● Click **Database Window.**

Another Method

The menu equivalent is <u>W</u>indow/<u>1</u> Personnel Records: Database. You can also click F11, or click the corresponding taskbar button, or click on any visible part of the Database window to switch to it.

● **From the queries object list, open the "Car Pool" query.**

● **Switch to Query Design view and maximize the window.**

● **Click**  **Show Table.**

Another Method

The menu equivalent is <u>Q</u>uery/Sh<u>o</u>w Table.

Your screen should be similar to Figure 3.33

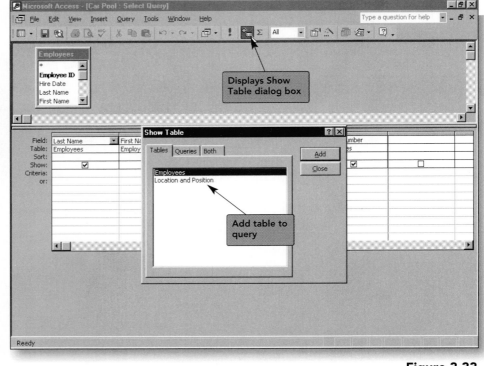

Figure 3.33

From the Query Design window, you need to select the name of the table you want to add to the query.

3 ● **On the Tables tab, select "Location and Position."**

● **Click** Add .

● **Close the Show Table dialog box.**

Your screen should be similar to Figure 3.34

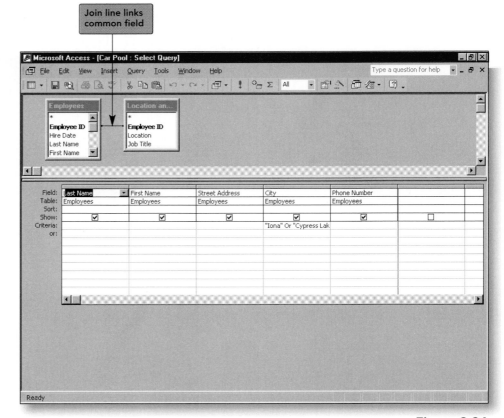

Figure 3.34

The field list for the second table is added to the Query Design window. The **join line** between the two field lists tells Access how the data in those tables are related. When you add multiple tables to a query, Access automatically joins the tables based on the common fields if one of the common fields is a primary key. This is the default join. If the common fields have different names, however, Access does not automatically create the join. Instead, you can create the join manually by dragging from one common field to the other. In this case, the join line indicates that the two tables have been temporarily joined with Employee ID as the common field.

Next you need to add the fields to the grid that you want to use in the query.

4 ● **Add the Location field to the design grid.**

● **To specify the location criterion, type the expression Fort Myers in the Location Criteria cell.**

● **Press** ⏎Enter.

Your screen should be similar to Figure 3.35

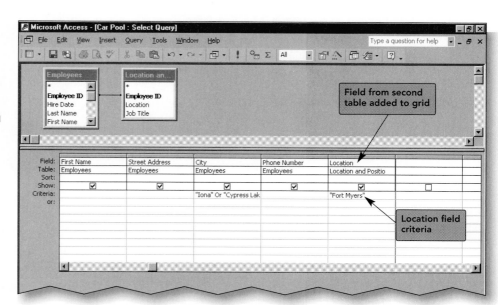

Figure 3.35

This is the only criterion that you need to add to your car pool query, so you can go ahead and display the results.

5 ● **Run the query.**

Your screen should be similar to Figure 3.36

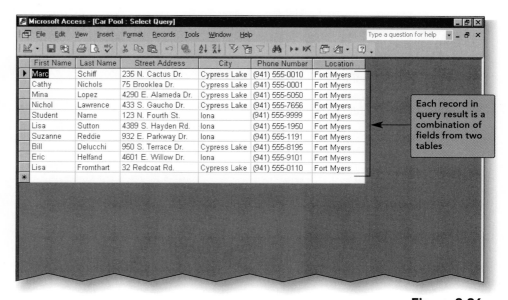

Figure 3.36

The query result shows there are 14 employees who live in either Iona or Cypress Lake and work at the Fort Myers location. Each record in the query result datasheet includes information from both tables. This is because of the type of join used in the query. There are three types of joins:

Join Type	Description
Inner join	Checks records for matching values and when it finds matches, combines the records and displays them as one record in the query results.
Outer join	Each matching record from two tables is combined into one record in the query results. One table contributes all of its records even if the values in its joined field do not match the field values in the other table.
SQL join	Records to be included in the query results are based on the value in one join field being greater than, less than, not equal to, greater than or equal to, or less than or equal to the value in the other join field.

In a query, the default join type is an inner join. In this case, it checked for matching values in the Employee ID fields, combined matching records, and displayed them as one record in the query result.

Next you want to sort the query datasheet by City and Last Name.

6 ● **Move the City column to the left of the Last Name column.**

● **Select the City and Last Name columns.**

● **Click** 🔼 **Sort Ascending.**

● **Move the City column back to its original location, after the Street Address column.**

● **Deselect the City column.**

Your screen should be similar to Figure 3.37

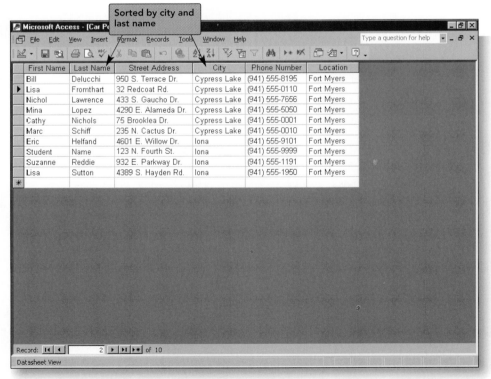

Figure 3.37

This is exactly what you need to give Julie for her car pool, so you decide to print and save the data.

7 • Print the table.

• Close the query, saving your changes.

• Close the "Location and Position" table.

Your screen should be similar to Figure 3.38

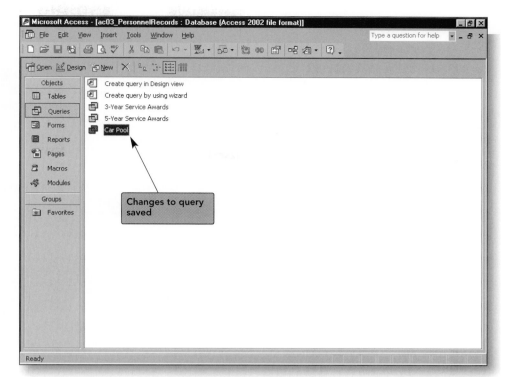

Figure 3.38

Note: If you are running short on time, this is an appropriate point to end your Access session. When you begin again, open the ac03_Personnel Records database.

Creating Reports

Brian showed Tami the printout you gave him of the employees who will get service awards. She sees many uses for the information generated by Access, including the ability to quickly analyze information in the database. As a start, she has asked you to create an address report for all employees sorted by name. You have already created and printed several simple reports using the Print command on the File menu. This time, however, you want to create a custom report of this information.

concept 4

Report

4 A **report** is printed output generated from tables or queries. It might be a simple listing of all the fields in a table, or it might be a list of selected fields based on a query. Access also includes a custom report feature that enables you to create professional-appearing reports. The custom report is a document that includes text formats, styles, and layouts that enhance the display of information. In addition, you can group data in reports to achieve specific results. You can then display summary information, such as totals, by group to allow the reader to further analyze the data. Creating a custom report displays the information from your database in a more attractive and meaningful format.

You will create the address list report using the data in the "Employees" table.

① ● **Open the Reports object window.**

● **Click** 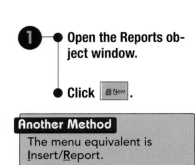 New .

Another Method

The menu equivalent is Insert/Report.

Your screen should be similar to Figure 3.39

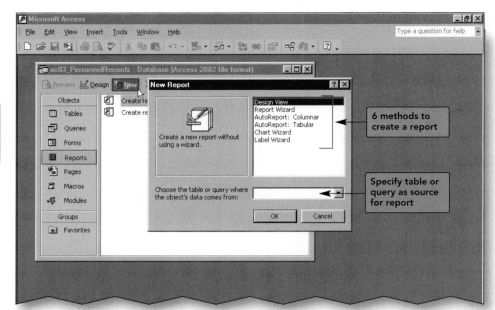

Figure 3.39

The New Report dialog box presents six ways to create a report. You can create a report from scratch in Design view, or by using the Report Wizard or one of the AutoReport Wizards. The Report Wizard lets you choose the fields to include in the report and helps you quickly format and lay out the new report. The AutoReport Wizard creates a report that displays all fields and records from the underlying table or query in a predesigned report layout and style.

Using the AutoReport Wizard

You decide to use the AutoReport Wizard to create a columnar report using data in the "Employees" table.

① ● **Select AutoReport: Columnar.**

● **Select "Employees" from the table selection drop-down list.**

● **Click** OK .

Your screen should be similar to Figure 3.40

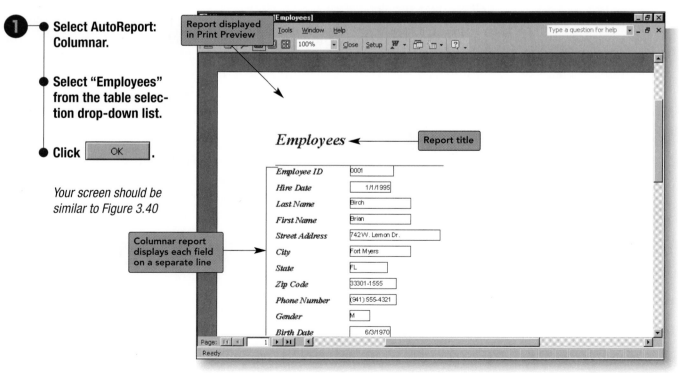

Figure 3.40

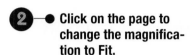

Your report may be displayed
with a different style. This is
because when creating an
AutoReport, Access
remembers the last
AutoReport style used on
your machine, then applies
that same style to the new
report. If the AutoReport
command has not been used,
the report will use the basic
style. You will learn how to
change styles later in this lab.

After a few moments, the report is created and displayed in the Print
Preview window. The AutoReport Wizard creates a columnar report that
displays each field on a separate line in a single column for each record.
The fields are in the order they appear in the table. The report appears in a
predefined report style and layout. The report style shown in Figure 3.40
uses the table name as the report title and includes the use of text colors,
various typefaces and sizes, and horizontal lines and boxes.

Just as you can in Table, Form, and Datasheet views, you can use the navigation tools and navigation buttons to move through the pages of a report.

● Click on the page to
   change the magnifica-
   tion to Fit.

Another Method

The menu equivalent is
View/Zoom/Fit to Window.

*Your screen should be
similar to Figure 3.41*

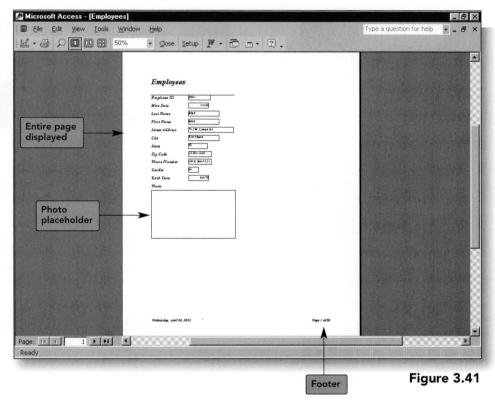

Figure 3.41

Now the entire page is visible, and although most of the text is too small to
read, you can see the entire page layout. The box is a placeholder for the
employee photo. The current date and page number appear at the bottom
of the page in the footer.

3 ● Click 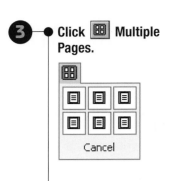 **Multiple Pages.**

● **Point to the page icons to highlight the number of pages to display and click when the menu indicates 2×3 pages are selected.**

Your screen should be similar to Figure 3.42

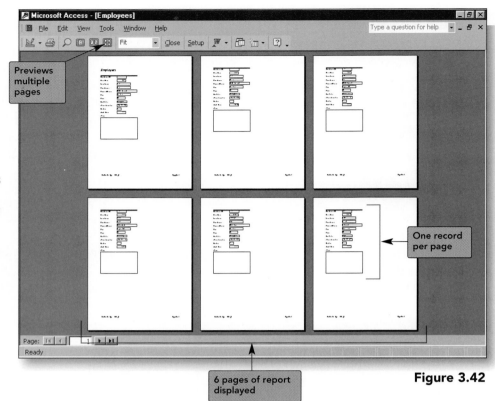

Previews multiple pages

One record per page

Page: [|◄] [◄] 1 [►] [►|]

Ready

6 pages of report displayed

Figure 3.42

Additional Information

The View/Pages command can be used to display up to 12 pages, and the 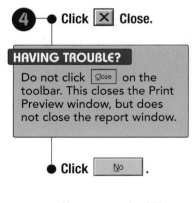 button can be used to display up to 20 pages of a report in the window.

The window now displays six pages of your report (two rows of three pages each, or 2×3).

After looking over the columnar report, you decide the layout is inappropriate for your report, because only one record is printed per page. In addition, you do not want the report to include all the fields from the table. So you will close this report file without saving it, and then create a different type of report that better suits your needs.

4 ● Click ☒ **Close.**

HAVING TROUBLE?

Do not click Close on the toolbar. This closes the Print Preview window, but does not close the report window.

● Click No .

Your screen should be similar to Figure 3.43

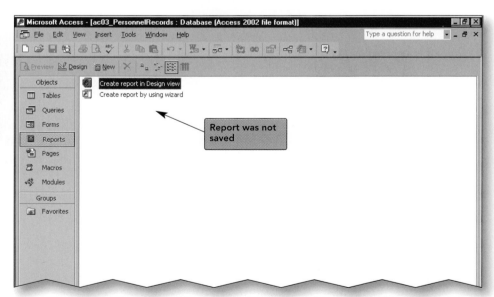

Report was not saved

Figure 3.43

Using the Report Wizard

You want the report to display the field contents for each record on a line rather than in a column. You will use the Report Wizard to create this type of report.

 **In the Reports object window, select Create report by using wizard.**

Your screen should be similar to Figure 3.44

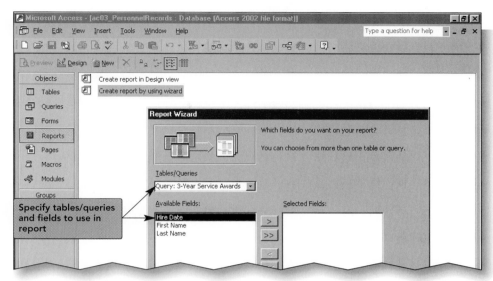

Figure 3.44

The Report Wizard consists of a series of dialog boxes, much like the Form and Query Wizards. As with those Wizards, in the first dialog box you specify the table or query to be used in the report and add the fields you want included.

2 **Select Table: "Employees" from the Tables/Queries drop-down list.**

Add the First Name field to the Selected Fields list.

Then add the Last Name, Street Address, City, State, Zip Code, and Phone Number fields in that order.

Additional Information

A report does not have to include all the fields from the table or query that is used to create it.

Your screen should be similar to Figure 3.45

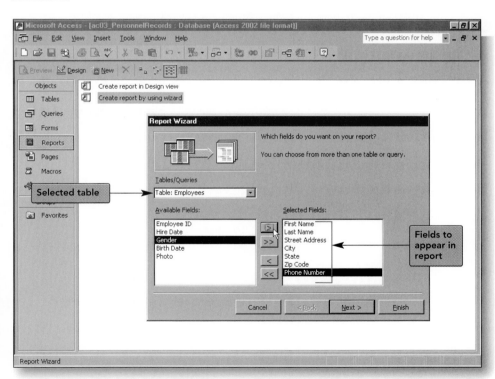

Figure 3.45

All the fields that you want included on the report are now displayed in the Selected Fields list, and you can go on to the next Wizard step.

*Your screen should be
similar to Figure 3.46*

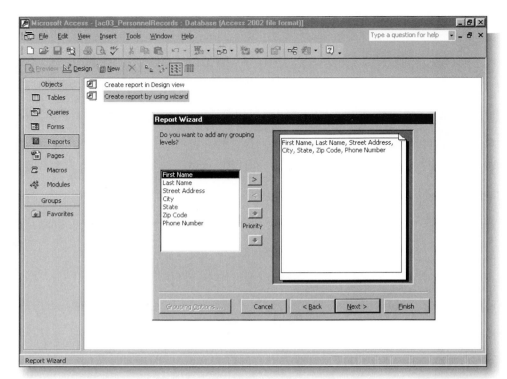

Figure 3.46

In the second Report Wizard dialog box, you specify how to group the data in the report. Tami does not want the report grouped by any category, so you do not need to do anything in this dialog box.

4 ● Click [Next >].

*Your screen should be
similar to Figure 3.47*

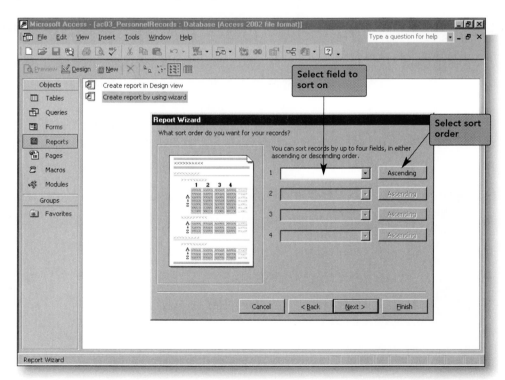

Figure 3.47

This dialog box is used to specify a sort order for the records. A report can be sorted on up to four fields. You want the report sorted in ascending order by last name and first name within same last names.

5 ● Select the **Last Name** field from the number 1 drop-down list

● Select the **First Name** field from the number 2 drop-down list.

Additional Information

You can click [Ascending] to change the sort order to descending. Alternately, when the current sort order is descending, the button displays [Descending], and you can click it to change to ascending sort order.

Your screen should be similar to Figure 3.48

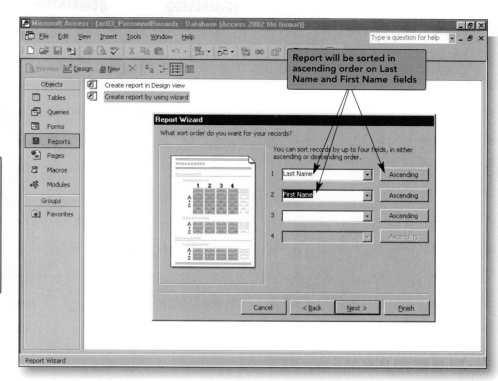

Report will be sorted in ascending order on Last Name and First Name fields

Figure 3.48

The sort fields and order are set and you can go on to the next Wizard step.

6 ● Click [Next >].

Your screen should be similar to Figure 3.49

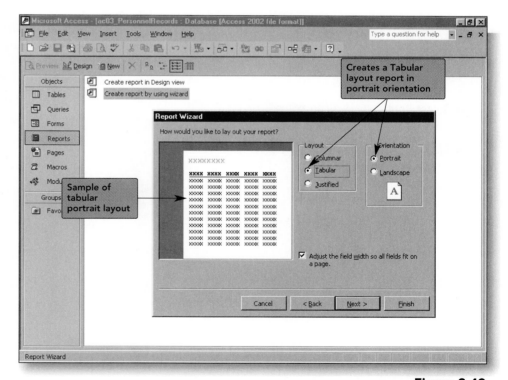

Creates a Tabular layout report in portrait orientation

Sample of tabular portrait layout

Figure 3.49

This dialog box is used to change the report layout and orientation. The default report settings create a tabular layout using portrait orientation. In addition, the option to adjust the field width so all fields fit on one page is selected. Because this report is only five columns, the default settings are acceptable.

7 ● Click [Next >].

Your screen should be similar to Figure 3.50

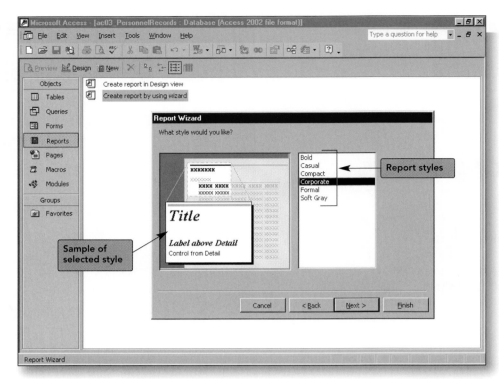

Figure 3.50

From this dialog box you select a style for the report. The preview area displays a sample of each style as it is selected.

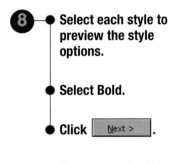

8 ● **Select each style to preview the style options.**

● **Select Bold.**

● **Click [Next >].**

Your screen should be similar to Figure 3.51

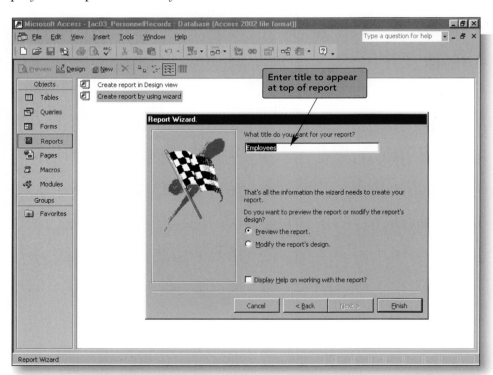

Figure 3.51

The last Report Wizard dialog box is used to add a title to the report and to specify how the report should be displayed after it is created. The only change you want to make is to replace the table name with a more descriptive report title.

9 ● **Type** Employee
Address Report.

● **Click** Finish .

*Your screen should be
similar to Figure 3.52*

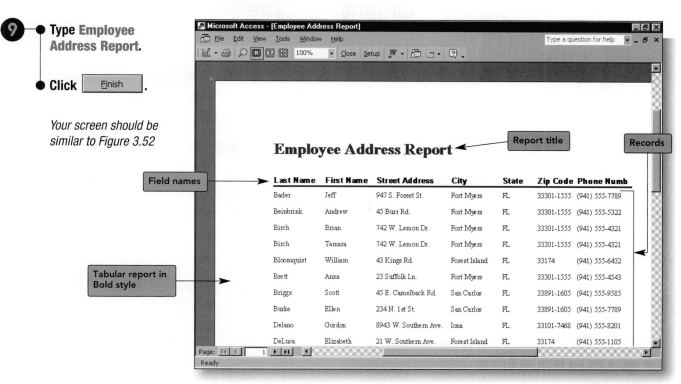

Figure 3.52

The program takes a minute to generate the report, during which time
Report Design view is briefly displayed. In a few moments, the completed
report with the data from the underlying table is displayed in the Print
Preview window in the selected Bold report style. The report title reflects
the title you specified using the Wizard. The names of the selected fields are
displayed on the first line of the report, and each record appears on a separate row below the field names. Notice that the Last Name field is the first
field, even though you selected it as the second field. This is because the
sort order overrides the selected field order.

Modifying the Report Design

You like the layout of this report, but you still want the Last Name field to
follow the First Name field. You also notice that the Phone Number field
name is cut off, so you need to change it so it displays correctly. To make
these changes, you need to modify the report design.

Formatting toolbar

Field List box

Report Design toolbar

1 Click 📊 ▾ View to switch to Report Design view.

Your screen should be similar to Figure 3.53

Toolbox toolbar

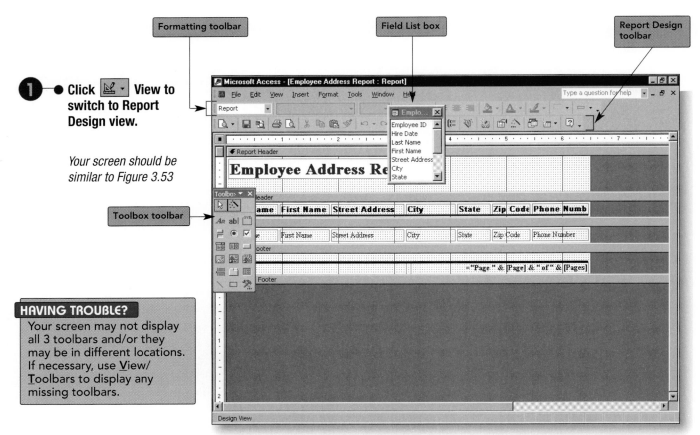

Figure 3.53

Additional Information

Use View/Field List or 🔲 to hide and display the Field List.

Additional Information

You can also use View/Toolbox or click 🛠 to hide and display.

The Report Design view is used to create and modify the structure of a report. This view displays three toolbars: Report Design, Formatting, and Toolbox. The Report Design toolbar contains the standard buttons as well as buttons that are specific to the Report Design view window. The Formatting toolbar contains buttons that allow you to make text enhancements. The Toolbox toolbar buttons are used to add and modify report design objects.

In order to have an unobstructed view of and work with the report design, you will move the Toolbox toolbar and close the Employees Field List.

Additionally, the Field List box containing the field names from the "Employees" table may be displayed. The Field List can be used to quickly add additional fields to the report.

2 • If necessary, close the Field List box.

• Move the Toolbox to the lower right corner of the window.

Your screen should be similar to Figure 3.54

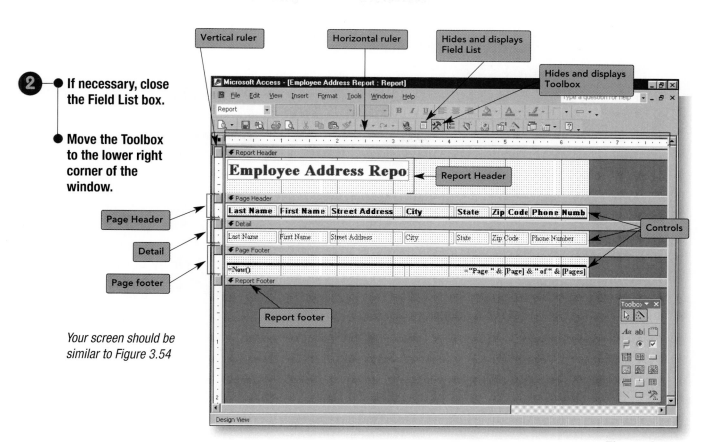

Figure 3.54

The report's contents are displayed in a window that is bordered along the top by a horizontal ruler and along the left by a vertical ruler. These rulers help you correctly place items within the window.

The Report Design window is divided into five sections: Report Header, Page Header, Detail, Page Footer, and Report Footer. The contents of each section appear below the horizontal bar that contains the name of that section. The sections are described in the following table.

Section	Description
Report Header	Contains information to be printed once at the beginning of the report. The report title is displayed in this area.
Page Header	Contains information to be printed at the top of each page. The column headings are displayed in this section.
Detail	Contains the records of the table. The field column widths are the same as the column widths set in the table design.
Page Footer	Contains information to be printed at the bottom of each page, such as the date and page number.
Report Footer	Contains information to be printed at the end of the report. The Report Footer section currently contains no data.

All of the information in a report is contained in boxes, called controls. You make changes to your report design by working with these controls.

5 **Controls** are objects on a form or report that display information, perform actions, or enhance the design. Access provides controls for many types of objects, including labels, text boxes, check boxes, list boxes, command buttons, lines, rectangles, option buttons, and more.

There are two basic types of controls: bound and unbound. A **bound control** is linked to a field in an underlying table. An example of a bound control is a text box that creates a link to the underlying source (usually a field from a table) and displays the field entry in the report or form. An **unbound control** is not connected to a field. Examples of unbound controls are labels, which can be taken from the underlying table associated with a text box or customized with descriptive titles or user instructions. Other unbound controls contain elements that enhance the appearance of the form, such as lines, boxes, and pictures. A text box can also be an unbound control if it is used for user input or to display calculation results.

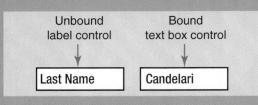

Selecting Controls

In this report design, the label controls are displayed in the Page Header section, and the text box controls are in the Detail section. You need to select the Last Name and First Name controls in order to modify their order.

1 ● **Click the Last Name label control in the Page Header section.**

Your screen should be similar to Figure 3.55

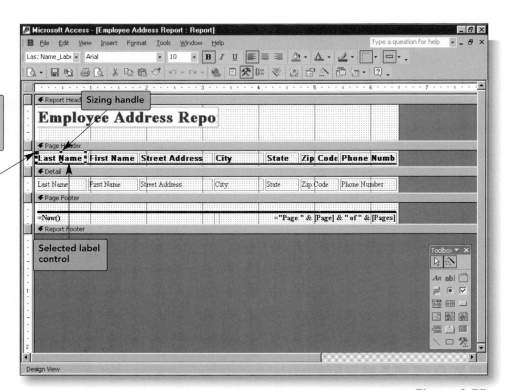

Figure 3.55

The Last Name label control is surrounded by eight small boxes called **sizing handles** that indicate the label control is selected. The sizing handles are used to size the control. In addition, a large box in the upper left corner is displayed. This is a **move handle** that is used to move the selected control.

You also want to select the Last Name text box control.

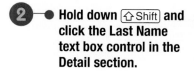

Hold down ⇧ Shift **and click the Last Name text box control in the Detail section.**

Your screen should be similar to Figure 3.56

Label and text box controls selected

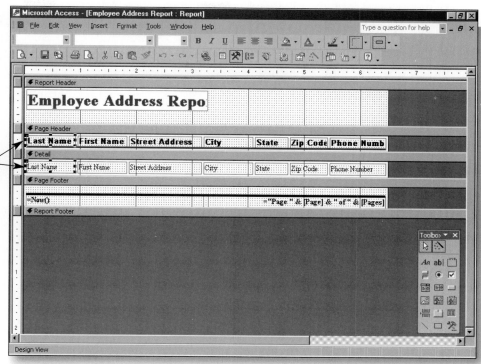

Figure 3.56

<table>
<tr><td>**Additional Information**</td></tr>
</table>

You can also delete controls by selecting them and pressing Delete.

Now both controls are selected. Once controls are selected, they can be moved and sized.

Moving Controls

Another Method

You can also move controls using Ctrl + the directional arrow keys.

You want to move the Last Name controls to the right of the First Name controls. Controls can be moved to any location in the Report design by dragging them to the new location. The mouse pointer changes to a 🖑 shape to indicate that a selected control can be moved. The grid of dots helps you position the controls on the form. It not only provides a visual guide to positioning and sizing controls, but controls are "snapped" to the grid, or automatically positioned on the nearest grid line.

Because you need to swap positions of the two fields, you will first move the Last Name controls to the right, and then you will move the First Name controls to the left.

1 • Drag the Last Name controls to the right so the right edge of the control is at the 2½" ruler position. (They should not completely obscure the First Name controls, which you will need to select and move next.)

HAVING TROUBLE?

Do not point to a sizing handle when dragging the control to move it, as this will size the controls.

• Select both First Name controls and drag them to the left edge of the grid.

• Select the Last Name controls again and drag them to between the First Name and Street Address controls.

Your screen should be similar to Figure 3.57

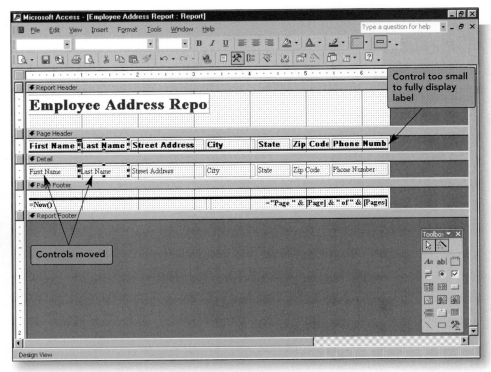

Figure 3.57

Sizing Controls

Next you will increase the size of the Phone Number label control. When you position the mouse pointer on a sizing handle, it changes to a ↔. The direction of the arrow indicates in which direction dragging the mouse will alter the shape of the object. This is similar to sizing a window.

1 • Select the Phone Number label control in the Page Header section.

• Point to the middle handle on the right end of the selected control.

• When the mouse pointer appears as ↔, drag the control to the right just until the entire field label is displayed.

Additional Information

The right edge of the form will automatically increase as you increase the size of the control.

Your screen should be similar to Figure 3.58

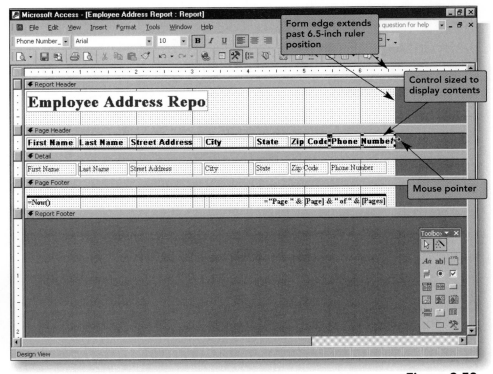

Figure 3.58

Printing a Report

When you are making a lot of design changes to a report, it is a good idea to periodically check how the printed output will look. If you need to make further adjustments, you can return to Design view. Other adjustments can be made using the print page setup options.

Changing Page Margins

You want to preview how the first few pages of the report will appear when printed.

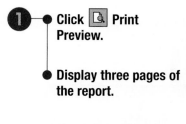 **Click** 🔍 **Print Preview.**

● **Display three pages of the report.**

Your screen should be similar to Figure 3.59

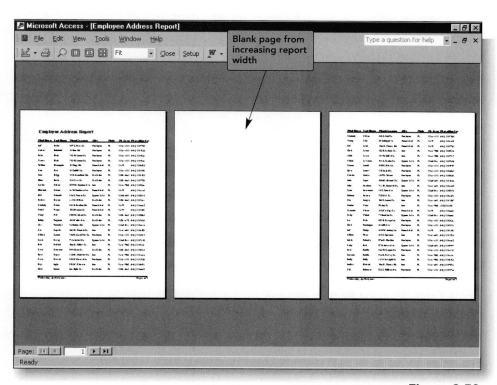

Figure 3.59

A blank page is displayed between the first and third page. This is because as you increased the size of the Phone Number label, the overall report width increased, making it too large to fully display across the width of the page using the default margin settings. The **margin** is the blank space around the edge of a page. You will decrease the right margin to allow the extra space needed to print the width of the report across the page.

2 Click [Setup].

● If necessary, open the Margins tab.

Your screen should be similar to Figure 3.60

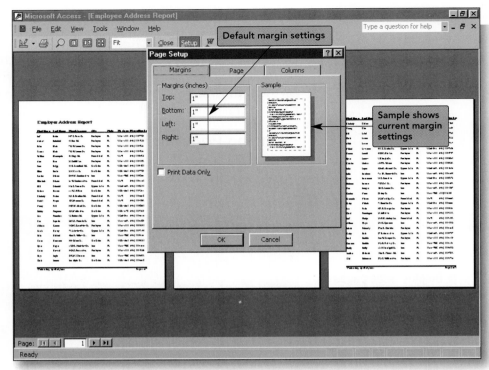

Figure 3.60

The default margin settings are 1 inch on all sides of the page. You will decrease the right margin to .75 inch. The sample will adjust to reflect the change as you enter it.

3 Enter **.75** in the Right text box.

● Click [OK].

Your screen should be similar to Figure 3.61

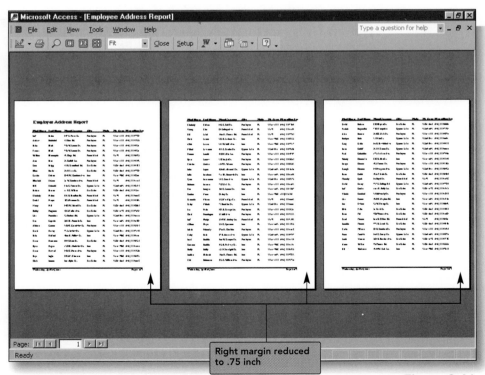

Figure 3.61

Now, everything looks good to you.

Printing a Selected Page

You decide to print out only one page and get Tami's approval before printing the entire report. Just like you can with a table or form, you can print all of the report or only specified pages. You are going to print the page containing your record.

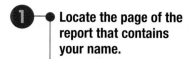 **Locate the page of the report that contains your name.**

Additional Information

The page number is displayed in the page indicator box. You can use the navigational keys on either side of this box to move from page to page.

● **Choose File/Print.**

Additional Information

The 🖨 Print button prints the entire report.

● **If necessary, select the appropriate printer for your system.**

● **Select Pages.**

Additional Information

The page number is displayed in the page indicator box.

● **Type the page number containing your record in the From and To text boxes.**

Your screen should be similar to Figure 3.62

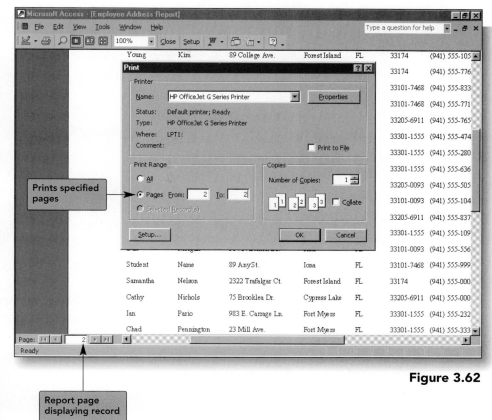

Figure 3.62

The page you want to print is now specified, and you are ready to send it to the printer.

2 ● Click [OK].

● Close the Report window, saving the changes you have made.

Your screen should be similar to Figure 3.63

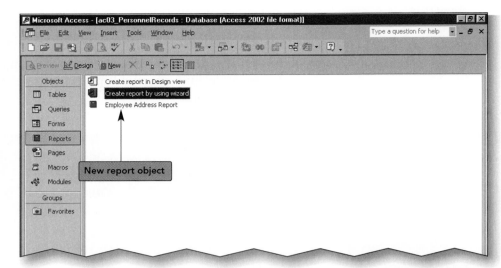

New report object

Figure 3.63

The Database window is displayed again, and the report object name is listed in the reports object list. The Report Wizard automatically saves the report using the report title as the object name.

Creating a Report from a Query

You have seen how easy it is to create a report from a table, so you would like to create a report from the "Car Pool" query.

1 ● Use the Report Wizard to create a report based on the "Car Pool" query using the following specifications:

- **Include all fields except Location.**

- **Sort on City first, then Last Name and First Name.**

- **Select a Tabular layout.**

- **Use the Casual style.**

- **Title the report Iona to Fort Myers Car Pool Report.**

When the Wizard finishes creating the report, your screen should be similar to Figure 3.64

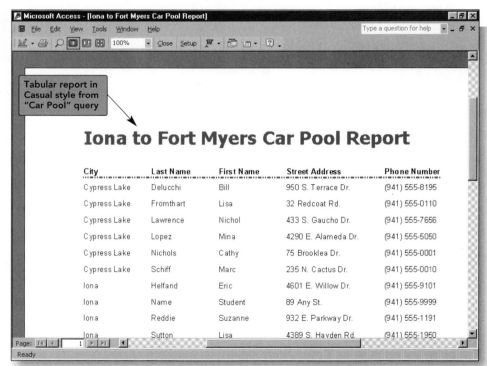

Tabular report in Casual style from "Car Pool" query

Figure 3.64

You will now do a little quick design work on this report and print it out.

2 ● **Use Report Design view to change the field order to First Name, Last Name, Street Address, City, and Phone Number order.**

● **Save the report.**

● **Preview, and then print the report.**

Your completed Car Pool report should look like that shown here.

Iona to Fort Myers Car Pool Report

First Name	Last Name	Street Address	City	Phone Number
Bill	Delucchi	950 S. Terrace Dr.	Cypress Lake	(941) 555-8195
Lisa	Fromthart	32 Redcoat Rd.	Cypress Lake	(941) 555-0110
Nichol	Lawrence	433 S. Gaucho Dr.	Cypress Lake	(941) 555-7656
Mina	Lopez	4290 E. Alameda Dr.	Cypress Lake	(941) 555-5050
Cathy	Nichols	75 Brooklea Dr.	Cypress Lake	(941) 555-0001
Marc	Schiff	235 N. Cactus Dr.	Cypress Lake	(941) 555-0010
Eric	Helfand	4601 E. Willow Dr.	Iona	(941) 555-9101
Suzanne	Reddie	932 E. Parkway Dr.	Iona	(941) 555-1191
Name	Student	89 Any St.	Iona	(941) 555-3333
Lisa	Sutton	4389 S. Hayden Rd.	Iona	(941) 555-1950

Thursday, April 05, 2001   Page 1 of 1

Compacting the Database

Additional Information

A file is fragmented when it becomes too large for your computer to store in a single location on your hard disk. When this happens, the file is split up and stored in pieces in different locations on the disk, making access slower.

As you modify a database, the changes are saved to your disk. When you delete data or objects, the database file can become fragmented and use disk space inefficiently. To make the database perform optimally, you should **compact** the database on a regular basis. Compacting makes a copy of the file and rearranges how the file is stored on your disk.

1 ● **Choose Tools/Database Utilities/Compact and Repair Database.**

● **Close the database and exit Access.**

LAB **3**

Analyzing Data and Creating Reports

Filter (AC3.4)

A filter is a restriction placed on records in the open datasheet or form to temporarily isolate and display a subset of records.

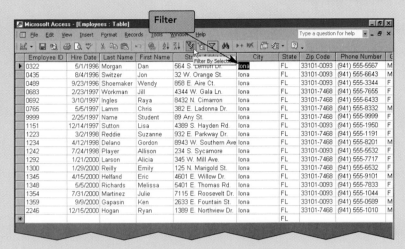

Query (AC3.11)

A query is a request for specific data contained in a database. Queries are used to view data in different ways, to analyze data, and even to change existing data.

Query

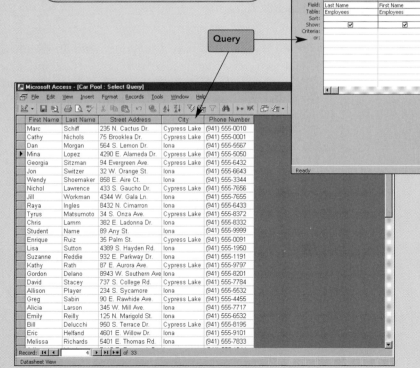

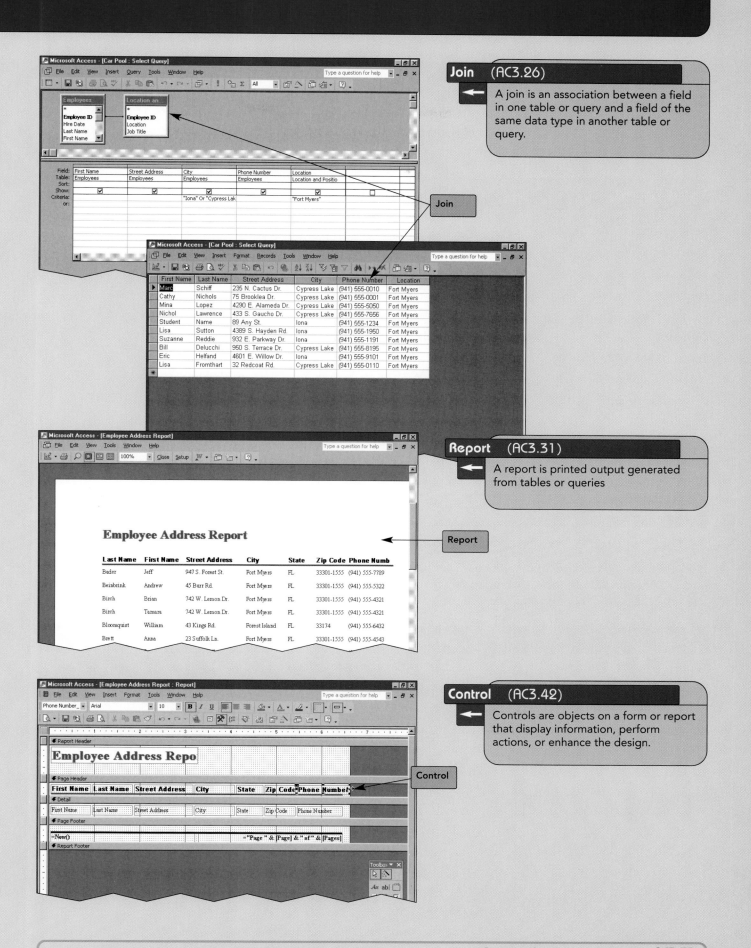

Join (AC3.26)

A join is an association between a field in one table or query and a field of the same data type in another table or query.

Report (AC3.31)

A report is printed output generated from tables or queries

Control (AC3.42)

Controls are objects on a form or report that display information, perform actions, or enhance the design.

key terms

AND operator AC3.8	design grid AC3.16	multitable query AC3.26
bound control AC3.42	field list AC3.16	OR operator AC3.8
cell AC3.16	filter AC3.4	query AC3.11
column selector bar AC3.16	Filter by Form AC3.7	query datasheet AC3.15
common field AC3.26	Filter by Selection AC3.6	report AC3.31
compact AC3.49	join AC3.26	row label AC3.16
control AC3.42	join line AC3.29	Show box AC3.16
criteria AC3.4	margin AC3.45	sizing handles AC3.43
criteria expression AC3.8	move handle AC3.43	unbound control AC3.42

mous skills

The Microsoft Office User Specialist (MOUS) certification program is designed to measure your proficiency in performing basic tasks using the Office XP applications. Getting certified demonstrates that you have the skills and provides a valuable industry credential for employment. After completing this lab, you have learned the following Access 2002 Microsoft Office User Specialist skills:

Skill	Description	Page
Creating and Using Databases	Open datase objects in multiple views	AC3.16, AC3.39
Creating and Modifying Queries	Create and modify Select queries	AC3.12
Viewing and Organizing Information	Create queries	AC3.11
	Sort records	AC3.30, AC3.36
	Filter records	AC3.4
Producing Reports	Create and format reports	AC3.31
	Preview and print reports	AC3.45

command summary

Command	Button	Action
<u>E</u>dit/Clear <u>G</u>rid		Clears query grid
<u>I</u>nsert/<u>R</u>eport	New	Creates a new report object
<u>V</u>iew/<u>D</u>esign View		Displays Design View window
<u>V</u>iew/<u>Z</u>oom/<u>F</u>it to Window		Displays entire previewed page
<u>V</u>iew/P<u>a</u>ges		Displays specified number of pages of previewed report
<u>V</u>iew/Toolbo<u>x</u>		Displays/hides Toolbox
<u>R</u>ecords/<u>F</u>ilter/<u>F</u>ilter by Form		Displays blank datasheet for entering criteria to filter database to display specific information
<u>R</u>ecords/<u>F</u>ilter/Filter by <u>S</u>election		Displays only records that contain the same value as in the selected field
<u>T</u>ools/<u>D</u>atabase Utilities/<u>C</u>ompact and Repair Database		Compacts and repairs database file
<u>F</u>ilter/Appl<u>y</u> Filter/Sort		Applies filter to table
<u>Q</u>uery/<u>R</u>un	!	Displays query results in Query Datasheet view
<u>Q</u>uery/Sh<u>o</u>w Table		Displays Show Table dialog box
<u>W</u>indow/Database		Displays Database window

screen identification

In the following Access screen, several items are identified by letters. Enter the correct term for each item in the spaces provided.

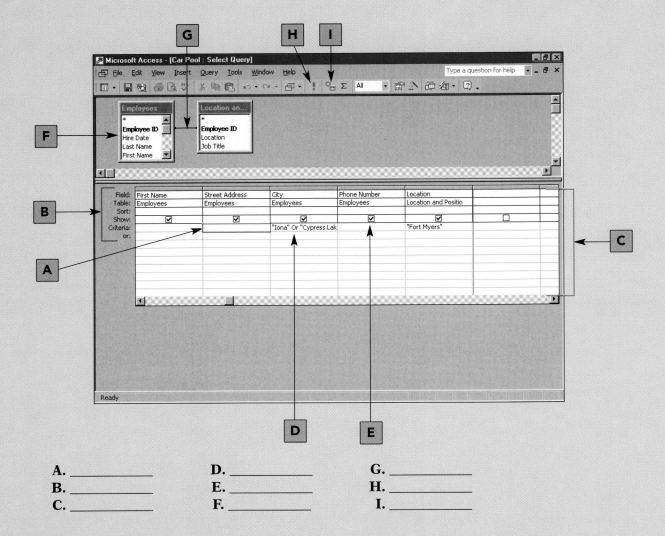

A. _____   D. _____   G. _____

B. _____   E. _____   H. _____

C. _____   F. _____   I. _____

matching

Match the numbered item with the correct lettered description.

1. ▣   _____ **a.** intersection of a column and row

2. query   _____ **b.** a control that is tied to a field in an underlying table

3. multitable query   _____ **c.** temporary restriction placed on displayed data to isolate specific records

4. criteria   _____ **d.** includes any records containing either condition

5. ▣   _____ **e.** object that links a form or report to the underlying table

6. filter   _____ **f.** runs a query and displays query datasheet

7. OR   _____ **g.** used to ask questions about database tables

8. bound   _____ **h.** query that uses data from more than one table

9. control   _____ **i.** set of limiting conditions

10. cell   _____ **j.** accesses Filter By Form feature

multiple choice

Circle the letter of the correct response.

1. A(n) _____ is a restriction placed on records in the open datasheet or form to quickly isolate and display a subset of records.
   a. filter
   b. query
   c. join
   d. property

2. AND and OR are _____.
   a. criteria
   b. operators
   c. elements
   d. properties

3. Select, crosstab, parameter, action, and SQL are different types of _____.
   a. action elements
   b. formats
   c. queries
   d. property elements

4. Inner, outer, and SQL are different types of _____.
   a. joins
   b. queries
   c. filters
   d. reports

5. All information in a report or form is contained in boxes called _____.
   a. filters
   b. criteria
   c. controls
   d. keys

6. A filter is created by specifying a set of limiting conditions or _____.
   a. forms
   b. controls
   c. criteria
   d. objects

7. The operator that broadens a search, because any record meeting either condition is included in the output, is _____.
   a. AND
   b. OR
   c. MOST
   d. ALL

8. A(n) _____ is a question asked of the data contained in a database.
   a. form
   b. inquiry
   c. request
   d. query

9. A(n) _____ is an association that tells Access how data between tables is related.
   a. join
   b. criteria expression
   c. query
   d. object

10. Bound and unbound are types of _____.
    a. buttons
    b. forms
    c. properties
    d. controls

true/false

Circle the correct answer to the following statements.

1. Multiple filter results can be saved.   True   False
2. The OR operator narrows a search.   True   False
3. Queries are used to view data in different ways, to analyze data, and to change existing data.   True   False
4. Values that tell Access how to filter the criteria in a query are called filter expressions.   True   False
5. Access includes a custom report feature to assist in creating professional-appearing reports.   True   False
6. Filters use reports to set limiting conditions.   True   False
7. The AND operator is assumed when you enter criteria in multiple fields.   True   False
8. A join line shows how different tables are related.   True   False
9. Reports are printed output generated from tables and queries.   True   False
10. Controls are text objects.   True   False

Concepts

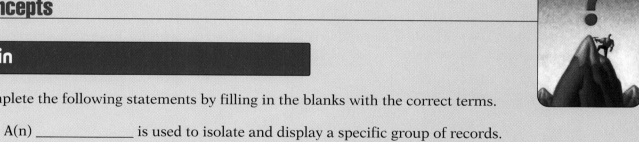

fill-in

Complete the following statements by filling in the blanks with the correct terms.

1. A(n) _____ is used to isolate and display a specific group of records.

2. The _____ operator narrows the search for records that meet both conditions.

3. The _____ operator narrows the search for records that meet either condition.

4. A(n) _____ is an association that shows how data between tables is related.

5. A(n) _____ retrieves specific data from one or more tables and displays the results in a query datasheet.

6. The _____ of the Query window is where the fields to be displayed in the query datasheet are placed.

7. Tables are joined by relating the _____ between the tables.

8. _____ are used to hold the report data.

9. Custom names in a report are _____ because they are not connected to a field.

10. The _____ comparison operator is used to find values that are less than or equal to another value.

lab exercises

discussion questions

Answer the following questions by preparing written responses.

1. Discuss what filters are and how they can be used in a database. When would it be appropriate to use a filter?

2. Discuss the differences between the AND and OR filter conditions.

3. Discuss what a query can do and some advantages of using queries.

4. Discuss the different types of controls. Give an example of how they can be used to create different report designs.

Hands-On Exercises

rating system
★ Easy
★ ★ Moderate
★ ★ ★ Difficult

step-by-step

Filtering a Database

★ 1. Maria Dell, the owner of the Simply Beautiful Spa, continues to be impressed with your work on the company's database (Step-by-Step Exercise 1 of Lab 2). She is thinking of offering a spa package that would include various anti-aging skin treatments and massages. To get an idea of how much interest there would be in this package among those who currently frequent the spa, Ms. Dell has asked you for a list of clients who are over the age of 35. She doesn't need a formal report right now, so you decide to just filter the existing table and print the filtered datasheet. The printed datasheet is shown here.

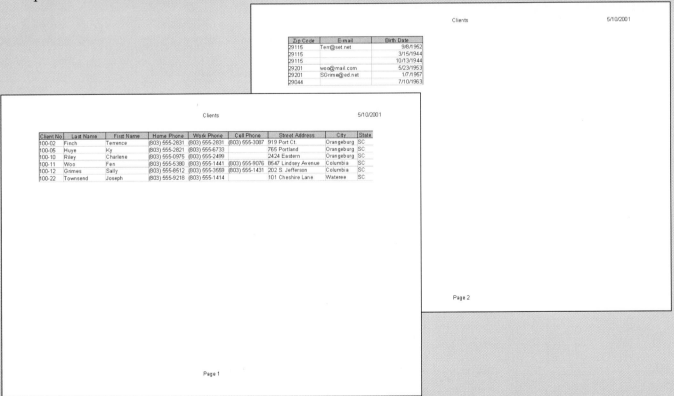

To filter the table, follow these steps:

a. Open the database file named ac02_Simply Beautiful that you modified in Step-by-step Exercise 1 of Lab 2. Open the table named "Clients."

b. Select Filter by Form and enter <1/1/65 in the Birth Date field. Apply the filter.

c. Enter your name in the last of the displayed fields and print the filtered datasheet in landscape orientation.

d. Remove the filter.

e. Close the table, saving the changes.

f. Compact and repair the database.

Locating Bimonthly Advertisers

★★ **2.** The data entry form for the Happenings database is is working well (Step-by-Step Exercise 2 of Lab 2). The printer you use for the Happenings newsletter, however, is raising his prices. You have been quite pleased with the quality of his work and would prefer not to have to go to someone else. Instead, you decide to contact the local merchants who are currently advertising in the newsletter bimonthly to see if they would be willing to increase the frequency of their ads. To do this, you want to create a datasheet that contains the contact information for these merchants, as shown below.

To produce this datasheet, you will perform a query on the "Advertisers" table.

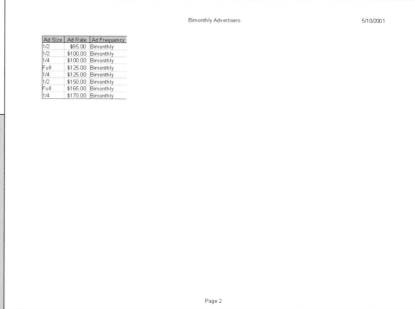

a. Open the database file named ac02_Happening Ads that you modified in Step-by-Step Exercise 2 of Lab 2. Select the Queries object.

b. Use the Query Wizard to run a select query on the "Advertisers" table. Include all the fields in the order listed. Title the query Bimonthly Advertisers.

c. In Query Design view, enter Bimonthly in the Ad Frequency criteria field. Run the query. Sort the Ad Rate field in ascending sort order. Print the query using landscape orientation.

d. Close the query, saving the changes.

e. Compact and repair the database.

Creating a Stock Report

★ ★ **3.** Evan, the owner of the Downtown Internet Cafe, has asked you to submit a daily report on all
★   low-quantity items so he can place the necessary orders. With the database you created in Step-
by-Step Exercise 3 of Lab 2, you can use it to mointor inventory levels and respond to Evan's
request. First you decide to run a query to find the low-stock items, and then you can generate the
requested report from the query. Your completed report should look similar to the report below.

To generate the query and
report, follow these steps:

a. Open the database file
named ac02_Cafe Supplies
that you modified in Step-
by-Step Exercise 3 of Lab
2.

b. Use the Query Wizard to
create a query based on
the "Inventory" table.
Include all fields except
Item # in their current
order. Name the query
Low Stock. In Design view,
enter the criteria to display only those records
with an On-Hand # that is
less than 25, and run the
query. Review the result-
ing datasheet.

Vendor Name	Better Beverages, Inc.
Contact	Pat Lawry
Phone	(206) 555-909
E-mail	bev@dial.com
Description	Sumatra coffee
# On Hand	11
Special Order?	N
Vendor Name	Better Beverages, Inc.
Contact	Pat Lawry
Phone	(206) 555-909
E-mail	bev@dial.com
Description	Guatamala coffee
# On Hand	0
Special Order?	N
Vendor Name	Central Ceramics
Contact	[Your Name]
Phone	(602) 555-192
E-mail	student@learn.com
Description	Coffee mugs
# On Hand	12
Special Order?	Y

Thursday, May 10, 2001   Page 3 of 5

c. Upon reviewing the
datasheet, you realize that
it is not in a very useful order. Also, since Evan typically places orders by phone, the address
information is not really necessary. Return to Design view and do the following:

- Apply an ascending sort to the Vendor Name column.
- Delete the four mailing address columns.
- Move the Vendor Name, Contact, Phone, and E-mail columns to the left of the Description
  column.

d. Run the query and review the resulting datasheet. Since the query now looks satisfactory
enough to create a report from it, close the Query window, saving the changes.

e. Use the Report Wizard to create a report based on the "Low Stock" query you just saved.
Include all the listed fields in the following order:

- Vendor Name
- Contact
- Phone
- E-mail
- Description
- # On Hand
- Special Order?

f. Select Vendor Name as the only sort field. Select the Columnar layout and Bold style. Name the report **Order Items**.

g. Preview and print the page of the report that contains your name in the Contact field, and then close the Report window, saving the changes.

h. Compact and repair the database.

Creating a Product Development Report

★★ 4. You are responsible for updating, maintaining, and using EduSoft's database (Step-by-Step
★ Exercise 4 of Lab 2). You are frequently asked to provide reports that show the company's curriculum software products from different vantage points and for different purposes. The most recent request was from product development, asking for a report that shows the math and science titles released over 3 years ago. They plan on using this report to gauge how many titles on those topics will need to be updated in the near future. The report you create for them will look similar to the report shown here.

To create the requested report, follow these steps:

a. Open the database named ac02_Learning that you modified in Step-by-Step Exercise 4 of Lab 2.

b. Use the Query Wizard to create a query based on the "Software" table. Include the following fields in this order: Title, Subject, Grade Level, Release Date. Name the query **Old Math and Science**.

c. In Query Design view, enter **Math** in the first Subject criteria cell and **Science** in the second (or) criteria cell. Enter **<1/1/98** in the Release Date criteria cell. Run the query and review the resulting datasheet. Close the Query window, saving the changes.

96-97 Math and Science Titles			
Release Date	**Subject**	**Title**	**Grade Level**
1/20/1996	Science	Try It I	K-2
6/4/1996	Science	Try It II	3-5
9/20/1996	Science	Try It III	6-8
6/14/1997	Math	Solve It I	K-2
9/3/1997	Math	Solve It II	3-5
12/15/1997	Math	Solve It III	6-8

Thursday, May 10, 2001   Page 1 of 1

d. Use the Report Wizard to create a report based on the "Old Math and Science" query you just saved. Include all the fields in the order listed. Select Release Date as the first sort field and Subject as the second sort field. Select the Tabular layout, landscape orientation, and Formal style. Name the report **96-97 Math and Science Titles**.

e. Center the Report Header control at the top of the page.

f. Preview and then print the report. Close the Report window, saving the changes you made.

g. Compact and repair the database.

Creating an Animal Adoption Report

★★ 5. The Animal Angels volunteers are successfully using the database you created to enter
★   information for all the animals picked up by the organization and boarded, placed in foster care,
      and/or adopted (Step-by-Step Exercise 5 of Lab 2). Meanwhile, you created another table
      containing information about the adoptive homes (including names, addresses, and phone
      numbers). The Animal Rescue Foundation management have now asked you for a report, shown
      below, of all animals adopted in the past six months and by whom, so the appropriate thank you
      notes can be sent. Your completed report will be similar to the report shown here.

To create the requested report, follow these steps:

a. Open the database file named ac03_Angels.

b. Open the Queries tab and create a query in Design view. Join the "Animals" and "Adopters" tables, and add the following fields to the design grid in the order listed below:

   - Type
   - Status
   - Adoption Date
   - Adopter First Name
   - Adopter Last Name
   - Adopter Street
   - Adopter City
   - Adopter State
   - Adopter Zip

c. Specify A as the Status criteria and >9/1/98 as the Adoption Date criteria. Run the query and review the resulting datasheet. Select an ascending sort in the Adopter Last Name column. Save the query as Adoptees and close the Query window.

d. Use the Report Wizard to create a report based on the "Adoptees" query you just saved. Include the following fields in the order listed below:

   - Adopter First Name
   - Adopter Last Name
   - Adopter Street
   - Adopter City
   - Adopter State
   - Adopter Zip
   - Type

e. Select Adopter Last Name as the first sort field and Adopter First Name as the second sort field. Select the Justified layout, landscape orientation, and the Casual style. Name the report Animal Adoption Report.

f. Center the Report Header control at the top of the page. Move the Adopter Last Name field before the Adopter First Name field.

g. Preview and then print the report. Close the report window, saving the changes you made.

h. Compact and repair the database.

on your own

Identifying a Product Developer

★ 1. The program manager for the EduSoft Company is requesting a list of software titles that were worked on by Teri O'Neill so he can use it for Teri's review. Open the database named ac02_Learning and the "Software" table you updated in Step-by-Step Exercise 4 of Lab 2. Filter the table to include only those records that have Teri O'Neill in the Developer field. Add your name to one of the software titles (e.g., [Your Name]'s Seeing Stars) and print the filtered datasheet.

Issuing W-2 Forms

★★ 2. As an administrative assistant at Lewis & Lewis, Inc., you are responsible for sending out W2 forms to all of the employees. Use the Lewis Personnel database that you updated in On Your Own Exercise 4 of Lab 2 and create a query that includes only the employee name and home address fields. Save the query as Home Address. Run and print the resulting query datasheet.

Expense Account Report

★★ 3. One of the department managers at JK Enterprises has requested a report showing who in her group has submitted an expense report but not yet been paid. In the JK Enterprise database, open the "Expenses" table you updated in On Your Own Exercise 2 of Lab 2. Locate a department that has at least two expense reports that have not been paid. (If there are none, change some of one department's paid fields from Yes to No.) Then run a query that includes all fields except the employee ID. Enter query sort criteria to find only records for employees who have not been paid, and for the department you chose earlier. Apply an ascending sort to the field containing the date the expense report was submitted. Save the query as Pending and then use the Report Wizard to create a report named Pending Expenses based on the query. Sort the report by the date submitted and then the name fields. Preview and print the report.

Thank You Card Report

★★ 4. The Animal Angels owners have finished sending thank you cards to those who adopted animals
★   in the last six months, and would now like to send cards to those who have provided foster care in the same time period. Using the same techniques you used in Step-by-Step Exercise 5 of this lab, create a query in the ac03_Angels database that joins the "Animals" and "Fosters" tables; includes the animal type, status, and foster home information; and specifies F and >9/1/98 as the Status and Foster Date criteria. Save the query as Foster and close the query. Then use the Report Wizard to create a report called Foster Angels based on this query. Include all fields except the Status field, with the foster home name and address information fields first and the Type field last. Preview and print the report. Compact and repair the database after closing it.

on the web

The owners of Golden Oldies have decided to expand their offerings to include out-of-print books as well as collectable record albums. Revisit the Web to obtain some book titles and resources and add the appropriate fields to the "Inventory" table of the Golden Oldies database you updated in On the Web Exercise of Lab 2. To create a list of only the new products, filter the table to include the client and book fields (not the record album fields), and print the filtered datasheet. Then create a query called **Complete Products** that includes the records for both product types (record and book), sorted by category. Use the Report Wizard to create a report that is based on the query; include the customer name, product type, category, and source fields; and sort it by customer last name. Preview and print the report.

Working Together: Linking Access and Word

Case Study

Brian, the co-owner of Lifestyle Fitness Club, recently asked you to provide him with a list of all employees who have at least 3 and 5 years of service with the Club. You queried the Employees table in the Personnel Records database and were quickly able to obtain this information. Now you want to include the query results with a brief memo to Brian.

You will learn how to share information between applications while you create the memo. Your memo containing the query results generated by Access will look like the one shown here.

Note: This tutorial assumes that you already know how to use Word and that you have completed Lab 3 of Access. You will need the database file Personnel Records you saved at the end of Lab 3.

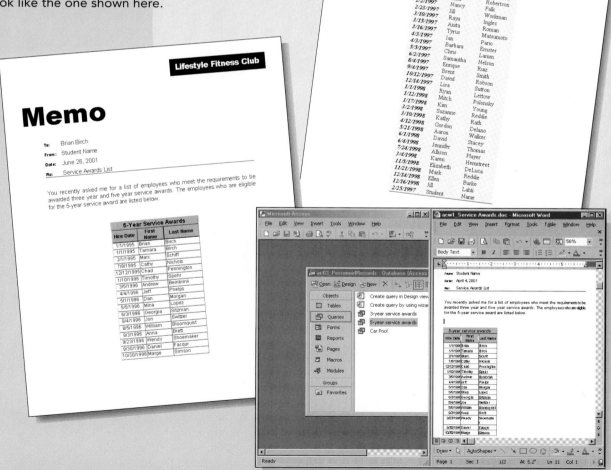

Copying Between Applications

You have already created the memo to Brian and just need to add the information from Access to the memo. All Microsoft Office applications have a common user interface such as similar commands and menu structures. In addition to these obvious features, they have been designed to work together, making it easy to share and exchange information between applications.

As with all Office applications, you can cut, copy, and paste selections within and between tables and objects in an Access database. You can also perform these operations between Access databases and other applications. For example, you can copy a database object or selection into a Word document. The information is inserted in a format the application can recognize.

Copying a Query to a Word Document

You will begin by copying the 5-year query results from Access into a Word memo. You can also use the same commands and procedures to copy information from Word or other Office applications into Access.

First, you need to open the memo document in Word.

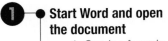
● **Start Word and open the document** acw1_Service Awards.

● **Maximize the application and document windows.**

● **If necessary, change to Normal view at Page Width zoom.**

● **In the memo header, replace Student Name with your name.**

● **Scroll the memo so you can see the body of the memo.**

Your screen should be similar to Figure 1

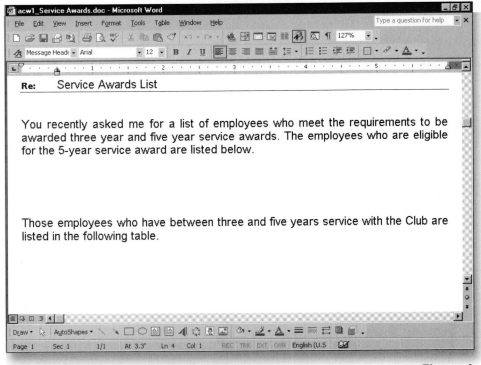

Figure 1

This document contains the text of the memo to Brian. Below each of the paragraphs, you want to display the appropriate list of employees. This information is available in the Personnel Records database file and can be obtained using the Service Awards queries you created and saved.

2

● **Start Access.**

● **If necessary, maximize the window.**

● **Open the** ac03_Personnel Records **database file.**

● **Open the Queries object list.**

Your screen should be similar to Figure 2

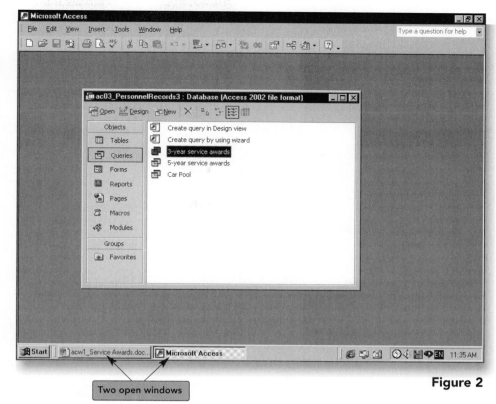

Two open windows

Figure 2

There are now two open applications, Word and Access. Word is open in a window behind the Access application window. Application buttons for all open windows are displayed in the taskbar.

You want to copy the output from the 5-Year Service Awards query below the first paragraph of the memo. You can use Copy and Paste or drag and drop between the Access and Word applications to copy a database object. To use drag and drop, both applications must be open and visible in the window. You can do this by tiling the application windows.

3 • Right-click on a blank area of the taskbar to open the shortcut menu.

HAVING TROUBLE?

If your taskbar is hidden, point to the thin line at the bottom of the screen to redisplay it.

• Choose Tile Windows Vertically.

• Click in the Access window to make it active.

Your screen should be similar to Figure 3

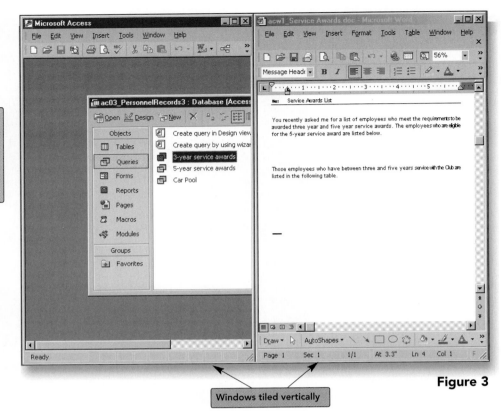

Windows tiled vertically

Figure 3

You can now see the contents of both the Access and Word applications and are ready to copy the query results to below the first paragraph of the memo.

4 • Select the 5-year Service Awards object in the Access Database window.

• Drag the selected object to the second blank line below the first paragraph of the memo.

• Click in the Word document to deselect the table.

Your screen should be similar to Figure 4

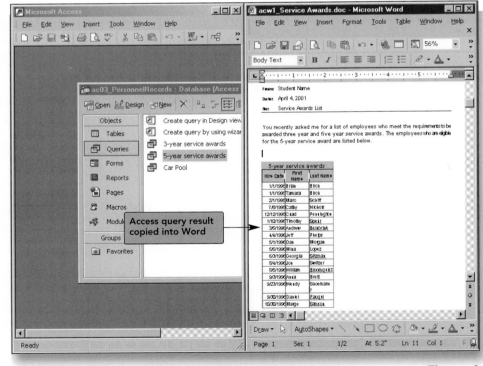

Access query result copied into Word

Figure 4

The query results have been copied into the Word document as a table that can be edited and manipulated within Word. Much of the formatting associated with the copied information is also pasted into the document.

Formatting Copied Data

You think the memo would look better if the Hire Date column of information in the table was centered. You also want to make the table wider so the entire contents of the last name are displayed on a single line, and you want to center it between the margins of the memo.

1 ● Click ▣ to maximize the Word window.

● Scroll the table to see Wendy Shoemaker's record.

● Increase the width of the table by dragging the right table border line to the 2.5 inch position on the ruler.

● Move to any row in the Hire Date column and choose Table/Select/Column.

● Click ≡ to center the Hire Date column contents.

● Choose Table/Select/Table to select the entire table.

● Click ≡ to center the table between the margins.

● Deselect the table.

Your screen should be similar to Figure 5

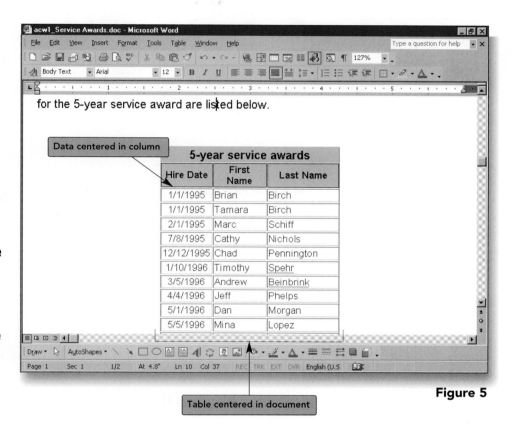

Figure 5

Editing a Copied Object

As you check the information in the table, you notice that Daniel Facqur's first name is misspelled. You want to correct this in both the memo and in the database table.

1 ● Edit the spelling of "Danial" to "**Daniel**" in the Word table.

● Click 🔲 to restore the Word window to tiled vertically.

● Switch to Access and open the "5-year Service Awards query."

● Correct the spelling of Daniel's name in the query results.

Your screen should be similar to Figure 6

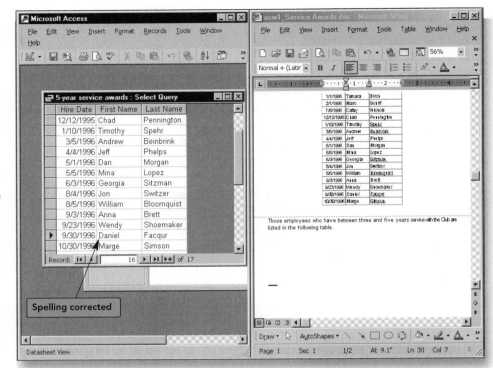

Figure 6

Now the information is correct in both applications.

Your first query table has been copied into the memo and formatted to fit the memo's layout. Next you need to insert the query results showing all employees who have more than 3 years and less than 5 years with the club. As you consider the memo, you are concerned that you may need to make corrections to the database again. If you need to, you want the memo to be automatically updated when you modify the query. To do this you will link the query object to the memo.

Linking between Applications

You will insert the query result into the memo as a **linked object**. Information created in one application can be inserted as a linked object into a document created by another application. When an object is linked, the data is stored in the **source file** (the document it was created in). A graphic representation or picture of the data is displayed in the **destination file** (the document in which the object is inserted). A connection between the information in the destination file to the source file is established by the creation of a link. The link contains references to the location of the source file and the selection within the document that is linked to the destination file.

When changes that affect the linked object are made in the source file, the changes are automatically reflected in the destination file when it is opened. This is called a **live link**. When you create linked objects, the date and time on your machine should be accurate, because the program refers to the date of the source file to determine whether updates are needed when you open the destination file.

Linking a Query to a Word Document

One way to create a link to the query is with the 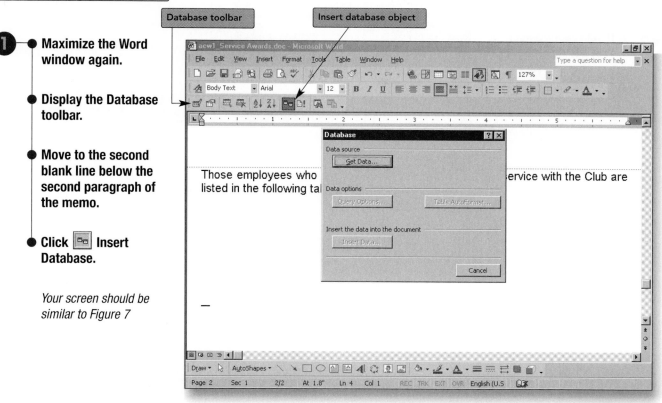 Insert Database button on the Database toolbar of Word. This is the method you will use to link the 3-Year Service Awards query table to the memo.

1 ● Maximize the Word window again.

● Display the Database toolbar.

● Move to the second blank line below the second paragraph of the memo.

● Click 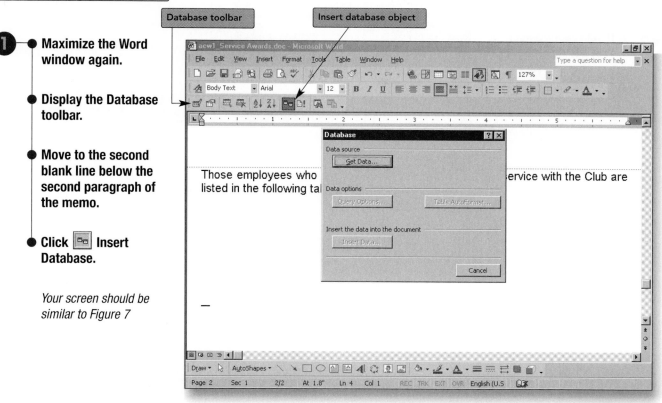 Insert Database.

Your screen should be similar to Figure 7

Figure 7

From the Database dialog box, you need to first select the database file to be inserted into the memo.

2 ● Click [Get Data...].

● Select the location containing your data files from the Look In drop-down list.

● Double-click the ac03_Personnel Records **database file.**

Your screen should be similar to Figure 8

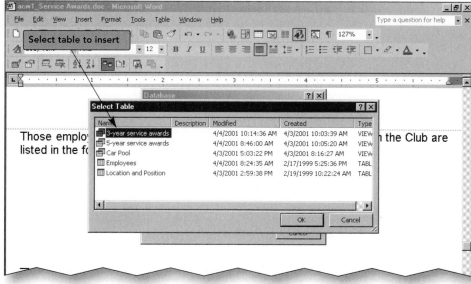

Figure 8

The Select Table dialog box automatically opens to the queries list for Personnel Records. This is because the last object you worked with in this database was a query (the 5-year Service Awards query table, which you just copied into the memo). From this list, you will select the 3-Year Service Awards query to be inserted in the Word document.

If necessary, select "3-Year Service Awards."

Click OK **.**

Your screen should be similar to Figure 9

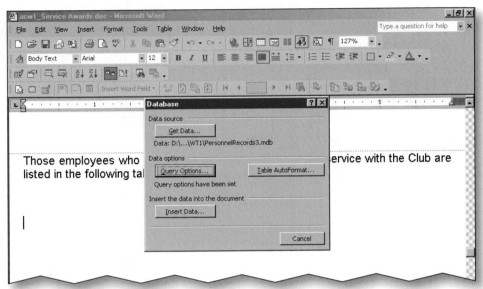

Figure 9

The Database dialog box is displayed again. The Query Options button enables you to modify the query settings. Since you want it to appear as it is, you do not need to use this option. The AutoFormat button lets you select a format to apply to the table. If you do not select a format style, the datasheet is copied into the document as an unformatted table.

Click Table AutoFormat... **.**

Your screen should be similar to Figure 10

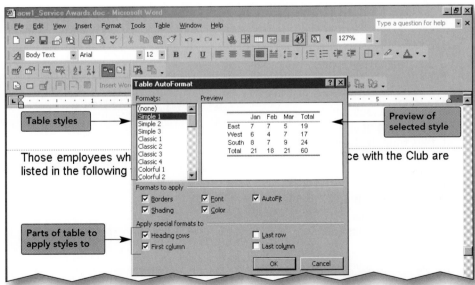

Figure 10

From the Table AutoFormat dialog box, you select the style you want to use and the parts of the table you want to apply it to. You want the formats applied to the heading rows and first column.

5

- If necessary, select the Heading rows and First column options as the only two areas to apply special formats.

- Select the Colorful 2 style.

- Click [OK].

- Click [Insert Data...] from the Database dialog box.

Your screen should be similar to Figure 11

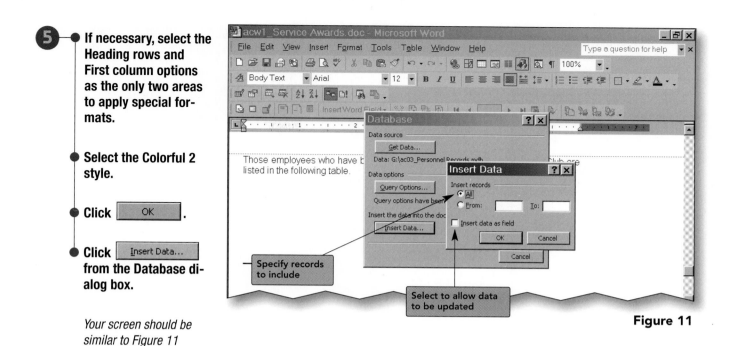

Specify records to include

Select to allow data to be updated

Figure 11

From the Insert Data dialog box, you specify what records to include in the inserted table and whether to insert the data as a field. Inserting it as a field allows the data to be updated whenever the source changes.

6

- If necessary, select **All**.

- Select **Insert** data as field.

- Click [OK].

Your screen should be similar to Figure 12

Query object inserted into Word document using selected AutoFormat style

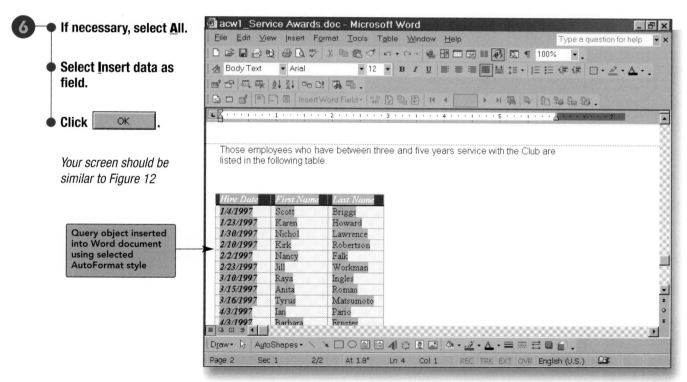

Figure 12

The link to the database file and to the query object is established, and the database table is inserted into the document in the selected format style. The table lists the 33 employees who have between 3 and 5 years with the club.

7 ● **Click above the table to deselect it.**

● **Scroll the memo to see the bottom of the inserted table.**

Your screen should be similar to Figure 13

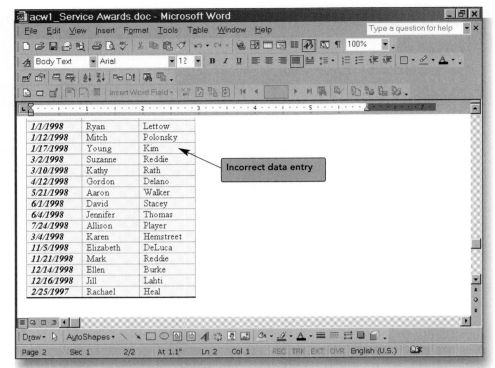

1/1/1998	Ryan	Lettow
1/12/1998	Mitch	Polonsky
1/17/1998	Young	Kim
3/2/1998	Suzanne	Reddie
3/10/1998	Kathy	Rath
4/12/1998	Gordon	Delano
5/21/1998	Aaron	Walker
6/1/1998	David	Stacey
6/4/1998	Jennifer	Thomas
7/24/1998	Allison	Player
3/4/1998	Karen	Hemstreet
11/5/1998	Elizabeth	DeLuca
11/21/1998	Mark	Reddie
12/14/1998	Ellen	Burke
12/16/1998	Jill	Lahti
2/25/1997	Rachael	Heal

Incorrect data entry

Figure 13

Now you notice that Kim Young's first and last names are reversed. You want to correct this in both the table in Access and in the memo.

Updating a Linked Object

Because you linked the Access object to the Word document, you can make the change in Access, and it will be automatically updated in the memo.

1 ● Restore the Word window to tiled vertically.

● Close the "5-year Service Awards" query.

● Open the "3-Year Service Awards" query in Access.

● Correct the Last Name and First Name fields in Kim Young's record.

● Move to any other record to complete the edit.

● Click 🖫 Save.

● Switch to the Word memo and click on the table to select it.

● Click 🖳 Update Field to update the table contents.

● Scroll the memo to confirm that Kim Young's name is now corrected in the table.

Your screen should be similar to Figure 14

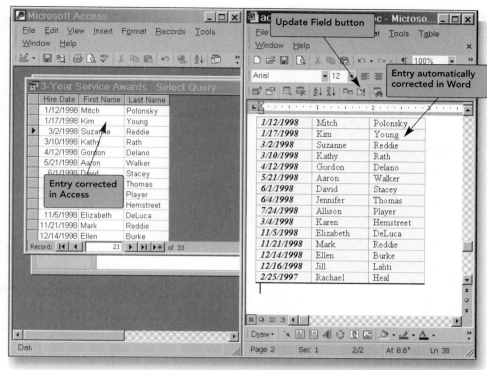

Figure 14

Additional Information
Edits made to a linked object in the destination file do not affect the source file.

The query results were regenerated and inserted into the document again. The last change you want to make is to center the table. Then you will save and print the memo.

2 ● From the taskbar shortcut menu, choose <u>U</u>ndo Tile.

● Close the Database and Mail Merge toolbars.

● Center the table on the page.

● Deselect the table.

● Preview both pages of the memo.

Your screen should be similar to Figure 15

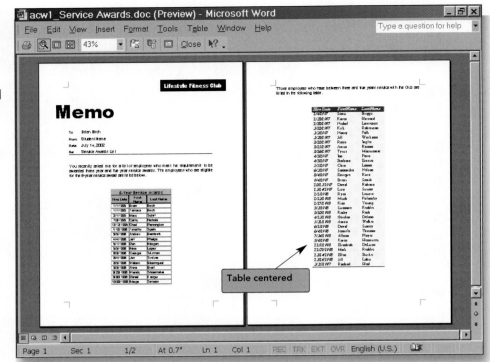

Figure 15

3 ● Save the memo as Service Awards Linked.

● Print the memo and exit Word.

● Maximize the Access window.

● Close the query and exit Access.

Your printed memo should look similar to the one shown in the Case Study at the beginning of this lab.

Working Together: Linking Access and Word

key terms

Destination file   ACWT1.6
Linked object   ACWT1.6
Live link   ACWT1.6
Source file   ACWT1.6

lab exercises

Hands-On Exercises

step by step

Spa Marketing Memo

★ 1. The Simply Beautiful Spa database has been used extensively (Step-by-Step Exercise 1 of Lab 3). Maria Dell, the owner, has asked you for a printed list of clients who are over the age of 35 to get an idea of how much interest there would be in an anti-aging spa package she is considering offering. You already filtered the Clients table to locate this information and now want to include the results in a memo to Maria (shown here).

   a. Open the ac02_Simply Beautiful database and the "Clients" table that you modified in Step-by-Step Exercise 1 of Lab 3. Apply the filter. (If you did not save the table with the filter, create the filter again by entering <1/1/65 in the Birth date field of the Filter by Form window).

To: Maria Dell
From: Student Name
Date: [Current Date]
Here is the information you requested on the spa clients who are over the age of 35.

Last Name	First Name	Street Address	City	State	Zip Code	E-mail	Birth Date
Finch	Terrence	919 Port Ct.	Orangeburg	SC	29115	Terr@set.net	09/08/1952
Huye	Ky	765 Portland	Orangeburg	SC	29115		03/15/1944
Riley	Charlene	2424 Eastern	Orangeburg	SC	29115		10/13/1944
Woo	Fen	8547 Lindsey Avenue	Columbia	SC	29201	woo@mail.com	05/23/1953
Grimes	Sally	202 S. Jefferson	Columbia	SC	29201	SGrime@ed.net	01/07/1957
Townsend	Joseph	101 Cheshire Lane	Wateree	SC	29044		07/10/1963

lab exercises

b. Hide the Client No., Home Phone, Work Phone, and Cell Phone fields.

c. Open Word and enter the following text in a new document.

TO: Maria Dell

FROM: [Your Name]

DATE: [current date]

Here is the information you requested on the spa clients who are over the age of 35.

d. Select the filter results and use Copy and Paste to copy them into the Word document.

e. Save the memo as Beautiful 35+ Clients. Close the document and exit Word.

f. Unhide the four fields. Remove the filter. Close the table and database.

Low Stock Memo

★★ **2.** Evan, the owner of the Dwontown Internet Cafe, continues to beimpressed with the Cafe's database (Step-by-Step Exercise 3 of Lab 3). Evan has asked you to send him a memo listing of all special-order items and how many of these items are currently in-stock right away. You are not sure how much detail he needs (he didn't say anything about placing any orders), and he is not available for you to ask him right now. You decide to go ahead and create the memo and link the query result to it. This way, you can easily revise the query and update the memo should it be necessary. The completed memo is shown here.

a. Open the ac02_Cafe Supplies database that you modified in Step-by-Step Exercise 3 of Lab 3.

b. Create a new query named "Special Orders" that will display items with Y in the Special Order? field, and include the On Hand, Description, and Vendor Name fields (in that order). Run the query. Save the query.

c. Open Word, and enter the following text in a new document.

TO: Evan

FROM: [your first name]

DATE: [current date]

The following table lists our current special-order inventory. Please let me know if you need additional information.

TO: Evan
FROM: Student Name
DATE: Current Date

The following table lists our current special-order inventory. Please let me know if you need additional information.

Special Order?	# On Hand	Description	Vendor Name
Y	30	Decaf Viennese	Pure Processing
Y	6	Business cards	Pro Printing
Y	1	Coffee mints	Tasty Delights
Y	45	Kenya coffee	Better Beverages, Inc.
Y	2	Ethiopian coffee	Better Beverages, Inc.
Y	0	Kona coffee	Better Beverages, Inc.
Y	12	Coffee mugs	Central Ceramics

d. Insert the query results into the Word document as a linked object and a field. Use an Auto-Format of your choice.

e. Size and center the table appropriately.

f. Change the # on Hand in the query for Decaf Viennese to 30 and for Kenya coffee to 45. Update the table in the memo.

g. Save the memo as Special Orders. Print the document. Exit Word.

h. Save the query. Close the table and database.

Software Memo

★ ★ **3.** The report you created for EduSoft listing the math and science titles released over 3 years ago
★ has been well received (Step-by-Step Exercise 4 of Lab 3). EduSoft's production development
manager has asked you to locate the same information for all titles. You will quickly modify the
query to get this information and include it in a memo to the manager (shown here).

a. Open the ac02_Learning database
and the "Old Math and Science"
query that you modified in Step-
by-Step Exercise 4 of Lab 3.

b. Modify the query to display all
titles that are over 3 years old.
Best fit the fields. Save the modified query as "3+ Products."

c. Open Word and enter the follow-
ing text in a new document.
TO: Kaitlin Mann, Product Dev.
Mgr.
FROM: [Your Name]
DATE: [current date]
Here is the information you re-
quested on the products EduSoft
released over 3 years ago.

TO: Kaitlin Mann, Product Dev. Mgr.
FROM: Student Name
DATE: Current date

Here is the information you requested on the products EduSoft released over 3 years ago.

Title	Subject	Grade Level	Release Date
Say It	Speech	K-2	01/20/1995
Spell It	Spelling	K-2	04/20/1995
Spell It II	Spelling	3-5	07/20/1995
Type It	Typing	K-2	01/15/1996
Read It III	Reading	6-8	03/20/1996
Try It I	Science	K-2	01/20/1996
Try It II	Science	3-5	06/04/1996
Try It III	Science	6-8	09/20/1996
Seeing Stars	Astronomy	3-5	11/07/1996
Rain or Shine	Meteorology	3-5	01/23/1997
Any Body	Anatomy and Biology	6-8	03/15/1997
Solve It	Math	K-2	06/14/1997
Solve It II	Math	3-5	09/03/1997
Solve It III	Math	6-8	12/15/1997
Tell It	Speech	K-2	01/20/1995

d. Insert the query results into the Word document as a linked object and a field. Use an
AutoFormat of your choice.

e. Open the "Software" table and add a new record to the table using the following information:
90-0102; Tell It; Speech; K–2; Story Telling; your name; 1/20/1995.

f. Run the query again.

g. Update the memo.

h. Size and center the table appropriately.

i. Save the memo as EduSoft 3+. Print the document.

j. Save the query changes. Close the table and database.

Command Summary

Command	Shortcut	Button	Action
File/New	Ctrl + N	🗋	Opens New File task pane
File/Open	Ctrl + O	📂	Opens an existing database
File/Close		✖	Closes open window
File/Save	Ctrl + S	💾	Saves database object
File/Page Setup/		Setup	Sets page margins and page layout for printed output
File/Print/Pages/From			Prints selected pages
File/Print Preview		🔍	Displays file as it will appear when printed
File/Print	Ctrl + P	🖨	Specifies print settings and prints current database object
File/Exit		✖	Closes Access
Edit/Undo	Ctrl + Z	↺	Cancels last action
Edit/Cut	Ctrl + X	✂ or ✖	Removes selected item and copies it to the Clipboard
Edit/Copy	Ctrl + C	📋	Duplicates selected item and copies to the Clipboard
Edit/Paste	Ctrl + V	📋	Inserts copy of item in Clipboard
Edit/Select Record			Selects current record
Edit/Select All Records	Ctrl + A		Selects all controls on a form
Edit/Find	Ctrl + F	🔭	Locates specified data
Edit/Replace	Ctrl + H		Locates and replaces specified data
Edit/Delete Rows		⇥	Deletes selected field in Design view
Edit/Primary Key		🔑	Defines a field as a primary key field
Edit/Clear Grid			Clears query grid
View/Design View		📐 ▾	Displays Design view
View/Datasheet View		▦ ▾	Displays table in Datasheet view
View/Form View			Displays a form in Form view
View/Toolbars/Task Pane			Displays task pane
View/Zoom/%		Fit ▾	Displays previewed database object at specified percentage
Insert/Rows		⇤	Inserts a new field in table in Design view

Command	Shortcut	Button	Action
Insert/Column			Inserts a new field in a table in Datasheet view
Insert/Object			Inserts an object into current field
Insert/Report			Creates a new report object
Filter/Apply Filter/Sort		▽	Applies filter to table
Query/Run		!	Displays query results in Query Datasheet view
Query/Show Table		▣	Displays Show Table dialog box
Format/Column Width			Changes width of table columns in Datasheet view
Format/Column Width/Best Fit			Sizes selected columns to accommodate longest entry or column header
Format/Hide Columns			Hides columns
Format/Unhide Columns			Redisplays hidden columns
Records/Remove Filter/Sort			Displays all records in table
Records/Data Entry			Hides existing records and displays Data Entry window
Records/Sort/Sort Ascending		⬇	Reorders records in ascending alphabetical order
View/Toolbox		⚒	Displays/Hides Toolbox
View/Zoom/%			Displays previewed document at specified percentage
View/Zoom/Fit to Window			Displays entire previewed document page
View/Pages			Displays specified number of pages of previewed document
Records/Filter/Filter by Form		▣	Displays blank datasheet for entering criteria to display specific information
Records/Filter/Filter by Selection		▽	Displays only records that contain a specific value
Records/Apply Filter/Sort		▽	Applies filter to table
Tools/Relationships			Defines permanent relationship between tables
Tools/Database Utilities/Compact and Repair Database		▣	Displays blank datasheet for entering criteria to display specific information
Window/Database			Displays selected window
		▣	Displays Database window

Glossary of Key Terms

action query   A type of query used to make changes to multiple records in one operation.

AND operator   A criteria expression used to narrow a search by specifying that a record must meet both conditions to be included.

AutoReport Wizard   Creates a report, either tabular or columnar, based on a table or query, and adds all fields to the report.

Best Fit   A feature that automatically adjusts column width to fit the longest entry.

bound control   A control that is linked to a field in an underlying table.

bound object   A graphic object that is stored in a table and connected to a specific record and field.

cell   The space created by the intersection of a vertical column and a horizontal row.

character string   A group of text characters.

clip art   A collection of professionally drawn images that is usually included with a software program.

column selector bar   In Query Design view, the thin gray bar just above the field name in the grid.

column width   The size of a field column in Datasheet view. It controls the amount of data you can see on the screen.

common field   A field that is found in two or more tables. It must have the same data type and the same kind of information in each table, but may have different field names.

compact   The database makes a copy of the file and rearranges how the file is stored on disk for optimal performance.

comparison operator   A symbol used in expressions that allows you to make comparisons. The > (greater than) and < (less than) symbols are examples of comparison operators.

control   An object in a form or report that displays information, performs actions, or enhances the design.

criteria   A set of limiting conditions.

criteria expression   An expression that will select only the records that meet certain limiting criteria.

crosstab query   A type of query that summarizes large amounts of data in an easy-to-read, row-and-column format.

current record   The record, containing the insertion point, that will be affected by the next action.

database   An organized collection of related information.

Database toolbar   Toolbar that contains buttons that are used to perform basic database features.

datasheet   Data from a table, form, or query that is displayed in row-and-column format.

Datasheet form   A form layout that is similar to a table datasheet, in that information is displayed in rows and columns.

data type   Attribute for a field that determines what type of data it can contain.

Default Value property   A property used to specify a value that is automatically entered in a field when a new record is created.

design grid   The lower part of the Query Design window, which displays settings that are used to define the query.

destination file   The document in which a linked object is inserted.

document window   The area of the application window that displays the contents of the open document.

drawing object   A simple graphic consisting of shapes such as lines and boxes that can be created using a drawing program such as Paint.

expression   A combination of operators, identifiers, and values that produce a result.

field   A single category of data in a table, the values of which appear in a column of a datasheet.

field list   A small window that lists all fields in an underlying table.

field name   Label used to identify the data stored in a field.

field property   An attribute of a field that affects its appearance or behavior.

field selector   A small gray box or bar in datasheets and queries that can be clicked to select the entire column. The field selector usually contains the field names.

field size   Field property that limits a text data type to a certain size or limits numeric data to values within a specific range.

filter   A restriction placed on records in an open form or datasheet to temporarily isolate a subset of records.

Filter by Form   A method that filters records based on multiple criteria that are entered into a blank datasheet.

Filter by Selection   A type of filter that displays only records containing a specific value.

Find and Replace   A feature that helps you quickly find specific information and automatically replace it with new information.

form   A database object used primarily to display records onscreen to make it easier to enter and make changes to records.

format   To enhance the appearance of the document to make it more readable or attractive.

Format property   A property that specifies the way data is displayed.

frame   A division of a window that can be scrolled separately.

graphic   A non-text element or object, such as a drawing or picture, which can be added to a table.

hyperlink   A connection to locations in the current document, other documents, or Web pages. Clicking a hyperlink jumps to the specified location.

identifier   A part of an expression that refers to the value of a field, a graphic object, or property.

join   Creates a relationship between tables by linking common fields in multiple tables.

join line   In the Query Design window, the line that joins the common fields between one or more table field lists.

landscape   Printing orientation that prints across the length of the page.

linked object   An object that is pasted into another application. The data is stored in the source document, and a graphic representation of the data is displayed in the destination document.

live link   A link in which, when the source document is edited, the changes are automatically reflected in the destination document.

margin   The blank space around the edge of a page.

menu   Method used to tell a program what you want it to do.

menu bar   A bar that displays the menu names that can be selected.

move handle   The large box in the upper left corner of a selected control that is used to move the control.

multitable query   A query that uses more than one table.

navigation buttons   Used to move through records in Datasheet and Form views. Also available in the Print Preview window.

Navigation mode   In Datasheet view, when the entire field is highlighted.

object   A table, form, or report that can be selected and manipulated as a unit.

operator   A symbol or word used to specify the type of calculation to perform in an expression.

OR operator   A criteria expression used to broaden a search by specifying that a record may include either condition in the output.

orientation   The direction the paper prints, either landscape or portrait.

picture   An illustration such as a scanned photograph.

portrait   Printing orientation that prints the report across the width of a page.

primary key   One or more fields in a table that uniquely identify a record.

query   Used to view data in different ways, to analyze data, and to change data.

query datasheet   Where the result or answer to a query is displayed.

record   A row of a table, consisting of a group of related fields.

record number indicator   A small box that displays the current record number in the lower left corner of most views. The record number indicator is surrounded by the navigation buttons.

record selector   Displayed to the left of the first column; it can be used to select an entire record in Datasheet view.

relational database   Database in which a relationship is created by having a common field in the tables. The common field lets you extract and combine data from multiple tables.

report   Printed output generated from queries or tables.

row label   In the design grid of Query Design view, identifies the type of information that can be entered in the row.

scroll bar   A window element located on the right or bottom window border that lets you display text that is not currently visible in the window. It contains scroll arrows and a scroll box.

selection cursor   A colored highlight bar that appears over the selected command in a menu as you point to it.

shortcut menu   A menu of the most common menu options that is displayed by right-clicking on the selected item.

Show box   A box in the Show row of the design grid that, when checked, indicates that the field will be displayed in the query result.

sizing handles   Small boxes surrounding a selected control that are used to size the control.

sort   To temporarily reorder table records in the datasheet.

source file   The document in which a linked object is created.

status bar   A bar displayed at the bottom of the document window that advises you of the status of different program conditions and features as you use the program.

table   Consists of vertical columns and horizontal rows of information about a particular category of things.

tab order   The order in which Access moves through a form or table when the [Tab⇆] key is pressed.

tabular form   A form layout in row-and-column format with records in rows and fields in columns.

task pane   A separate, scrollable pane displaying shortcuts to frequently used features.

toolbar   A bar of buttons commonly displayed below the menu bar. The buttons are shortcuts for many of the most common menu commands.

unbound control   A control that is not connected to a field in an underlying table.

unbound object   A graphic object that is associated with the table as a whole, not with a specific record, and does not change when you move from record to record.

Undo   A feature used to cancel your last action.

validation rule   An expression that defines the acceptable values in a validity check.

validation text   Text that is displayed when a validation rule is violated.

validity check   Process of checking to see whether data meets certain criteria.

value   A part of an expression that is a number, date, or character string.

view   One of several windows or formats that Access provides for working with and looking at data.

workspace   The large area of the screen where different Access windows are displayed as you are using the program.

Supplied/Used File	Created/Saved As
Lab 1	
ac01_Friend1 (graphic)	Lifestyle Fitness Employees: Employees (table)
Step-by-Step	
1.	Beautiful: Clients (table)
2.	Happenings: Advertisers (table)
3.	Supplies: Vendors (table)
4.	Adventure Travel: Travel Packages (table)
5. ac01_Whitedog (graphic)	Animal Rescue: Tracking (table)
On Your Own	
1.	Music Collection: CD Catalog (table)
2.	Lewis Personnel: Phone List (table)
3.	Patient Information: Patient Data (table)
4.	JK Enterprises: Expenses (table)
On the Web	
1.	Golden Oldies: Inventory (table)
Lab 2	
ac02_EmployeeRecords	Employee Data Form (form)
Step-by-Step	
1. ac02_Simply Beautiful	Client Info (form)
2. ac02_Happening Ads	Advertiser Information (form)
3. ac02_Cafe Supplies	Vendor Info (table)
4. ac02_Learning	EduSoft Titles (form)
5. ac02_AA	Angel's Animals (form)
On Your Own	
1. Adventure Travel (from Lab 1)	Packages (form)
2. JK Enterprises	JK Expenses (form)
3. Patient Information (from Lab 1)	Administration (form)
4. Lewis Personnel: Phone List	Human Resources (form)

Supplied/Used File	Created/Saved As
On the Web	
1. Golden Oldies (from Lab 1)	Collectibles (form)
Lab 3	
ac03_Personnel Records	Car Pool (query)
	3-year Service Awards (query)
	5-year Service Awards (query)
	Employee Address Report (report)
	Iona to Fort Meyers Car Pool Report (report)
Step-by-Step	
1. ac02_Simply Beautiful	
2. ac02_ Happening Ads	Bimonthly Advertisers (query)
3. ac02_ Cafe Supplies	Low Stock (query)
	Order Items (report)
4. ac02_ Learning	Old Math and Science (query)
	96-97 Math and Science Titles (report)
5. ac03_Angels	Adoptees (query)
	Animal Adoption Report (report)
On Your Own	
1. ac02_Learning	
2. Lewis Personnel (from Lab 2)	Home Address (query)
3. JK Enterprise (from Lab 2)	Pending (query)
	Pending Expenses (report)
4. ac03_Angels	Foster (query)
	Foster Angels (report)
On the Web	
1. Golden Oldies (from Lab 2)	Complete Products (query)
Working Together	
acw1_ServiceAwards	
ac03_Personnel Records	Service Awards Linked (document)
Step-by-Step	
1. ac02_Simply Beautiful	Beautiful 35+ Clients (document)
2. ac02_Cafe Supplies	Special Orders (query)
	Special Orders (document)
3. ac02_Learning	3+ Products (query)
Old Math and Science (query)	EduSoft 3+ (document)

MOUS Skills

Access 2002 Core Certification

Standardized Coding Number	Activity	Lab	Page	Lab Exercises Step-By-Step	Lab Exercises On Your Own
AC2002-1	**Creating and Using Databases**				
Ac2002-1-1	Create Access databases	1	AC1.8	1,2,3,4,5	1,2,3,4,5
Ac2002-1-2	Open database objects in multiple views	1	AC1.25	2,3,4	
		2	AC2.40	1,2,3,4,5	1,2,3,4,5
		3	AC3.16,AC3.39	3	
Ac2002-1-3	Move among records	1	AC1.36	1,2,3,4,5	1,2,3,4,5
		2	AC2.6	1,2,3,4,5	1,2,3,4
Ac2002-1-4	Format datasheets	2	AC2.30		
Ac2002-2	**Creating and Modifying Tables**				
Ac2002-2-1	Create and modify tables	1	AC1.10,AC1.23	1,2,3,4,5	1,2,3,4,5
		2	AC2.8	1,2,3,4,5	1,2,3,4
Ac2002-2-2	Add a predefined input mask to a field				
Ac2002-2-3	Create Lookup fields				
Ac2002-2-4	Modify field properties	1	AC1.18	1,2,3,4,5	
		2	AC2.8	1,2,3,4,5	
Ac2002-3	**Creating and Modifying Queries**				
Ac2002-3-1	Create and modify select queries	3	AC3.12	2,3,4,5	
Ac2002-3-2	Add calculated fields to select queries				
Ac2002-4	**Creating and Modifying Forms**				
Ac2002-4-1	Create and display forms	2	AC2.32	1,2,3,4,5	1,2,3,4
Ac2002-4-2	Modify form properties				
Ac2002-5	**Viewing and Organizing Information**				
Ac2002-5-1	Enter, edit, and delete records	1	AC1.27,AC1.47	1,2,3,4,5	1,2,3,4,5
		2	AC2.39	1,2,3,4,5	1,2,3,4
Ac2002-5-2	Create queries	3	AC3.11	2,3,4,5	2,3,4
Ac2002-5-3	Sort records	2	AC2.27		
Ac2002-5-4	Filter records	3	AC3.4	1	1

Standardized Coding Number	Activity	Lab	Page	Lab Exercises	
				Step-By-Step	On Your Own
Ac2002-6	**Defining Relationships**				
Ac2002-6-1	Create one-to-many relationships				
Ac2002-6-2	Enforce referential integrity				
Ac2002-7	**Producing Reports**				
Ac2002-7-1	Create and format reports	3	AC3.31	3,4,5	3,4
Ac2002-7-2	Add calculated controls to reports				
Ac2002-7-3	Preview and print reports	3	AC3.45	3,4,5	3,4
Ac2002-8	**Integrating with Other Applications**				
Ac2002-8-1	Import data to Access				
Ac2002-8-2	Export data from Access				
Ac2002-8-3	Create a simple data access page				

Index